UPLIFTED

A Collection *of* Stories
from Asian Hustle Network

Journeys *of* Abundance,
Community *&* Identity

by Geena Chen

ASIAN HUSTLE NETWORK

This book is dedicated to our friends, family, AHN community, and all the go-getters looking to be inspired to dive into the entrepreneurial world.

Praise *for*
UPLIFTED

"*Uplifted* made me feel so seen. The entrepreneurial journey, as a young Southeast Asian woman, has left me feeling alone at many times. Reading the stories of these inspiring fellow Asian founders gave me a sense of connection, inspiration, and solidarity."

—*Vanessa Pham*
Cofounder & CEO of Omsom, Forbes 30 Under 30

"The passionate, eye-opening, and often hilarious stories in this anthology are a celebration of our collective Asian American entrepreneurial experience. I cried and cheered for the intimate recounting of these stories. From our confusion, pain, and failures, we can rise with victory. Read this to discover our remarkable contributions to American society."

—*Jane Hyun*
Leadership Strategist and Author of *Breaking the Bamboo Ceiling: Career Strategies for Asians*, Co-Author of *Flex*

"*Uplifted* sketches the breadth and gravity of Asian American dreams, connecting the dots between immigrant survival, career advancement, and community care. In their detail and diversity, these stories reinterpret 'Hustle' away from toxic grind culture and into a deeper, more sustainable vision of shared creation."

—*jason chu*
Rapper/Activist, Asian American cultural expert

"Bryan and Maggie are storytellers and historians of the modern immigrant hustle experience. They are community leaders with a pulse on what it means to be Asian American today—the first generation pursuing the new American dream."

—*Andrew Chau*
Cofounder & CEO of Boba Guys, Angel Investor

"Reading the different stories highlighted in *Uplifted* brought tears of gratitude to my eyes. More than a moment, this book is part of a larger cultural movement, fueled by everyday people who are unrelenting in the belief that our community's stories matter. Each story in this book is a testament to the courage it takes to expand upon our conceptions of who and what makes Asian America. Reading this served as an inspiring reminder that, with the love and support of community, we each have the power to write and rewrite the story of our lives."

—*Cassandra Lam*
CEO & Cofounder of The Cosmos

"The stories in *Uplifted* dive beneath the surface to show us the factors, both visible and invisible, that are shaping the entrepreneurial success stories we'll be hearing about in the decades to come. I laughed, I cried, and above all, I was inspired."

—*Laura Huang*
Professor at Harvard Business School and Author of *Edge: Turning Adversity into Advantage*

"Although I am not Asian, I find the stories in *Uplifted* to be really compelling. Each is at once unique and universal, a tale of someone who, by chasing after their dreams, discovers what they most value. They bring to mind the journeys of my own grandparents, Jews who escaped persecution in Eastern Europe over a century ago and came to America where they lived out their own version of the hustle. Thank you for sharing these inspiring and beautifully told stories."

—*Joel ben Izzy*
Storyteller and Author

"The stories in this book present a timely, hard-won guide for Asian American entrepreneurs looking to leverage their one-of-a-kind culture, community, and identity to build sustainable businesses with real-world impact. Read on to discover the truth of entrepreneurship without all the hype and the human connections that bring it all together. Pay attention and prepare to be moved into action."

—*Raad Ahmed*
Founder and CEO at Lawtrades, Writer at RaadAhmed.com

"Having worked in my parents' fabric shop starting at the age of 5, I figured that was a normal childhood for every kid growing up in America. It was not until I reached adulthood that I realized that that hustle was deeply cultural and in some ways, otherized me. However, in recent years, through communities like Asian Hustle Network, I saw my own childhood experiences in the countless stories of other members and didn't feel so alone anymore. *Uplifted* is a deeply personal and inspiring collection of many of these stories that serves as a tribute to the sacrifices and hard work of those that came before us as well as a poignant reshaping of our 'American Dream.'"

—*Bao Nguyen*

Dorector, *BE WATER*, an award-winning documentary chronicling the life of legendary actor and martial arts master, Bruce Lee

"Reading this book is like a gift to our soul and each story makes us walk away as a better person."

—*Nanxi Liu*

CEO & Founder of Enplug, Partner of XFactor Ventures, Forbes 30 under 30

"As Asians we are often overlooked, but our stories need to be shared. In *Uplifted*, we are able to learn the stories of the Asian American Dream. These stores talk about preserving and honoring Asian culture, while breaking the rules to progress into American culture."

—*Andy Nguyen*

Restaurateur who has reshaped the millennial age F&B industry

"I wish I had access to this book in my early teens. Growing up in an Asian community, I would rarely see any spotlight on the successes or achievements of our community. We are known as people who are 'behind the scenes' or 'working in silence.' This book highlights and amplifies the voices of twenty-one successful Asian entrepreneurs to inspire the next generation of entrepreneurs. However, the true beauty of this book is the ability to capture the essence of the Asian American community, collectivism, and the beauty of uplifting one another."

—*Sandy Lin*

Founder of Small Business Tips and TEDx Speaker

"Reading *Uplifted* transformed the way I think about my Asian identity from something to overcome to something that links me to a family of creative and ingenious hustlers."

—Jane Won
Writer and Educator

"I believe one of the most precious gifts that you can give someone is to let them know they are not alone. As a Taiwanese immigrant raised in the South, I am used to being othered. I remember dealing with racism on a regular basis to the point that I thought being invisible was a good thing. I didn't have a community to go to, so I buried my pain and trauma so that I could get on with my life. Now that I'm in my 40s and I see the restorative healing power of communities, I wish I had a book like this to let me know that I wasn't alone and WE are not alone."

—Ti Chang
Cofounder and VP of Design at CRAVE, Design Activist

"*Uplifted* is simultaneously an energy shot and a salve to both invigorate and soothe the soul. This book stirred something deep in me. I'm in awe of the struggle and resilience chronicled in these stories, and am inspired to dig deep to build my own success. For anyone who feels lonely or weary on their uncharted path, this book is a reminder that you are in a constellation of friends, family, community, and even strangers who are there to hold you if you need."

—Raina Sun
Life Coach at Raina Sun Coaching

"A collection of motivational and inspiring stories from our community. Wherever you are on your entrepreneurial quest or self-discovery journey, these diverse and impactful stories power us to foster advanced work—a daringly bold step to inspire purpose in this world."

—Michelle Hanabusa
Founder & Creative Director of WEAREUPRISERS and Cofounder of Hate Is A Virus

"Wow. These are such incredible stories that I'm surprised and devastated I haven't heard them before. Geena's ability to amplify the voices of Asian American people opens the imaginative floodgates of what is possible. *Uplifted* tells the stories that we've all been looking for as Asian Americans and as entrepreneurs. I have never felt so inspired and so seen."

—*Alina Liu*
Founder of No-Waste Club

"Like so many Asian Americans, I've felt invisible for so much of my life. Conditioned to keep my head down and hustle as a kid, it took me well into adulthood to feel comfortable with my own voice and to speak my truth. *Uplifted* is a celebration for me. This book offers a chance to bear witness to some remarkably talented and courageous Asian American business leaders, and to expose how much their narratives contribute to America's success as we know it today. I walked away from this book hopeful and inspired. I'm more motivated than ever to keep scaling my venture and to keep speaking my truth as a proud Asian American."

—*Eric Bahn*
Cofounder & General Partner at Hustle Fund, a venture capital fund investing in hilariously early founders

COPYRIGHT

Writing & Interviewing
Geena Chen

Cover & Book Design
Gabrielle Widjaja (Gentle Oriental)

Copyediting & Sensitivity Reading
Crystal Shelley (Rabbit with a Red Pen Editorial Services)

Printing
Printed in Canada by the Prolific Group

All rights reserved. © 2021 Asian Hustle Network ®, Inc. First Edition. Intellectual property rights extend to this book's manuscript as well as the front and back cover design. No part of this book may be used or reproduced in any manner whatsoever without the written permission of Asian Hustle Network, Inc. except in the case of quotations no longer than 2 sentences in length embodied in articles, social media promotion, and reviews. For permissions and other information, please contact *team@asianhustlenetwork.com* or visit us at *www.asianhustlenetwork.com*.

ASIAN HUSTLE NETWORK

CONTENTS

17		Introduction	Geena Chen
	CHAPTER 1		
27		Donut Princess	Mayly Tao
	CHAPTER 2		
43		Forgiveness	Jason Wang
	CHAPTER 3		
57		How I Became a Memelord	Tai Tran
	CHAPTER 4		
73		Forged through Failure	1: Jason Wang 2: Shawn Tsao
	CHAPTER 5		
101		Building Nguyen Coffee Supply	Sahra Nguyen
	CHAPTER 6		
117		Queenly	Trisha Bantigue
	CHAPTER 7		
137		Losing Everything — Twice	David Nguyen Jack Nguyen
	CHAPTER 8		
151		A Voice for the AAPI Community	Dion Lim

CONTENTS

	CHAPTER 9	
163	My First American Dollar	Mony Nop

	CHAPTER 10	
179	Rising Above Abuse	Urooj Alam

	CHAPTER 11	
193	Rocking the Boat	Lucia Liu

	CHAPTER 12	
203	Inventor, Reinventing	Seibo Shen

	CHAPTER 13	
217	Dorm Room Hedge Fund	Christina Qi

	CHAPTER 14	
229	A Taste of Home or a Source of Discovery	Sandro Roco

	CHAPTER 15	
245	Celebrating Disability Pride	Tiffany Yu

	CHAPTER 16	
255	Fighting Harassment and Hate	Tammy Cho

	CHAPTER 17	
273	Sabobatage	Eric Y. Chen

	CHAPTER 18	
289	Building Asian Hustle Network	1: Maggie Chui 2: Bryan Pham

For sure, there is no entrepreneurial success story without the individual who makes it all happen. But this narrative only tells half the story.

The other half—which is to say, the secret to actually making it in the hustle—is that we are being uplifted while also uplifting others. We exist in community, and we depend upon each other.

INTRODUCTION

On Hustling & What It Means to Us

The hustle: some love it, some love to hate it, and some are ambivalent about it. It's a word that's been commodified, glorified, racialized, and vilified. Since its etymological origins in the 1600s (a Dutch word meaning to shake and toss), its meanings have multiplied: to move quickly, to coerce, to swindle, to sell sex and drugs, and perhaps the most mundane of them all: to work hard, and do *whatever it takes*, to survive. Yet for all the buzz and culture that exists around the word, hustling is as everyday as the air we breathe. Pretty much everyone hustles—we simply have to.

For Asian Americans, the hustle holds a special place in our journeys, if not our identities. For our ancestors who arrived as early US immigrants from China, Japan, India, the Philippines, and Korea in the 1800s, hustle was their sole rite of passage—one that could potentially turn into a source of livelihood and pride.

But eventually, our ancestors' hustle on the vast railroads, mines, and farms of the US was no longer needed. Painted as a threat to other laborers, our ancestors would suddenly be banned from the nation by exclusionary laws. (Ready for a mouthful?) One Asian ethnic group at a time, through the Page Act (1875), the Chinese Exclusion Act (1882), the Asiatic Barred Zone Act (1917), the Johnson-Reed Act (1924), and the Tydings-McDuffie Act (1934), Asians were forbidden from entering the country, owning property, testifying in court, applying for citizenship, and more. Once welcomed for their hustle, they were soon rejected on the same basis.

Decades later, the Immigration and Nationality Act of 1965 allowed Asians back into the US, but only those who were highly skilled in science, technology, and medicine. Said another way, it was our hustle, again—but only a certain brand of hustle that served a strategic US national interest—that allowed Asians to slip through the cracks of exclusionary laws.

Allowed here only because of their chosen expertise and work ethic, how could the hustle not remain a centerpiece of Asian identity? And that's just the immigrant side. For our ancestors who arrived in the US as refugees, escaped from imperialist wars and disasters, the hustle would inevitably await the minute they got off the boat.

Hustling has been a fundamental building block of identity for Asians in diaspora, one whose meaning has flip-flopped through the centuries and therefore stirs up conflicting emotions—pride and solidarity on one hand, shame and exclusion on the other.

In *Uplifted* and in Asian Hustle Network, we use the word "hustle" to reclaim the intimacy of sincere striving—the blend of fear, desire, and effort that bring us closer to each other in our human experience. Chasing our dreams in the face of fear, being scrappy and creative with what we have, and treating others with kindness and abundance: these are some of the themes reflected in the eighteen stories of twenty-one individuals in *Uplifted*.

A history of uplifting each other

Student activists in Berkeley, Yuji Ichioka and Emma Gee, coined the term "Asian American" in 1968 on the heels of the civil rights movement. Inspired by the Black Power Movement and the protests against the Vietnam War, the two founded the Asian American Political Alliance to unite Filipino, Chinese, and Japanese American students on campus. At that time, Asian people in the US mainly identified with their ethnic backgrounds. Especially with intra-Asian conflicts ongoing in their homelands,

Asian Americans didn't adopt the title as a natural consequence of geographic proximity. "Asian American" was meant to counter "Oriental" (a pejorative label appointed by non-Asian people), and its first moral meanings were rooted in anti-racism, anti-imperialism, and social justice.

Over time, the term came to embody not just a shared moral lens, but also a shared struggle. In 1982, when two auto workers in Detroit murdered Vincent Chin, a Chinese American man that the killers had mistaken as Japanese, the Asian American movement gained steam. A new understanding emerged: that regardless of differences between Asian ethnic groups, the external perceptions that grouped Asians together would mean our struggles overlapped and thus required solidarity to overcome.

Today, Asian Americans still face shared obstacles, which impact people differently based on ethnicity, gender, sexuality, ability, family history, and many other factors. These obstacles are as commonplace as racism and income inequality, and as uniquely Asian American as the model minority myth, the bamboo ceiling, the fetishization of Asian women, and centuries' worth of imperialist wars in our homelands, both Western and intra-Asian.

Yet, while our shared obstacles are one reason for our unity as Asian Americans, they are far from the only reason. With the Asian American identity being just over fifty years old (aka young), we're still in the process of figuring out what it means, what we stand for, and what we're working towards. In Asian Hustle Network and in *Uplifted*, we focus on the creativity and resilience that appear on the flipside of our shared challenges as a reason for unity.

For centuries, we have innovated in the face of overt barriers to secure our survival by drawing on community, cultural knowledge, and scrappy creativity. Barred from land ownership, mainstream media, banking, and education, the earliest Asian communities in the U.S. set up their own newspapers, credit unions, and schools. To provide financial support to community members starting up their own businesses, different Asian communities set up rotating credit unions known by different names depending on language and ethnicity: ko, tanomoshi, hui, gye, paluwagan, and more.

Drawing on cultural knowledge, early Japanese, Filipino, Korean, Chinese, and Indian farmers brought local Californian flora and fauna to market as delicacies, where other early Californians had only seen them as part of the region's "wilderness": dried kelp and seaweed, brined fish and squid, and other specialty crops that weren't seen as marketable before.[1]

To exploit a loophole in the Chinese Exclusion Act in which restaurant owners could sponsor relatives to enter the U.S. when few others could, Chinese immigrants with zero years of restaurant experience opened restaurants together by the thousands. So many, in fact, that the number of Chinese restaurants increased tenfold between 1910 and 1930. In 2015, they numbered more than the total number of McDonald's, Burger King, Wendy's, and KFC restaurants in the US, combined.[2]

Individuals with outsized impact, like American actress Tippi Hedren and Cambodian American donut mogul Ted Ngoy, paved the way for thousands of Southeast Asian families to make a living as refugees. Tippi Hedren was an American actress who visited a Northern Californian Vietnamese refugee camp in the 1970s, flew out her manicurist to train twenty women, and found them high-paying jobs at salons around Los Angeles—thus writing the beginning of the Vietnamese American nail salon story into existence. Ted Ngoy, who makes an appearance in Chapter 1, started a chain of successful donut stores in California and sponsored hundreds more Cambodian refugee families to start their lives in the US, following the Cambodian Genocide.

Countless other stories, perhaps known only to the people who lived them, offer proof (but no record) of how Asian migrants helped each other relocate to and build a livelihood in America. Why so few records? We can guess that some didn't want to relive their experiences, and many more may not have thought their stories unique or worth telling. But today, the rising tide of first- to fifth-generation Asian Americans, uplifted by those who came before them, are doing even more to uplift each other—with the act of storytelling playing no small role.

Why *Uplifted?*

In recent years, here are some of the concepts in our culture that we've seen break down, from mythologized to mere myth: the idea of being "self-made," the promises of grind culture, and the American Dream itself. At the heart of all these ideas, there's the belief in a rugged sort of individualism that says we can do it all alone—at the expense of our mental health, our relationships, and the land—especially in the world of business and entrepreneurship.

For sure, there is no entrepreneurial success story without the individual who makes it all happen. But this narrative only tells half the story. The other half—which is to say, the secret to actually making it in the hustle—is that we are being uplifted while also uplifting others. We exist in community, and we depend upon each other.

Each of the individuals in the pages to follow honors the fact that they have been uplifted—by their cultural heritage, family, community, and even their greatest failures and shame. Tammy Cho (Chapter 16), community leader and cofounder of nonprofit Hate Is A Virus, was uplifted by her parents working from five in the morning to midnight every day for nineteen years to give her and her sister a better future—and she uplifts them in turn when she sells her tech company at age twenty-one. Sahra Nguyen (Chapter 5), founder of Nguyen Coffee Supply, was uplifted by a knowledge of her own history and the youth organizers that shaped her activism. Today, she is uplifting robusta coffee growers in Vietnam, the people along her supply chain, and the land of her home country itself. Jason Wang and Shawn Tsao (Chapter 4), cofounders of the food delivery app Caviar that sold for over $100 million two years after its founding, were uplifted by their friendship with each other and their three other cofounders through the lowest of times.

In other words, the path to success is about as unique to each individual as their very fingerprints, and the unifying factor is not some productivity tip, trick, or tactic touted by the latest who's who. Instead, it is the energy we keep flowing between us, and the gratitude that blooms from recognizing it.

Why now?

As the notion of a "traditional" career breaks down and is being rewritten year after year in our increasingly uncertain times, the ingenuity and creativity central to hustle culture are only becoming more indispensable. For aspiring entrepreneurs of all backgrounds who pick up this book, we aim to provide honest insights from successful people. Where possible, we name the numbers behind the financial risks they took, get concrete about mental health challenges, and zoom in on the inner workings behind critical decisions, all while providing rich behind-the-scenes visuals from their journeys.

We hope to give readers a physical manifestation of the community in book form: a collection of voices like a friend cheering them on, whether they're starting a new business, reflecting on their entrepreneurship journeys of the past, or simply yearning for more in life.

Asian Americans are re-examining their identities, their stories, and their sense of community in the wake of a pandemic and a time when anti-Asian hate flipped once again from covert to overt. We wrote this book to help them feel less alone in their journey of self-exploration, whether they're starting an entrepreneurial venture or not.

And for people outside the Asian community seeking a greater understanding of the vast and diverse community that is Asian America, our book is one that aims to tell our stories as they are, for ourselves: beyond the gaze of dominant culture and in our full, complex humanity.

Part of telling our stories in their full, complex humanity also means that we free ourselves from being race representatives. It means that from our editorial perspective, we aren't grooming and censoring the stories entrusted to us by these 21 individuals so that they coalesce into a sweeping thesis about Asian Americans. Asians, people of color, and other communities on the margins are put into boxes all the time, so we aim to avoid doing that. Asian American and diasporic Asian experiences are infinitely diverse and laden with possibility—to represent them is impossible, and it's a burden that unnecessarily stops too many from telling their stories at all.

So, no matter who you are, we hope you enjoy these eighteen stories of twenty-one inspiring individuals in the first Asian Hustle Network book, *Uplifted*. As different as each story is, we hope that the underlying notes of the human condition in each will resonate with you and encourage you to look with curiosity and kindness upon your own story—what it looks like today, and how you'll continue to craft it.

Geena Chen
June 2021

Footnotes

[1] "Asian American Businesses, 1848 to 2015: Accommodation and Eclectic Innovation" by Lane Ryo Hirabayashi. Published October 2017 and accessible at nps.gov/articles/upload/07-Essay-7-Asian-American-Business.pdf.

[2] "The Untold Story of Chinese Restaurants in America" by Heather R. Lee. Published May 20, 2015 and accessible at scholars.org/brief/untold-story-chinese-restaurants-america.

About Asian Hustle Network

Asian Hustle Network comprises over one hundred thousand Asian-identifying people worldwide who form community around chasing their dreams and who deepen their relationships to their identities and communities while doing so. Far from being limited to stories about hustling for income, fame, or glory, our members have shared thousands of anecdotes over the past year that uncover the many sides of hustling that make life worthwhile: as a way to explore one's values, identity, passion, and community, as well as overcoming odds when popular opinion is stacked against them. In its first year of existence as both an online and in-person community, we learned—through celebrating each other's successes, connecting each other to greater resources and assistance, and challenging each other to grow—that caring for one another is the only thing that makes abundance real.

Bryan Pham & Maggie Chui,
Cofounders of Asian Hustle Network
June 2021

CHAPTER 01

DONUT PRINCESS

The story of *Mayly Tao*, the *Donut Princess*, who continues her great-uncle Ted Ngoy's Cambodian American donut shop legacy

INTRO   Mayly Tao spent her childhood working in her parents' humble donut shop, one of hundreds dotting LA's street corners. Every weekend starting at five in the morning, Mayly would be mixing batter and frying dough, anticipating her future as a TV news reporter. Never did she think that her degree in communications from UCSD would land her back in DK's Donuts and Bakery in Santa Monica, launching innovations that would rock the donut world.

   The "DK" in DK's Donuts stands for "Donut King"— her great-uncle Ted. Ted Ngoy, called Uncle Ted in the story, immigrated to the US with his wife, Christy, and their three kids as Cambodian Genocide refugees in 1975, following President Gerald Ford's signing of the Indochina Migration and Refugee Assistance Act. This was a watershed immigration policy that funded the arrival of over two hundred thousand Vietnamese, Cambodian, Lao, and Hmong people to the US over two years.

After Ted spent a year working nearly twenty-four hours a day as a janitor, gas station attendant, electronics salesperson, and trainee at California's then-largest donut franchise, he opened his first donut shop. A year later, he bought another—and then another. By the early 1990s, California had become home to over 2,400 Cambodian-owned donut shops with a presence so strong that Massachusetts-based chain Dunkin' Donuts gave up on expanding into California. As Ted grew his donut dominion, he sponsored the journeys of over one hundred Cambodian refugee families to the US. He paid their airfare, housed them, taught them to bake and run payroll, and leased his shops to them.

Today, 80 to 90 percent of California's independent donut shops are owned by Cambodians who used Uncle Ted's lessons to make a living in a new country. Mayly's family's is one of them.

My grandma and I slept in the same room until I turned sixteen. She used to watch wrestling in bed and then snore until the roof came off. She embodied comfort to me, though she never hugged me or said "I love you." Instead, like so many other Asian grandparents, her signature phrase was "Did you eat yet?"

The kitchen was her sanctum. "No helping out," she would say as she shooed me away. "If you learn this, then you'll have to do it. Go play!"

From the doorway, I would peek at her as she sat cross-legged on the floor, grinding Cambodian and Chinese herbs in her black mortar. Then she would stand up to taste her broth on the stove with a wooden ladle, add a pinch of something, and taste it again. Vegetables soaked in the sink; she peeled each leaf one by one off its stem, chopped, and stir fried.

She cooked a traditional Teochew pork bone broth soup for seven hours. She simmered potatoes, Cambodian eggplant, and fall-off-the-bone chicken thighs into a curry for three hours. She

DONUT PRINCESS 29

Mayly Tao

The idea to create LA's first Donut Bouquet was based on my own preference for receiving customized and delicious gifts.

stir-fried ong choy with ground pork and served a side of bitter melon pork soup. Every day was a feast for the whole family. In the mornings, she woke before me to make a fresh noodle or rice dish, and she watched me eat before school.

She gave me immense comfort in the endless variety of her food. That's the same feeling I knew I wanted to give to others—the same feeling of home.

. . .

My grandparents immigrated to Cambodia from Southern China with my mom and her six siblings, in search of greater opportunities. But in 1975, the Khmer Rouge took over and forced thousands of families like mine out of their homes by gunpoint and into countryside concentration camps. In the four years to follow, the Khmer Rouge killed over two million Cambodian people—a quarter of the population—while forcing others to work the land under constant threat of punishment. My mom and her family eventually escaped the concentration camps through jungles laden with bombs and bodies. They hid until the war ended in 1979.

By that time, Cambodian refugees only needed the name, address, and phone number of a sponsor to gain entry into the US. Sponsored by her sister's ex-husband, my mom arrived in San Francisco with six siblings and her parents. There, she earned a penny for every item she sewed as a seamstress, while her siblings worked other jobs. Over several years, they lived seven people to a room and pooled their savings to purchase their own donut shop in LA: DK's Donuts, owned by Ted Ngoy's family.

In those same years, Ted had sponsored his nephew—my dad—to come over from Cambodia. After climbing into Uncle Ted's passenger seat in the LAX parking lot, my dad swiveled his neck to locate the unfamiliar, sweet smell: stacks and stacks of fresh maple bars in the backseat, the first American donuts he'd ever seen. Uncle Ted was in his prime of building his donut empire, teaching fellow refugees his business system, and leasing his shops out. With Uncle Ted's training over the next few months, my dad learned to bake and to run his own shop.

Arranged marriages were still common back then, and word reached Uncle Ted that "a very hardworking, trustworthy, and beautiful woman" had begun working at one of his shops. Uncle Ted drove my dad three hours out of LA just to meet her. Within fifteen minutes of their first meeting, Uncle Ted and my dad went to my grandpa's house to ask for my mom's hand in marriage. My mom and dad married shortly after and ran DK's Donuts together from 1981 until their divorce in 2006.

"She gave me immense comfort in the endless variety of her food. That's the same feeling I knew I wanted to give to others—the same feeling of home."

My mom has stood by me every step of the way, demonstrating her beauty from the inside and savvy business ideas. We are the perfect duo.

My parents are the hardest workers I've ever known. My dad woke up at two in the morning to bake, and he worked twelve hours straight. My mom started at four in the morning and didn't finish work until ten at night—she worked at both DK's and a Chinese restaurant she owned next door.

They were strict with me: no bad grades at my private Catholic high school, no hanging out with friends, no wearing makeup—and no showing emotion, especially crying. They taught me from a young age to speak with customers, buy supplies at Costco, and pay bills. Unless I spoke Teochew to my mom, she wouldn't answer. I spent the Christmas holidays alone, even though my birthday is December 25. Our lives revolved around business.

. . .

My parents are Buddhists, believing in a cycle of karma and contribution. Seeing them practice these principles throughout my life, I wanted to be a teacher or social worker when I grew up. But my parents urged me to explore professions that paid better, such as TV news reporting. I took their advice to heart and studied communications at UC San Diego for four years, making the two-hour drive home every weekend to help my parents at the shop.

After graduating and completing a news station internship that I hated, I realized that I had no passion for news reporting. I wasn't used to the lack of creative freedom, the dominance of network ratings over every decision, and the world of approvals, when things could get done much quicker in a smaller organization.

Around the same time, I returned home to visit and noticed how much my mom had aged. My older brother was back helping at the shop, and my dad had returned to Thailand after my parents' divorce. For the first time, my mom looked me in my eyes and asked, "Can you come back and help?"

When I returned to the shop in 2013, my soul felt defeated. My parents had worked their entire lives to give me the best education possible so I could explore other occupations—yet here I was, back at square one. I felt like I'd wasted four whole years and so much money working toward something I wasn't passionate about. Yet, I knew that if I was going to dedicate my life to something, it needed to have meaning. Being a news reporter

"For the first time, my mom looked me in my eyes and asked, 'Can you come back and help?'"

I'm proud to bring my family's stories to light and to share incredible experiences together. My mom and I return to Cambodia often to give back to the community there.

"In 2013, DK's Donuts resembled every other LA donut shop: slightly janky, with an old-school sign, a customer base of early-morning regulars who worked in hospitals and auto shops and schools, and a limited menu—the wildest products being apple fritters, cinnamon rolls, and bear claws. But, looking around, I also saw cheery walls, loads of family charm, and bright rows of donuts that our loyal customers had loved for decades.

'This is such a cool place,' I said. 'People need to know about it.'"

This store has been here for 40 years, and my family's legacy will live on forever.

wouldn't be fulfilling for me . . . but building an empire in honor of my parents definitely sounded more appetizing.

In 2013, DK's Donuts resembled every other LA donut shop: slightly janky, with an old-school sign, a customer base of early-morning regulars who worked in hospitals and auto shops and schools, and a limited menu—the wildest products being apple fritters, cinnamon rolls, and bear claws. But, looking around, I also saw cheery walls, loads of family charm, and bright rows of donuts that our loyal customers had loved for decades.

"This is such a cool place," I said. "People need to know about it."

I came up with three strategic pillars for my new mission. First, I was going to use everything I'd learned from college and studying abroad to upgrade the shop. Second, I wanted to leverage an unlimited reach through modern technology and tell everyone about DK's Donuts, aka "Donut Heaven"—almost like the Disneyland of Donuts. And finally, I wanted to make my family proud, while being my full self.

Working in the marketing and PR department at UCSD, I learned the importance of storytelling. I instantly commissioned someone to design a logo that would set us apart from other donut shops: a hot-pink donut with sprinkles, which felt universal, playful, and recognizable across languages, cultures, and nationalities.

At the time, I didn't use my parents' story as a focal point of my narrative—that was something I discovered later. I always stressed the quality of the donuts and prided myself on giving visitors an impeccable experience. Working between eight and twenty hours a day, I channeled my grandma's hospitality in every donut I served.

I made T-shirts, rebranded our donut boxes and store signage, and created a social media community of donut lovers through Instagram and Facebook. Since we were a small business, I never had a budget for marketing, so I had to get creative. When I created *@dksdonuts* on Instagram, I paired iPhone photography with relatable captions about getting up before sunrise, craving donuts at midnight, and sharing events that bigger brands and corporate teams invited us to celebrate.

I researched trends in the food industry and understood that experiential retail was the future. We needed to make something that would be "the first and only in LA." By coincidence, one of our regulars mentioned a new pastry that had taken New York by storm—a combination croissant and donut, or Cronut. New Yorkers were standing in line for hours to try it, or paying a hundred dollars to have it delivered.

I wanted DK's to be the first to bring the Cronut to LA, so I approached my mom and said, "Look, there's this pastry in New York that I think we can do even better. Let's figure out the recipe together."

She looked at me. "No. Hard no."

The next day, even though I'd never tasted an actual Cronut, I tried to create my own recipe in the kitchen. After my mom saw what I was doing, she rolled up her sleeves and upgraded my creation. Her version tasted irresistible, and I knew others would love it. We named it the DKronut (pronounced "d'Kronut") and decided on three flavors: glazed, house cream, and Nutella. For the next two weeks, we placed the DKronuts on the top shelf next to our bestsellers, and we waited.

We sold a paltry ten a day in the first few days. So, I started hyping it to all my regulars. "This pastry is really, really tasty. It has layers like a croissant, but it's doughy like a donut. You *have* to try it!"

Some did try their first DKronut and liked it, but they said, "Five dollars? Is this made of gold?" (At that time, our donuts cost between one and three dollars.)

My mom was losing patience with this experiment. "If we don't sell out a full tray in one day after three weeks, we'll have to stop making it."

How could I tell more people that we had this pastry? It had all the buzzwords: *first in LA, croissant donut, family-owned.*

I started by emailing a few of my favorite publications. To my surprise, a writer at Thrillist wrote back. We arranged a time for him to pick up a box of croissant donuts.

"Hey, Mom," I said, "I've got this really special person coming in later. Can you please pack six for him? And don't charge him."

". . . Don't charge him?"

"No, Mom, it's fine. He works at Thrillist. Let's have him try it and see what he thinks. Maybe he'll like it, and maybe he'll write about it."

That weekend, I went away and didn't get my hopes up. But when I arrived home at ten o'clock on Sunday night, his article had come out: "Attention, everyone: Cronuts are now in Santa Monica."

. . .

The next day, I started work at four in the morning. By five, the phone began ringing. "Do you have the croissant donut? We'd like a dozen."

Then another call. "We heard you have the Cronut. We want two dozen."

Pretty soon, we were drowning in orders, and the phone was still ringing. By seven, we had lost control. People were lined up outside, waiting two hours for their Cronut high.

My mom and I went into overdrive. Because the croissant donut takes a few days to make—the dough needs time to rise, and then you have to cut, fry, bake, garnish, and serve—we hired more people and streamlined production. Still, for the next two years, we worked twenty-hour days to keep up with demand.

Despite the grueling hours, my mom always had a giant bowl of noodles or rice ready for me at lunchtime so that we could eat quickly and return to the customers waiting outside. In that time, we met celebrities, journalists, and reporters I never thought I'd meet. We were featured in *USA Today* and *Food and Wine*, and we were even on BBC. We expanded our DKronut selection from three to twenty-five flavors, including Thai tea, green tea, cookie crumble, blueberry, and maple bacon. People freaked out about the last one: "Bacon on a donut?!"

Then, we received a letter from Dominique Ansel, the creator of the Cronut. He had trademarked the name, and he was unhappy about our use of "DKronut."

"Oh my god, a cease and desist from Dominique Ansel Group. What are we going to do?" I asked my mom and my brother. "We didn't steal anything from them. We should just change the name."

"You should call it Mayly's Donut!" my mom suggested.

"No, Mom. Nobody knows how to spell my name in the first place . . . No, no."

We decided to rename it the Double Decker O-Nut (O-Nut for short) and resolved the drama. After the O-Nut, we launched the Wow-Nut: half waffle, half donut, mixed in a cast-iron pan, deep fried, and garnished like a donut. We formulated flavors like

"Today, we've invented over 120 items on our menu. When people enter DK's, I want them to feel like they entered Grandma's house—like they have a whole buffet of donuts to choose from."

This was the second time I was featured on the Food Network. You can see my mom's reaction in the back.

red velvet crumble with cream cheese frosting, ube Hawaiian coconut glaze with freshly toasted coconut, and fresh strawberries and cream. Each combined the crisp of a waffle with the softness of a donut.

No longer just an everyday stop for people going to work, DK's became a standalone destination and a treat for important milestones. I started creating special experiences through custom letter donuts, inspired by the rise in personalized gifts. After I visited Texas, I created Texas-size donuts, where I wanted to bring the "everything's bigger in Texas" motto to California. I also knew from my communications program the importance of visual arts, even if the art subject was a donut. I created Donut Princess Los Angeles, where I branded LA's first donut bouquet as a thoughtful, boutique gift for celebrations. I created more donuts that were photogenic or that played into food lovers' nostalgia: cereal donuts, Flamin' Hot Cheetos donuts, spicy donuts, the galaxy donut, and more.

Today, we've invented over 120 items on our menu. When people enter DK's, I want them to feel like they entered Grandma's house—like they have a whole buffet of donuts to choose from. Like they have been famished from their journey and can expect something paired with homemade and hospitality.

. . .

It's been eight years since I rejoined my family at DK's. I look back, and I still can't believe all that's happened. I was so committed to putting my head down and working that I couldn't notice the larger changes. Neither could my mom. "It was like a dream," she says now. "It felt like we hit the jackpot."

After I stepped into DK's, I tripled the sales. We changed our production to make our donuts fresher and more frequently. We expanded our services to delivery, overnight shipping, and on-demand online ordering, which blew up the business. We added another baker purely for our specialty donuts.

I grew our Instagram from zero followers to over eighty thousand followers worldwide, who drool over our creations and inquire about nationwide delivery. We brought more customers in, but we kept our regulars. We gave people a novel experience, which turned DK's into a foodie hot spot in LA—if you're west of the 405, I guarantee you've heard of us.

Customers tell me, "You changed this place. *Thank you.*"

Before, I'd deflect the compliments, but now I'm in a state of mind to acknowledge them—only because I feel like I've finally fulfilled my third strategic pillar: to make my family proud.

My dad started to message me things like "I'm so proud of you."

My mom would brag and say, "Mayly just came in and knew what she was doing. She's the best."

My family was the driving emotional force behind everything I did. They endured, sacrificed, and dedicated their lives to my brother and me, without ever complaining. I started thinking about my grandparents, who are of Teochew descent, who left Southern China to find a new opportunity in Cambodia. I thought about my parents and their horrific journey from Cambodia to the US. Now it's my time to give back to them—to give them things they've never had before. This is what motivates me to get up every day.

Connection with ancestors has always been in my blood because of my Teochew traditions. We celebrate death anniversaries and our own Day of the Dead, which we call Chinese Halloween.

When we celebrate Chinese New Year, we make the favorite foods of the dead, burn fake money and fake clothes, and pray. Every year, it hits differently. Every year, the ceremony brings me back to this fact: time is precious. This life ends, and then you go on to your next life.

My grandma who raised me is ninety-one today. She's the last grandparent I have. I think, *Dang, what would I give to be able to ask Grandpa a hundred questions—or even one?* Children of refugees don't inherit heirlooms, like a vase or jewelry passed down by a great-great-grandma, because in war-torn countries, those artifacts are currency for survival. My grandma gave up her last diamond earrings to the Vietnamese soldiers who took her family over the Cambodian border in a tank. It's up to us to find other ways to keep their stories alive.

Last year, as we began spending more time at home during the pandemic, I decided to fulfill my childhood dream of writing a book about my mom's journey fleeing the Khmer Rouge. I sat her down, a recorder on the table and a notepad in my hands, and began asking questions. I want to document my parents' stories so that I'll have an answer when my kids ask me what their grandma's life was like.

As for my uncle Ted Ngoy, his story has been told in a different way. Four years ago, several filmmakers expressed interest in Uncle Ted's story, and I connected Taiwanese American filmmaker Alice Gu with my family to create *The Donut King*, a documentary that chronicles Uncle Ted's personal journey and the power of his legacy through hundreds of other Cambodian donut shops in the US. In 2020, the film launched to critical acclaim and earned a 97 percent rating on Rotten Tomatoes.

I ended up visiting Uncle Ted in Cambodia—for a signing of his book, a segment we shot with VICE, and *The Donut King*. Being with Uncle Ted is like hanging out with a grandpa. He speaks English and Chinese, and offers so much wisdom. "You're the future of our family," he tells me. "You're carrying the torch. You make me so happy. You fill me up with love."

I see myself as the Donut Princess, inspired by Uncle Ted's legacy as the Donut King. I want to lift up others the way he did for many Cambodian refugees—by being a role model for the next generation, documenting my family's stories as they make peace with their traumas, and inspiring others to do the same.

"My family was the driving emotional force behind everything I did. They endured, sacrificed, and dedicated their lives to my brother and me, without ever complaining... Now it's my time to give back to them—to give them things they've never had before. This is what motivates me to get up every day."

Uncle Ted serves an inspiration to all—his life is one like a rollercoaster. He always tells me how proud I make the family as his great niece. We're riding in a TukTuk around Phnom Penh, Cambodia, where he currently resides.

Further information and resources:

- Check out the delectable creations from DK's Donuts and Bakery at *DKsDonuts.com* or on Instagram *@dksdonuts*.

- Read BBC's article on Ted Ngoy's rags-to-riches-to-rags-to-riches story, "The Donut King who went full circle—from rags to riches, twice," which was published in November 2020. You can find it at *bbc.com/news/stories-54546427*.

- Watch *The Donut King*, a documentary directed by Alice Gu. In addition to detailing Ted Ngoy's extraordinary personal journey, *The Donut King* is a tribute to the reverberating power of his legacy—one that continues to touch Mayly's and hundreds more Cambodian donut shop families across the US today.

CHAPTER 02

FORGIVENESS

The story of *Jason Wang*, the founder of *FreeWorld*, a tech-enabled nonprofit aimed at ending generational poverty and recidivism through asset ownership and high-wage careers for people with criminal records across the US.

CONTENT WARNING
Child abuse, sexual violence, suicidal ideation

INTRO When people first set their eyes on Jason Wang, they don't usually think, *That guy probably went to a maximum-security prison*. But he did. A gang member at age fifteen, Jason received a twelve-year sentence to a prison in Texas and spent the next three years in a repetitive, violent, and gray microcosm of the world he had known. Yet, as shrunken as his life had become, his inner world was expanding.

Under the facilitation of group therapists in their rehabilitation program, Jason and the other juveniles imprisoned with him took turns reenacting their crimes with props, and they wrote version after version of their life stories on paper. Over three years of this introspection, aided by hundreds of books and the unfailing love of his mother, Jason began to understand how a cycle of poverty and abuse had shaped his choices, which then shaped his story—a story that drives his life's purpose today.

I'll never forget the day I was arrested in front of my mom. Two squad cars pulled up from behind me, guns drawn, as I was making my way into our garage. My mom usually slept during the day, but we were making so much commotion that she came down to see what was going on.

"What are you doing? That's my son!" she screamed as the officer cuffed me.

They started to explain the charges they were filing against me.

"You must have the wrong kid. My son would *never* do that," she said. I had hated her so much up to that point, yet she had leapt to my defense at the drop of a hat. *She loves me*, I realized, for the first time I could remember. The officers pushed me into the back seat.

. . .

My parents came to the US as adults—my dad from China and my mom from Malaysia—searching for better opportunities. They met while working and getting paid under the table at Chinese restaurants in New York.

A lifelong entrepreneur, my dad dreamed of opening businesses. Unfortunately, he borrowed money from a Chinese gang to start a trucking business. A few months in, the business went under. It wasn't long before a few of the gang members found my dad, with photos of his family in their hands, and threatened to slaughter all of us unless he paid.

He decided to flee. From New Jersey to New York to Georgia, we lived in apartments that crawled with rats and rang with the sounds of sirens and gunshots at night. Wherever we moved, my parents would pick up restaurant jobs, until we ended up in Carroll, Iowa. By then, my dad had finally saved enough money to start his own Chinese restaurant. Starting from when I was five, my dad made me work in the restaurant from the end of the school day until my bedtime. During lulls, my mom would unfurl huge Chinese menus, write math problems on the back, and make me solve them.

We were some of the few people of color in Carroll, along with a Black family and a Mexican family. Not only did I get picked for being different at school, but I also suffered my dad's terrible temper at home. When he was angry, he would throw tables, chairs, and anything he could get his hands on. He chased me around the kitchen with a butcher knife and wanted to stab me. He tried to run me over with his car. He would often tell me, "You're good for nothing," "You'll never amount to anything," "You're not my son," and "I don't love you." When we had huge blizzards at fifteen degrees below zero in the Iowa winter, he would strip me down, kick me while I was on the floor, and then throw me naked into the snow. I was six, seven, eight years old at the time.

Because my mom never stuck up for me when my dad was abusing me, I grew up hating her. I loathed both of them so much that when I was six years old, I suspended myself out of our apartment window, two floors above our restaurant, knowing that if I killed myself in the restaurant's parking lot, my dad would lose business and make less money. He cared about money most, so that's how I could hurt him, right?

Me as a child, featured in a local newspaper.

One day, when I was eleven, my dad sprung a piece of news on my mom: "I've got a wife and three kids in China, and they're gonna come live with us starting tomorrow." Unbeknownst to us, he had been in an arranged marriage when he was eighteen. For the past twelve years, he had actually been working on sponsoring them to come to the US.

That day, my mom drove to the middle of the woods to kill herself. The only thing that stopped her was the thought of me growing up without a mother. She gritted her teeth, came back home, and lived with my dad's ex-wife, as well as his ex-wife's daughter and her husband, in our two-bedroom apartment.

The other family stayed in one bedroom, while my parents were in another. I lived in the living room, my grandma in the kitchen. A few months later, my mom filed for divorce and took my grandma and me to Texas to begin our new life. There, she got a minimum wage job moving boxes for fourteen hours a night.

By this point in my life, I hated the world. Angry, abused, and convinced that I was good for nothing, I thought, *Fuck it. I'm just gonna do whatever the hell I want.* At age thirteen, I joined a gang, and that led to me making a terrible decision.

At age fifteen, I committed aggravated robbery, a first-degree felony, and was arrested.

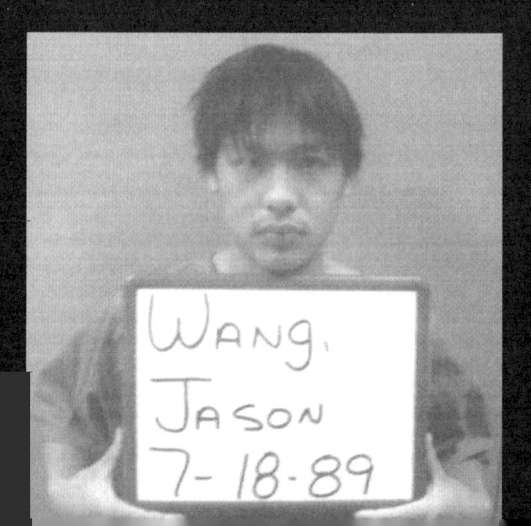

My mugshot when I was incarcerated at the age of 15.

...

My mom immediately took out her entire life savings of $10,000 to hire the best lawyer she could afford. He took her money and never returned her calls.

For two and a half months, I sat in a holding cell and awaited my court date.

Finally, the day came. In the courtroom, the judge looked down at me and said, "Jason, because of the seriousness of your offense, I'm going to sentence you to twelve years in prison."

All the feeling in my body floated away. My mom and my grandma wailed in the background, but nothing registered. I was in total shock. Later that night, though, as I lay down alone, I burst into tears. At age fifteen, twelve years felt like the rest of my life.

I arrived at a juvenile corrections facility called the Texas Youth Commission, the first Asian person there in ten years. The second I stepped in, I received a garbage bag with my toothbrush, sandals, bedsheets, pillow, and blanket. Then I went into the Pod.

The prison had housing built like warehouses, and in each warehouse there were four Pods, arranged two by two. Bunk beds lined all four walls for twenty-four people, although we were overcrowded to thirty sometimes. In the middle of the four Pods, facility staff would sit in a control room with one-sided glass.

This open-bay dormitory configuration is the most dangerous way to incarcerate people because you can't seal off the Pod's inhabitants from each other. Here were ten- to twenty-year-old kids with pent-up energy, who had gone through some traumatic shit and were furious at the world. As a result, we fought and rioted nearly every day—not because people in prison are predisposed to hurt each other, but because of the hopelessness induced by the harsh conditions, lack of programming, and corrupt correctional officers.

Meanwhile, my mom and grandma would travel fourteen hours every weekend to see me. My mom would finish her night

" Meanwhile, my mom and grandma would travel fourteen hours every weekend to see me. My mom would finish her night shift, drive in her minivan for as long as she could, pull over, and sleep in a bed in the back while my grandma served as a lookout. After sleeping for an hour or two, my mom would drive the rest of the way, just to see me for two hours. Then she would make the journey home."

Me visiting with my mom at the prison's education building.

8/20/05

Visitation with my mom and grandma while at Evins Regional Juvenile Facility.

10/21/06

shift, drive in her minivan for as long as she could, pull over, and sleep in a bed in the back while my grandma served as a lookout. After sleeping for an hour or two, my mom would drive the rest of the way, just to see me for two hours. Then she would make the journey home.

Every time she and my grandma came to visitation, they cried their eyes out. My mom used to say, "Even though *you're* physically in prison . . . mentally and emotionally, I'm in prison with you."

. . .

I knew that the key to my success in prison would be getting out of the Pod. Being in a room with thirty people who have nothing to do all day is gonna mean trouble. So, even though we were only allowed to have one job on campus, I sweet-talked my way into four. I cleaned the education building, worked in the kitchen, worked in the administration building, and mowed the grass on a riding lawnmower, all for twenty-five cents an hour.

When I wasn't working, I was reading. My mom sent me thick packets of mail every week. At first I thought they were from my homeboys or the girls I used to date. But instead, she was sending me math homework and books, with topics ranging from geology to the stock market to real estate to religion. Keeping me occupied with reading was her way of protecting me from trouble.

For three and a half years, I was that dude who read in the corner of the prison every day. I had fought and gained respect, and nobody screwed with me. Over three years, she curated and sent me hundreds of books like a personal librarian. I began asking her to print song lyrics and full-color photos of food, too.

Singing songs in my head and becoming my own radio, closing my eyes and tasting the food on the page—in the grey world of prison, how else do you recreate a sense of sanity?

Earning my GED.

Over time, I lobbied for the correctional officers to give me access to materials and a classroom in the prison. I started a GED program to teach others to read and do math, and I started a Bible study class on Sundays. Through the GED classes, I realized that the kids around me were hungry to learn. And on the yard, everybody would act super tough, but in the Bible study class, we were eventually singing hymns together at the top of our lungs.

Don't get me wrong though—this was a really shitty time. Everyone was pissed off, the whole place was corrupt, and the few who were released came right back. You know how in the movies they'll show characters crossing off days from a calendar? Yeah, don't do that. It makes time feel longer.

In 2006, a scandal broke out in the news. The world found out that not only were correctional officers abusing and sexually assaulting kids, but the whole system was extraordinarily corrupt. The state started holding public hearings to listen to guards and those imprisoned in the facility. Amazingly enough, they allowed me and six others to attend the hearings. Though we were shackled and in our jumpsuits, we went out in public for the first time to testify in front of the state Senate on national news.

A month later, I got transferred to a better facility only four hours away from my mom. I didn't serve the full twelve-year sentence in the end. In Texas, a unique law allows kids under eighteen who committed first-degree felonies to be released to supervision after a minimum of three years in prison, if they behave well.

I served the rest of my three and a half years. Then I entered into the free world.

> "As an eighteen-year-old newly out of prison, I would drive home from work with the windows down and the music blaring, and I would cry my eyes out. Driving a car, listening to music, feeling the wind through my hair—holy shit... I was free."

. . .

As an eighteen-year-old newly out of prison, I would drive home from work with the windows down and the music blaring, and I would cry my eyes out. Driving a car, listening to music, feeling the wind through my hair—holy shit... I was free.

I enrolled in UT Dallas and sat in the front row of every class. It blew my mind to see kids slacking off on Facebook in the back. My appreciation for life had magnified more than anyone else I saw around me, and I took advantage of everything I could. I got a full scholarship to school, worked two jobs, and used my savings to start my first businesses and buy homes to turn into investment properties and Airbnbs.

. . .

My second business, Byte Size Moments, was one of my biggest failures. Say you wanted to buy me a gift but couldn't deliver it in person. You could go to the Byte Size Moments website, pick a box of chocolates for me, and record a video to go along with it. Someone in a Byte Size Moments T-shirt would then hand-deliver the chocolates to my doorstep and play your video, all while wearing a concealed camera to record my reaction. We would then compile all the videos for both the giver and receiver.

The emotion was what drove me to believe we had a great product. We partnered with the military, and when overseas soldiers would send a teddy bear and a video to their families for Valentine's Day, the families on the other end would receive the gift dry-heave weeping. How often does a customer break down in tears of gratitude?

Yet, we could never make our revenue model work. We had high churn, because the second time anybody wearing a Byte Size Moments T-shirt arrives at your door, you know what to expect. And, of course, the secret recording aspect was weird in itself.

For two years, I put all the money I'd earned in management consulting and the stock market into the business. When our funds began approaching zero, I started pitching to angel investors in Texas—each of whom ushered me out the door when they found out about my criminal history. I went to Silicon Valley next, hoping that investors there might be more open minded.

I was so persistent in cold-calling and randomly showing up at venture capital firms that I would eventually land a meeting with a partner. But once I'd heard no two hundred times, my spirit just broke. *We don't actually have a business,* I realized, long overdue. *And worst of all, I don't know how to make payroll.*

Realizing that five people had essentially thrown away two years of their lives to help me chase my dream, with nothing to show for it, killed me inside. I turned to alcohol, I became suicidal, and I ended up homeless at one point. Ultimately, I found myself lying down in the street in front of my house in the middle of the night, crying my eyes out, and thinking about getting hit by a car or jumping off a bridge. The reason I'd held on to the failing business for so long was because its identity had become intertwined with mine—declaring the business a failure would be a public declaration that I was a failure, too.

But eventually, I moved through the stages of grief, from denial to acceptance, and shut it down.

I had lost everything. I had even sold all my possessions to pour the money into the business. But rather than go back into management consulting or another six-figure job that I hated, I decided to take another risk. I had nothing to lose.

With $36,000 in credit card debt, I moved to New York and took a fundraising job at a nonprofit that helped people with criminal histories. I fell in love with the work and never looked back. I don't give a shit about money anymore. All I care about is this: Am I doing what I've been put on earth to do? And that's helping people with criminal histories.

Three years later, with the help of Matt Mochary, Jason Green, and Andy Bromberg (our first Board of Directors), we founded FreeWorld. The board's generosity ensured that we had 3 years of funding lined up to make this dream come alive.

> "I had lost everything. I had even sold all my possessions to pour the money into the business. But rather than go back into management consulting or another six-figure job that I hated, I decided to take another risk. I had nothing to lose."

. . .

Given a choice between a job applicant with a record and one without, most companies will choose the person without a record. FreeWorld gives people with criminal histories access to high-wage careers in industries that are so short-staffed that they have no choice but to hire for skill alone.

There are over three and a half million trucking jobs available in the United States. We can train somebody to get their license, and therefore a job, within thirty days. Driving in a truck all day is unappealing for most people, but for our graduates, who have spent eleven years on average in prison, it's a chance to see the world. Within the first year, they make about $50,000. By year two, they're making $70,000. By year three, they can make $80,000. If they choose to buy their own truck and become owner-operators, they can make anywhere between $150,000 to $200,000. At every stage, these numbers represent a living wage and a path to breaking the cycle of poverty.

To avoid being dependent on philanthropic donations, FreeWorld operates an income share agreement, or ISA. If a person makes a certain minimum salary, they pay 10 percent over a set period of years. If they don't make the minimum, they don't pay a thing. It incentivizes us as well as them to continue doing well.

Since December 2019, we've been getting consistent payments every month, so we feel like we've hit product-market fit. Every FreeWorld graduate can pay for two or three future graduates. That means, for each new participant in the program, we can put a roof over their heads if they're homeless, provide them transportation through a partnership with Lyft, collect any missing identification documents for them, and provide job training and job placements for three years.

But the real power behind FreeWorld is teaching our graduates how to build wealth. Within six months, we get them from an average credit score of 467 up to 697. If they have student loans, restitution, child support, or any debts that have gone to collections, we wipe them out. We work to make them whole and, more radically, help them become wealthy.

In the US, the average Black family has a total net worth of $17,000, while the average white family has a net worth of $171,000. Most of our graduates are Black and Brown. We're helping them learn to budget and invest, purchase a first home, and pass wealth on to their kids. That's what's most exciting for us.

. . .

For a long time, I held immense guilt and sadness when I thought about all the people I hurt. No matter what I do in life, I know that I can never pay it back. I have thought about reaching out to my past victims and apologizing, either through writing a letter or meeting with them in person. . . but I ended up choosing not to.

Because I'm scared.

I'm scared that I might be reopening a wound that has scabbed over in the past twelve years. Maybe they've moved on. Maybe they'll be angry. Maybe they'll want to do something to me and my family in retribution.

It's been a long journey, but over time, I've learned about forgiveness, closure, and moving on in life. I can't change the past, but that knowledge fuels me to do the work that I do today. And part of that work is simply being honest about my story.

My story is imprinted in everything I do. If people can empathize with it, maybe they'll look at others with criminal histories with a bit more empathy than they do today, too.

Me visiting a prison through a program called Defy Ventures.

In the two years since FreeWorld's founding, Jason has helped 120 people with felony records get jobs in the trucking industry, with a median salary between $50,000 and $80,000. They have a 100 percent employment rate, and zero returning to prison so far. Further information and resources:

- To support Jason's work at FreeWorld, check out *JoinFreeWorld.com*.

- To hear Jason tell his story in his own voice, we love his interview on episode 22 of the Rock the Boat podcast titled "Jason Wang, from Convict to CEO." You can listen to it at *GoRockTheBoat.com*.

- The median wealth statistic comes from a Brookings study, "Examining the Black-white wealth gap," by Kriston McIntosh, Emily Moss, Ryan Nunn, and Jay Shambaugh, published on February 27, 2020. You can read about the study at *brookings.edu/blog/up-front/2020/02/27/examining-the-black-white-wealth-gap*.

CHAPTER 03

HOW I BECAME A MEMELORD

The story of *Tai Tran*,
founder of *Asians Never Die*

INTRO   What does it mean, culturally, to be Asian, anyway? It's not like there's an Asian language, Asian flag, or "Asian food"—despite many restaurants claiming to serve it. And given that Asia is really a swath of landmasses and oceans comprising over forty-eight countries, countless ethnic and religious groups, and more than half the world's population, defining the "Asian" cultural experience with any semblance of seriousness feels impossible.

Maybe that's why Tai Tran does it by making memes.

The online Facebook and Instagram community called Asians Never Die started as Tai's hobby meme account, where he documented the struggles of squeezing the Sriracha from a near-empty bottle, drying reused Ziploc bags on the dish rack, or growing up with haircuts shaped by his mother's mixing bowls. But the account soon became a global community of people adding their own humorous and imperfect takes on what it means to be Asian. Through stories of lived experiences, the notoriously heterogeneous Asian community came closer to understanding its own staggering diversity—and unity—one involuntary chuckle at a time.

But before he became a meme mogul with over a million followers, Tai struggled to make sense of what it meant to be Asian in America . . .

My parents came to the US as refugees from war-torn Vietnam and settled in San Jose, California. Our family of six crammed into a small, roach-infested two-bedroom, surviving through government welfare programs like food stamps and Section 8. I wore thrifted clothes and Payless shoes to school, sticking out among the other kids with their nice JanSport backpacks and Nikes—so being Asian on top of that only seemed to add to my struggles.

The non-Asian kids from the neighborhood would bully us and shout slurs at us just because we were Asian. We looked different and ate different food, and my parents barely spoke English. But I was born in the US, so why was I being treated like a foreigner? Other kids would call me Tie, Tay, Tea, Tang, and Ching Chong as they pulled their eyelids up in a slant. "Look, it's Tie and Chin!" they would say about me and my best friend Chinh, while they put their fists around an imaginary tie knot and pulled it up to their chins.

Man, how come I can't have a cool name like Jason or Brad or Chad? I thought. I felt embarrassed when teachers had a hard time pronouncing my name during roll call.

I would look to TV shows and movies to learn about what it meant to be American. That's where I saw white families celebrating Thanksgiving, unwrapping beautiful gifts, and decorating Christmas trees, living a classically American life.

But how come we ate pork fried rice instead of turkey for Thanksgiving? Or wrapped our remote controls in saran wrap instead of letting them be? I simply wanted to fit in with what I thought was American—not the Long Duk Dong, nerdy, emasculated, uncool Asians represented on TV.

Even in my Asian family, I felt like an outcast. Not only am I super energetic and a middle child—the neglected ones, I see you!—but I'm also left-handed. About 10 percent of the world is left-handed, but in my parents' Chinese and Vietnamese cultures, left-handedness is unacceptable. It even went as far as my mom sitting next to me and trying to convert me, forcing me to write with my right hand and hitting my left hand anytime I messed up, saying "Left hand is bad!"

In elementary school, as parent-teacher conferences approached, I anxiously imagined my teachers shaking their heads and reinforcing my parents' worst nightmares, saying, "Tai is such a bad student." I didn't feel like I was a bad student. Sure, it took me hours to read a couple of pages, and I was never booksmart, but mostly, I just couldn't sit still and put my head down. I always wanted to move around the classroom, entertain others, and make funny faces like I'd been practicing in the mirror after my hero Jim Carrey.

I was never the best-looking guy, or the coolest, or the most gangster—but I knew that people would like me and accept me if I could make them laugh. More than anything else, and even to this day, I wanted to feel accepted for who I really was.

Everything changed once I started middle school. This was the '90s in the Bay Area: the subculture identity of AZN Pride was just forming. Asian youth had their own style, fashion, lingo, and a sense of community around it all. Kids wore big baggy pants, rocked jade necklace Buddhas, had slicked-back hair dyed bleach blond, or grew out their bangs. Tommy Hilfiger, Nautica, and Polo were all the rage at that time, though my parents couldn't afford them. The Asian community was big into boba life, the car-tuning world, and raving. And with AIM, Yahoo! Messenger, and Asian Avenue on the rise, Asians were connecting to online communities around the world.

Unlike my elementary school, which was majority Hispanic, my middle school was 40 percent Asian. And from the first day, I started hearing about this cool clique called "the Asian Wall."

A red brick wall outside our middle school, the Asian Wall was the everyday gathering spot of forty to sixty of us Asian teens. During school, we would get picked on because we were smaller and outnumbered, but at the Asian Wall, nobody would mess with us.

Messing with one of us meant messing with all of us—that's what emboldened us to be ourselves. For the first time, I felt like it was cool to be Asian, like we are dope, too.

By high school, the Asian Wall had morphed into "Asia." Asia was one of many sets of otherwise ordinary picnic benches that were nevertheless racialized in absurd ways by us high schoolers. Walking along the side of the building, you could pass through "Asia," "Africa," "Mexico," and "The Islands." A circle of over a hundred Asians gathered around Asia every day: you had your ABCs, your fresh ones from overseas, your mixed ones, and your token Black and white friends who felt more connected with Asian culture than their own. The mixture of Asians included Chinese, Vietnamese, Filipinos, and Cambodians. At lunch, we hung out in a big circle, talked about cars and girls, and looked at the latest *Import Tuner* and *Turbo* magazines. We would sneak into the bathroom and smoke cigarettes, thinking we were the coolest.

Being a cool Asian back then was all about trying to be a badass with don't-F-with-me energy. I had friends who joined Asian gangs, which were plentiful in the '90s and early 2000s. They got into fights, sold drugs, hung out at coffee shops, and stole car parts, but thankfully, my parents swayed me away from that life. Or they whooped my butt so much that I was afraid of doing things that would upset them.

Through it all, we grew to appreciate a sense of shared culture. When you came to hang out at my house, your shoes would be off without me asking. When you met my parents, you knew to say hello and be respectful. With people who were culturally different, I wouldn't mind explaining these things, because bridging cultures together is what the US is all about. But with my Asian friends, we never had to explain our unspoken rules. That made our friendships easier, and I started feeling safe. For the first time, I didn't need to change myself to be part of the majority culture.

> "For the first time, I felt like it was cool to be Asian, like we are dope, too."

. . .

When high school graduation rolled around, Asia disbanded. I left home for the first time to go to UC Riverside, six hours south in California. It was the only school that accepted me due to my lower-than-stellar academic performance. I joined an Asian fraternity, made new friends, and did what a normal college student did: partied, gained new experiences, and almost got kicked out of school twice.

When I barely graduated with a business economics degree four years later, with high hopes of pursuing my dream job and making a stable income to support my family, the economic recession of 2008 put a stop to those dreams. It seemed like everybody around me was losing their jobs and homes. I moved back in with my parents and took the only odd jobs I could find: selling cars at three different dealerships, and even selling vitamins through network marketing for a few months.

Times were terrible. I finally had the college degree that my parents thought would solve all our financial problems with the promise of a stable job. While my friends who went to prestigious schools like UC Davis, UC Berkeley, and UCLA started prestigious jobs at Facebook, Google, and Apple . . .

"I sell cars," I admitted in countless social settings over the next year and a half.

"He sells cars," my parents lamented to their friends, wishing it wasn't so, yet unable to advise me.

Finally, nearly two years after graduation, I joined a tiny startup: a platform called MyTime, which was like Yelp, where you could read reviews and book appointments with hair stylists or dog walkers. Every day, I commuted almost two hours each way from San Jose to San Francisco for less than $30,000 a year. As a college graduate in the Bay Area with a few years of sales experience, that was nothing to brag about—but I knew I needed to get out of the world I was in and take a chance on something that would lead me down a better path.

Half a year later, I started working at a different startup closer to home, which made me much happier. I worked with one of my fraternity brothers and even got to go to Vietnam for the first time. But three years later, in 2016, the company went belly-up. I was unemployed. Again.

In the two years prior, I'd started dabbling on YouTube and making funny videos here and there, after being inspired by other Asian YouTubers entertaining us with their skits and videos. But because I lacked focus and a support circle, I gave up on it quickly. A few years later, the phenomenon known as memes started to take over the social media world—a format that turned photos and captions into quick comedy bits that friends would share with each other. Memes floated around Reddit, Facebook, and Instagram, but not many of them were Asian-centric.

Why don't I create memes focused on Asian culture, something that our community can relate with? I thought. That's when the idea sparked. I remember the moment vividly: on January 2, 2016, while lying in my bed on a Saturday morning after the New

Year, I created an Instagram page called "Asians Never Die." A few swipes of my thumb later, I had posted my first meme.

I don't remember my first meme, but I remember the first one that went viral: the four types of Asian boyfriends. Yes, it's a blanket statement—I know not all guys are like this! But to me, that's what comedy is all about: Are the blanket statements and stereotypes relatable? Can they start a more meaningful conversation?

I simply searched "Asian guys" in Google Images, grabbed four random photos, and captioned them. There was the gangster with tattoos and a shaved head, the K-pop guy who looked like the perfect oppa, the artsy and creative guy, and the comedy guy, which was a picture of the comedian David So. I consider myself this last type: not very handsome, but an awesome personality! As soon as I posted it on Instagram, people started tagging

"'I sell cars,' I admitted in countless social settings over the next year and a half.

'He sells cars,' my parents lamented to their friends, wishing it wasn't so, yet unable to advise me."

Where Asian parents said they found you..

When I was acting up as a child, my parents would tell me that they found me in the trash can and I wasn't really their kid. I guess in their frustration, they used it as a way to make me feel guilty and to learn from my bad behavior.

"As Asian Americans, we don't see our stories told in the mainstream, but there are so many interesting things to discover about how we grew up.

We're this in-between of Eastern and Western culture, with unique upbringings as immigrant refugees. I wanted to capture the humorous sides of our childhood."

Are they called egg rolls? Spring rolls? Lumpia? Who cares, it ain't a party without a tray of these.

The Asian party starter pack. You have to have karaoke and some gambling involved.

their friends in the comments. "You're the oppa!" "You're the gangster!" The thread kept growing until it received thousands of likes and comments. So of course, I began creating "the four types of Asian girlfriends" next.

I posted memes five to six times a day in the beginning.

My wife would turn over in bed at three in the morning and ask, "What the hell are you doing?"

"I'm still making memes!" I would respond with my phone screen on my face in the pitch black.

When I make a meme, I take inspiration from everyday life, recalling my own memories or observing my friends and family. Say I go to a family party, and my drunk uncle is dancing awkwardly and singing his ass off in karaoke. That's a meme. I take a picture of him, and later in bed in the middle of the night, I'm arranging it next to other objects in an app called PhotoGrid and slapping on a caption, whether it be an Asian family party starter pack—those were big in 2016—or simply "Drunk uncle karaoking: must-have at party."

My formula has never changed. If it makes *me* laugh or makes *me* feel some type of way, then I believe others will relate, too. If *I* don't find something funny, I don't post it, no matter what. The success of Asians Never Die hinges on wrapping emotion and memory in picture or video form, and making it relatable enough for people to share with their circle of friends.

"Dude, that's so funny. *My* family grew up wrapping the remote control!"

"*My* family grew up reusing Walmart bags as trash bags!"

"I got spanked with slippers, too!"

As Asian Americans, we don't see our stories told in the mainstream, but there are so many interesting things to discover about how we grew up. We're this in-between of Eastern and Western culture, with unique upbringings as immigrant refugees. I wanted to capture the humorous sides of our childhood.

Why the name "Asians Never Die"? On the surface, the name is a nod to the saying "Asian don't raisin," which is a stereotype that Asians look way younger than they actually are. But the phrase "Asians Never Die" is also about never forgetting your culture and roots and where your ancestors came from. For example, Vietnamese is my second language—I speak it at a conversational level. I sometimes think, *Will my son even speak Vietnamese? Will he want to learn? How do I teach him if my Vietnamese is elementary?* I've also wondered, *Will my son know how to use chopsticks? Or will he eat pho with a fork and spoon? Will he even want to identify as Asian? What does being Asian even mean?*

I and many others had struggled with our upbringing as Asians trying to fit into a Western world—to be accepted by a culture that didn't want to accept us. So, we formed our own identity: Asian American. And now, the physical bubble of Asian Americans I had in middle school and high school has morphed into a digital bubble that's over 400,000 strong on Instagram and over one million strong on Facebook.

> "All of us squat, right? There's the kimchi squat, for people who squat while making kimchi, or old Asian men who squat and smoke cigarettes."

...

When I first started Asians Never Die, it was purely my comedic outlet to entertain my friends. Nine months after I started the page, I took a full-time job to support myself financially, as making memes wasn't going to pay the bills.

I was back to the corporate grind. From eight in the morning to six at night, I worked my full-time job, but as soon as the work day ended, I was working on my passion of entertaining people online. I was swiping my thumb furiously on BART, making memes, posting at least once or twice a day, and commenting back and forth until midnight. Engaging with the community was key to growing the page, which went from a thousand followers to five thousand, then a hundred thousand. I was elated, feeling like I was finally onto something.

I never planned for it to become my full-time thing. But after the first year, Asian businesses started noticing our growth and messaging us about collaborations and sponsorships. They were talking about paying me to spread the word about their products and services.

"What?" I yelped. I didn't even understand what a sponsored post was back then. "Babe, look at this message," I said, showing it to my wife.

The first sponsored post was for twenty-five dollars—far from a life-changing amount of money. But it was the catalyst that would change Asians Never Die from a personal passion project into something I could do full time without having to grind it out at a traditional job.

On my birthday, my wife gifted me a custom-printed Asians Never Die T-shirt. Simple as it was, white text on a black tee, I had never thought to make one myself.

I posted a photo on our Facebook and Instagram, and the comments erupted. "Yo, that's so cool. I want one!" "Do you have it in small? Do you have sizes for women?" "Do you have a hoodie version?"

"This is just a shirt that my wife commissioned," I typed back.

"Yeah, well, you should sell it," they responded.

I made a small run of twenty-five shirts, created a post, and sold out within twenty-four hours. *Holy shit*, I thought. *People want to buy shirts from me?*

Then we made another hundred and sold out in two days. In the beginning, I didn't know anything about e-commerce, but I learned along the way, from Shopify to shipping. Our merchandise operation started in my bedroom closet, where I hung our first tees in a neat row according to size. It steadily grew into my garage, then my dad's house, then a small office. Merchandise

How the merch journey began. My wife gave me a screen printed shirt for my birthday that read "Asians Never Die."

> "Going from a cushy, six-figure tech job to . . . memes? How long would that last?"

My dad helping to package up our merch and ship it to our customers. It's a family affair.

became such a big part of our company that we outgrew even that and moved into a 1,500 square foot warehouse office.

Our most popular merch is a play on the brand Anti Social Social Club, which we parodied as Asian Squat Social Club. Asian Squat is something a lot of people resonate with. All of us squat, right? There's the kimchi squat, for people who squat while making kimchi, or old Asian men who squat and smoke cigarettes. Once again, I made a small batch, posted it, and boom! That's been our hottest seller since day one. Because of that design, I created another page called Asian Squat Social Club, thinking it would be funny if people sent me photos to repost of them squatting all around the world in the merch. We have 17,000 followers in that club now, with people wearing our gear and squatting in Tulum, Taipei, Tasmania . . . I've shipped them to every continent—even to an address in the North Pole! (Santa?)

Our merch, advertising, and sponsorships grew until one day, my side income was identical to my full-time income. It was get-

Asian Squat Social Club

It's a lifestyle. One of our most popular designs that created a movement to Asian Squat around the world.

ting more difficult to juggle a full-time job, a full-time business, and a full-time wife.

"Why don't you just quit your job and do Asians Never Die full-time?" my wife suggested after two years of me trying to balance both.

Going from a cushy, six-figure tech job to . . . memes? How long would that last? Would the revenue be stable enough for me to quit my job? What would my parents think? I was terrified even entertaining the idea—but I said, "Fuck it. What do I have to lose? I can always find a job."

I took the leap of faith and submitted my resignation letter. It was the best decision I've made.

. . .

In this new digital media industry, monetization can come from brand sponsors, ad sponsors, companies you work with directly, products you can sell, or even peer-to-peer platforms such as Patreon. But there is no stable paycheck. You can make a lot one month and nothing the next month. Even though I ran the company lean and paid myself a minimal salary for two years, I still spent many sleepless nights wondering if I needed to start driving for Uber or DoorDash to pay the lease and all the bills.

When I opened my first office in 2018, it was a small 350-square-foot place with me and one assistant. The next year, our apparel and content creation team outgrew that spot, and we moved into a 700-square-foot place. The next year, we relocated to a 1,500-square-foot office-warehouse. We built a studio to create content and loaded up on thousands of products, excited for our breakout year in 2020—and then COVID hit in March and shut everything down. That's when the panic set in. All the pop-up events we booked got canceled. All the content we planned was abruptly paused. Our online sales dropped dramatically because of people losing their jobs and not wanting to spend on unnecessary things. I also had a son who was due to come out the next month.

The fears of losing everything I built kept me up at night. These are the risks you take when you pursue the road less traveled.

With no investors or financial backing, we had invested everything we made back into the company to take it to the next level. I ultimately made the decision to close down our office, which we had just settled into, and go back to square one: my bedroom, where it all began. I packed everything, sold what we could, and moved our operations back home.

Through it all, I asked myself again and again, *Why did I start Asians Never Die?* The answer was to entertain and create a community that Asians around the world can go to and share a memory and a laugh, to know that there are others like us. To know that we should be proud to be Asian and to never forget our culture and roots while we create our own identity in this

"The fears of losing everything I built kept me up at night. These are the risks you take when you pursue the road less traveled."

Meeting one of my idols, Joe Jitsukawa from JK Films.
I watched his skits growing up in the mid 2000s when YouTube was starting. It was an honor to be a guest on his podcast.

new home. Asians Never Die is a museum of lived experiences, a platform that enables people to share more of their own stories and to continue the meaningful conversation around what it means to be Asian American.

From AZN Pride in the '90s to the evolution of the digital age of YouTube, Facebook, and Instagram in the 2000s, we're using these platforms to tell our stories—written by us, and acted with our faces. Finally, we are using our voices, and people are listening. We have found mainstream success in *Fresh Off the Boat*, *Crazy Rich Asians*, and *Minari*, and now we have our own Marvel superhero, Shang-Chi. I am excited to see the progress of our community. Where we go from here is still unknown, but I hope that Asians Never Die has been, and continues to be, a small part in pushing the Asian American movement forward.

Boba life.

The key to a girl's heart. Popcorn chicken and some boba milk tea.

Further information and resources:

- Visit Asians Never Die at *AsiansNeverDie.com* and on social media at @asiansneverdie.

CHAPTER 04

FORGED THROUGH FAILURE

The story of *Caviar*, one of the foundational food delivery startups that made it possible to order food other than cheap pizza in 2012, which is now owned by DoorDash

Part I: *Jason Wang*
Part II: *Shawn Tsao*

PART 1: JASON WANG

INTRO

If you're a young person today who's about to enter the job market, does the pinnacle of success sound like going to a good college, getting a stable job, paying off your loans, and retiring comfortably at sixty-five?

Probably not. Both the feasibility and the sway of that particular dream over young people's hearts went up in flames throughout the millennial generation's coming of age (the late '90s to now), and the new rules of career planning are still being rewritten.

Like so many of the entrepreneurs in this book, Jason Wang grew up in the heat of this culture shift for young entrants to corporate America. With Chinese immigrant parents who encouraged him to pursue a stable career in accounting, Jason nonetheless graduated right into the aftermath of the 2008 financial crisis and Occupy Wall Street, then witnessed the tech startup scene in the Bay Area burgeon for the first time since the dot-com crash. After spending just enough time in corporate America to become fully disillusioned with its promises, Jason wound up building Caviar, one of the foundational food delivery startups in 2012, and sold it just two years later for over $100 million.

> It all began, as he would say, with his induction into the world of food beyond his parents' home cooking (normally an unextraordinary rotation of chicken, rice, and vegetable plates). In middle school, Jason had a bite of his first legendary burrito at Gordo Taqueria in his one-square-mile hometown of Albany, California. And unbeknownst to him, the pursuit of delicious food would define his life pursuits from then on . . .

Growing up, when I wasn't gaming on my dad's Compaq computer, watching anime, practicing piano and saxophone, or doing schoolwork, I would be selling something. In elementary school, I used to cut out coupons from coupon books and sell them to my friends at church. At age thirteen, I registered a Pokémon website and a Cardcaptors website called Cardcaptors.com, then recruited a team of teenagers around the world on AOL Instant Messenger to write content for the sites. We didn't know what we were doing, but the Cardcaptors website received thirty thousand page views a day at its peak. Then we added those old-school Double-Click banner ads that paid one dollar per one thousand impressions, which was a great allowance for an eighth grader . . . until the actual Cardcaptors company mailed me a cease and desist. From there, I became the first student in my high school to get a debit card, so I opened an eBay account, sold my classmates' belongings for them, and took a 15 percent cut. That hustle helped pay my college tuition.

Once I started at UC Berkeley, though, I stopped hustling completely. My parents had immigrated to the US from China when I was one, mainly so that I could go to an American college and live the American dream. Like many immigrants in the '80s, my dad brought us to the States for his studies, first for his master's degree in optometry at the University of Houston and then for his PhD at UC Berkeley. My mom had been a doctor in China, but she started over in the States, washing dishes for a couple of dollars an hour at Chinese restaurants while studying English and nursing. They had given me a happy childhood and hoped that I would get a stable job as an accountant.

For four years, I put all my ideas on the back burner and focused on getting my CPA. When I landed my first internship at one of the Big Four accounting firms in my sophomore year, my parents were thrilled: "You'll have a stable career that can last the rest of your working professional life!" My peers and I were preparing to graduate amid the worst financial crisis of our time. Everyone around me seemed to be pursuing the same fields—accounting, banking, or consulting—so I went with the flow. Everyone did.

. . .

After graduation, I tried the banking world at Merrill Lynch first: strict and formal while sitting in a cube all day crunching numbers and making PowerPoints. By day one, I was already looking for another job. Nine months later, I started at Google, which was much more chill and fun, with great benefits . . . But at the end of the day, I just hated working in a corporate job. Waking up every day knowing that any contribution I made would be nothing more than a rounding error to the bottom line of these companies, I felt painfully unmotivated and devoid of life.

The journey to extend this by another five to ten years—or worse, until I turned sixty-five—promised to be long and excruciating.

Around that time, my cousin became the first successful entrepreneur in our family. He had surprised everyone when he suddenly quit his engineering job at Lockheed Martin and began building a fantasy sports app, which Yahoo! later bought and turned into the Yahoo Fantasy Sports app. Up to that point, no one in my family had thought of entrepreneurship as a viable path. But I'd seen his whole journey play out, and my wheels were turning.

"Let's partner on a business together," I said to my dad one day, while I was still at Google.

For all my dad's love of stability, he had, in fact, thrown away twelve years of optometry training to teach himself programming and join a startup when I was in middle school—the peak of the dot-com bubble in 1999. Smartphones didn't exist yet, dial-up was the fastest internet, and every web company was on the verge of going public. But when the bubble burst on the heels of his startup going IPO, his stock became worthless.

At this point, fifteen years into my dad's strictly nine-to-five government job teaching programming at UC Berkeley, my mom kept finding him asleep on the couch late at night with the TV still on. He'd become as bored as I had, and similarly entranced by my cousin's success, he agreed to build something with me.

With my dad on the engineering side and me on the business side, we created a Craigslist app for the Windows Phone that became the number one productivity app on Windows. With $500 a day in ad revenue beginning to come in from the app, we grew optimistic, thinking we could pivot into making apps full time.

Then, a few things happened: the Windows Phone died out, Craigslist sent a cease and desist to developers to stop scraping their data, and we shut our project down. But I'd gotten the itch to build again. *That was a lot of fun*, I thought. *What's next?*

. . .

After the cease and desist, I was still at Google, head spinning with new ideas. One of my friends, who worked an engineering job fifteen minutes down the street at EA SPORTS, would come to the Googleplex for free dinner all the time. He was a traditional guy who liked the corporate life, so he never budged as I pitched him startup ideas nonstop. But one day, wanting to get his mind off a recent breakup, he finally gave in.

In 2011, the daily deals site Groupon was set to be the biggest internet company IPO since Google's IPO in 2004. Because I love to eat and to get deals, our first startup idea was inspired by Groupon—but instead of offering coupons across activities, products, food, and travel, we planned to focus solely on restaurants.

Since college students also love to eat and to get deals, we first launched our concept, Munch on Me, at UC Berkeley. Students signed up to claim one food freebie per week on our website; in turn, our restaurant partner could market their promotion, with the idea that some of these new customers would return. For our first deal, we partnered with a Berkeley restaurant called Saigon

"The four of us quit our jobs that summer to focus on Munch on Me full time. That was the start of it all— the catalyst that changed our lives."

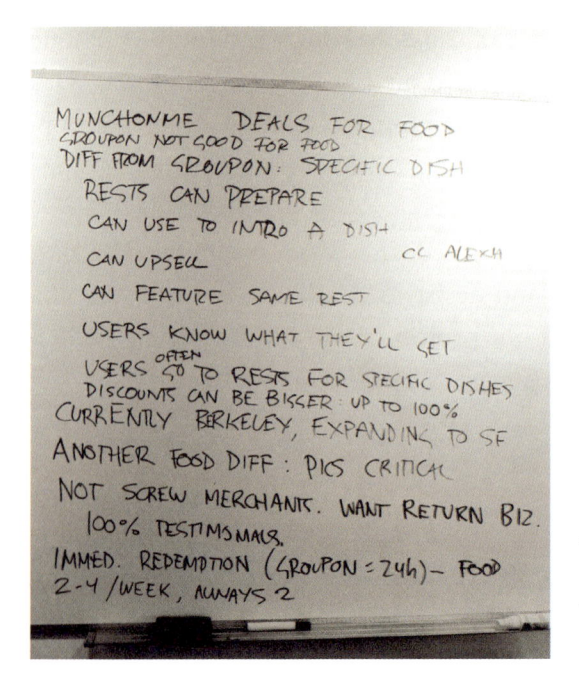

The birth of Munch On Me, a daily deals website for food at restaurants.

Eats to give away their Asian Taco. In one week, we signed up four thousand users, or 10 percent of campus. Saigon Eats had a line like they'd never seen before. They quickly sold out of tacos and had to hang up a sign asking people to come back the next day.

With a successful proof of concept, I scouted all my smartest friends and colleagues to help grow Munch on Me. We became a team of ten cofounders. The first thing we did was raise $4,000 with our pocket money and spend half of it on a lawyer we found online, who lost our corporate book and incorporated us incorrectly, so we had to redo it all. Then, less than a week after launching Munch on Me, Y Combinator founder Paul Graham and some of his partners came to speak at UC Berkeley about entrepreneurship. Even though we were alumni by then, we attended. During the Q and A, I stood up in the auditorium and pitched my idea for Munch on Me on the spot.

One of them encouraged us to apply to Y Combinator. They liked our team and early traction, and they believed, like most people back then, that daily deals companies could thrive in their own verticals on the tails of Groupon's success. We applied to Y Combinator's summer 2011 batch, while we continued to work full-time jobs and run weekly deals.

We snuck into popular Berkeley classrooms at the crack of dawn and taped flyers on the back of every seat. We slipped flyers onto car windshields, under doors, and into bathroom stalls. Eventually, we grew our user base to twenty thousand people, around half of UC Berkeley's population.

When Y Combinator accepted us later that spring, they invested $20,000 for 7 percent of the company. Today, that would be considered minimal, but it was normal back then—and more funding than we'd ever seen. By then, we had naturally whittled down our chaotic founding team from ten to four cofounders. The four of us quit our jobs that summer to focus on Munch on Me full time. That was the start of it all—the catalyst that changed our lives.

. . .

At its peak, Munch on Me expanded from Berkeley to LA, San Diego, Seattle, New York, and Boston, with over thirty people on our team. But then, Groupon IPOed, and its stock tanked. One by one, the five hundred Groupon clones of the world, including us, started to fail. After Y Combinator, I talked to over a hundred investors, but we were only able to raise $25,000 from one angel investor—the only Asian American, who wanted to invest in an Asian American founding team. With his funds, we ran Munch on Me for nearly a year, making meaningful revenue but no profit.

Our team of thirty started to quit one by one, until we were down to five team members, and ten dollars in our business bank account.

We knew we had to pivot. In November 2011, we ran the last deal ever on Munch on Me and began to shut it down. I tried

"Our team of thirty started to quit one by one, until we were down to five team members, and ten dollars in our business bank account."

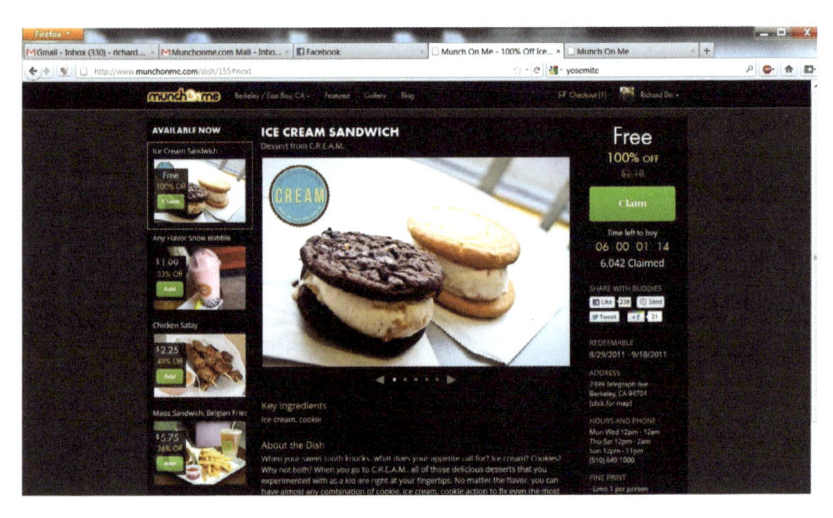

6,042 Free CREAM ice cream sandwiches claimed.

selling the company to players like Groupon and LivingSocial. In early 2012, a former competitor called CollegeBudget bought Munch on Me, which had been reduced to a glorified email list of fifty thousand active purchasers of deals, for $10,000.

Finally, we had money in the bank, but we knew that if we ran out again, we were done—and all five of us hated the idea of returning to corporate America. Hyperconscious of our burn rate at all times, we became the most frugal team I knew of. Every day, we ate the same $5 footlongs from Subway for lunch. Every night, I ate the same $1.99 chicken and rice plate from Oakland Chinatown for dinner. Our one-room office in San Francisco's Financial District was already discounted to $800 a month because we rented from an old-school Chinatown landlord who didn't want to work with anyone else. But to buy ourselves more time, we put an extra desk and chair in there and rented the "office space" to other startups for $500 a month on Craigslist.

The idea to pivot into a food delivery startup, which later became Caviar, emerged as the result of one too many five-dollar footlongs. Tired of eating the same lunch for months, one of our cofounders, Shawn, tried to get a sandwich from a popular shop across town called Ike's Place. Those days, before rideshares were widespread, the three-mile trip took forty-five minutes on Muni, one hour in line, and another forty-five minutes back—in total, two and a half hours for one sandwich.

So we called Ike's. "Hey, can you guys deliver? We want to order five sandwiches to the Financial District. We'll pay you a delivery fee."

"Nope, we don't do that," they answered.

Back then, it turned out that only mediocre pizza places or Chinese, Indian, or Thai shops had a delivery driver on staff. Could we become the first company to offer on-demand delivery from people's favorite restaurants in San Francisco? We knew it could be a huge opportunity. From there, we began the monthslong journey of convincing just one restaurant from a sea of nonbelievers to try it with us . . . And thus, Caviar was born.

"Four people depended on me, and one of my cofounders' parents called me and said, "You're crazy. My son needs to go back to his job. How much longer will you keep doing this?"

That was our lowest point. Some of us had dropped out of school, and some had left our stable jobs. We were about to lose everything we had worked for in the past year and a half—and now we would face our parents, who would tell us 'I told you so.'"

A funny day.

We thought we were getting acquired by a Japanese Groupon clone. So we dressed up in suits and went out to lunch. They asked us a bunch of questions and we never heard from them again.

In the six months between shutting down Munch on Me in December 2011 and launching Caviar the following May, I questioned everything I was doing, but I never let it show. Otherwise, everyone else would begin to doubt.

Four people depended on me, and one of my cofounders' parents called me and said, "You're crazy. My son needs to go back to his job. How much longer will you keep doing this?" That was our lowest point. Some of us had dropped out of school, and some had left our stable jobs. We were about to lose everything we had worked for in the past year and a half—and now we would face our parents, who would tell us "I told you so."

But at the same time, because we had met while pledging the same Asian fraternity at Berkeley, this was nothing out of the ordinary. We just felt like five Asian dudes struggling together in college again. Our bond made the company special in the early days. Even with my best friends in high school, I'd never gotten to the point where I could say that I'd do anything for someone else and actually follow through. But I felt that way about my cofounders, and vice versa. Others saw that and wanted to be part of it, too.

In 2011, when it was rare to see any Asian American founders, let alone a group of five, we stood out and naturally attracted others who felt like they were different—especially other Asian Americans. In fact, three Asian Americans owned the first restaurant that finally agreed to partner with us, HRD Coffee Shop. And with the first partnership in place, in May 2012, we launched Caviar.

The launch itself was uneventful. We literally put a picture of a burrito on our website and messaged thirty friends on Google Hangouts with "Hey, what are you doing for lunch tomorrow? Want a burrito from HRD? I'll pick it up and deliver it to you." We simply wanted to test the idea. Even though HRD Coffee Shop was a marquee restaurant in San Francisco with notoriously long lines for lunch, would people really pay a $9.99 delivery fee plus 18 percent of the order, on top of a burrito that was already $10, just to get it delivered?

It turned out the answer was yes, especially for those who worked in downtown San Francisco. A few days later, I emailed every Y Combinator founder from 2011 and prior. Over twenty of them wanted to test Caviar for their company lunches, especially after learning that we could deliver from Ike's Place. Our turning point came when I signed Kabam, a gaming company that provided dinner for hundreds of employees every weekday. With a budget of $15 per employee, each Kabam order was a few thousand dollars. Though our $9.99 delivery charge was a flat rate, the 18 percent fee was what made us what we called "ramen profitable," even after paying our drivers. We could operate without stressing about money anymore, and we could enjoy ramen—a milestone that had eluded us throughout building Munch on Me.

...

In the two years between launching Caviar and selling it, we worked seven days a week and grew by 20 percent every month. From the outside, Caviar looked seamless: you could order food, track it in real time, and get it delivered. But inside, chaos ensued. We were essentially building three businesses at once: a product for our drivers on mobile, a product for our restaurants on tablet, and an app for our customers on Android, iOS, and the web. We couldn't onboard engineers fast enough. Instead of the wild algorithms people thought were routing their orders, humans behind spreadsheets manually assigned orders. The fax machines at our partner restaurants clogged up with fifteen orders at once, and it felt like everything was crashing.

Our exit came unexpectedly in 2014. We were only two months into raising $13 million in our Series A. For the first time, we increased our cofounder salaries from $0 to $60,000 and began ramping up our hiring. We received a surprise email from

Top: Our first courier appreciation night. We were all about community and treating all of our stakeholders with respect.

Bottom: Our small SF team at 923 Market St.

a customer named Jeff, who had ordered Caviar every day before suddenly disappearing. We soon found out why he had dropped off: he had started working as a marketing lead at Square, which provided free lunch.

Hey, loyal customer here, Jeff wrote. *We'd love to meet up and discuss something we're building called Square Order, where you can order ahead and pick up from restaurants. You guys already have delivery, and we love Caviar.*

"It's Jeff!" we said, and agreed to meet.

When the possibility began to set in, we realized we could move much faster if Square acquired us. The food delivery space was heating up with competitors like DoorDash, Uber Eats, and even Amazon at the time, and Square had plenty of engineers, which we sorely needed to keep up with our growth.

After three months of due diligence, we closed a deal to sell Caviar to Square in August 2014. And with that, we landed ourselves right back into stable, salaried jobs as middle managers with health benefits at Square.

"I'm back in this role again," I said to myself, transported back to 2009. "Man . . . I can't wait to get out."

Jason and his cofounders stayed at Square for two years and left in August 2016. From there, Jason planned to travel the world with his partner for one year, but he ended up enjoying it so much that he no longer has an end date. In between his travels, which have involved eating one hundred tacos in a week on a road trip across Mexico, mountaineering on the Seven Summits of the world, and chasing storms with the man who holds the Guinness World Record for most tornados seen, Jason has continued to spearhead new projects with various members of his old team at Caviar.

Together, they've opened restaurants like Rooster & Rice, a Thai khao mun gai concept in the Bay Area; Halal Guys, a New York–based franchise, on the West Coast; and many more. And they do it all while taking time every day to mentor and invest in a new generation of entrepreneurs in food and tech to give others the same opportunities they had while building Caviar.

PART 2: SHAWN TSAO

INTRO Shawn grew up hating failure—a quality that he and his cofounders at Caviar share. Yet, it was only through failing day in and day out, in ways both big and small, that the team broke through and found success. We spoke with Shawn to get another perspective on the Caviar story, as the second youngest on the team, a first timer in the tech industry, and Caviar's operations and design lead.

Failure was never an option while growing up with parents who had lived through the Cultural Revolution. My dad had escaped the pig farm he labored on because of a cello and violin scholarship, and my mom had fended for herself without her own mother from the age of twelve. For them, even small failures could mean the difference between life and death. So, when they left China together and started raising me—first in my birthplace of Tokyo and then in Torrance, California, where we moved when I turned five—they made it clear that they wouldn't just forbid failure, but that I also had to be the best at anything I wanted to do.

They were on my ass all the time to make sure I was getting As in every class, consistently testing into the advanced level for piano, and becoming a well-rounded person for college admissions through sports and other extracurriculars.

As a child, I asked them, "Ugh, why you gotta be so strict?" When I looked around me, I saw all my white friends getting money just for getting one A on their report card. "Dad, I got straight As. What do I get?"

"Straight As? That's the minimum," he said. "Why would you get a reward for getting the minimum?"

Looking back, I'm grateful to even have both of my parents. I'm grateful that they forced me to be on top of my shit all the time, while allowing me to discover what I wanted—to be an architect. As a kid, I loved drawing, playing Legos, and creating mock designs for buildings and homes in Photoshop and Illustrator with my mom, who was a designer herself.

Even though my parents never pressured me into a specific career path, they weren't necessarily happy about me going into architecture. Sometimes, they would show me newspaper and magazine articles featuring this or that celebrity architect. "See how much they get paid?" my dad would say, poking his finger at the headline. "Nothing!"

But they still supported me as I took architecture classes at community college during high school, majored in architecture at UC Berkeley, and spent my summers drawing bathrooms and living rooms or nearly cutting off my finger making models for various internships.

. . .

I could have finished my architecture degree at UC Berkeley early, but I chose to stay on campus another year to intern at an architecture firm, work for the Cal football team, and generally take it easy before starting my full-time job.

One day, my friends Jason and Tony came up to me in our fraternity house. "Hey, we want to do this daily deals startup company," they said. "We'd love for you to join and help us.

We need a business-sided person to do sales. Also, someone who knows design."

"What is a startup company?" was my response.

Even though I lived in Silicon Valley, I had been so ingrained in architecture that I was truly unaware of the tech industry engulfing everything around me.

"Well, we're a company," Jason said, "and we're called Munch on Me. We're trying to be like Groupon, but only for restaurants."

That I understood. Back then, Groupon, LivingSocial, and other daily deal sites were the bee's knees, and Jason wanted to be just like them. *Oh, wow. You want to be this billion-dollar company?* I thought, not knowing that Groupon would later sink.

I agreed. "Sure, I'll help. You don't need to pay me. I'm happy just to help my friends."

At first, I helped out here and there, making the art for their marketing flyers, drawing avatars for the app, and occasionally pitching restaurants in Berkeley. But a couple of months in, Munch on Me got into Y Combinator, and Jason poached me again—this time, to join the team full time.

By then, I had learned enough about the tech world to understand how Y Combinator's stamp of approval suddenly made Munch on Me a "real" company. I'd saved up a year's worth of runway from four years of working for the Cal football team, and I was extremely fortunate to have parents in a stable financial situation. In the worst case, I could move back in with them in Torrance, and that security made a significant difference. Not everyone has that cushion.

In my mind, I had nothing to lose. Many of my friends were graduating Berkeley with high-paying job offers: up to $100,000 a year with a $10,000 sign-on bonus for investment bankers, and even higher for my software engineering friends. Meanwhile, I had a $30,000 offer from an architecture firm, no sign-on bonus. Being an architect had been my dream up to that point, but I ended up turning down my offer.

With Munch on Me, the idea of building something big out of something so small attracted me more than anything else. And I was optimistic about our team; I knew we could build something bigger than ourselves.

> "From Jason and Tony, I really learned how to hustle. To be extremely confident in myself, even though I was hearing no left and right. We were working to convince just *one* person."

. . .

The first time I saw Jason hold a meeting for all of his Munch on Me partners, there were twenty cofounders. I don't even know how he collected that many intelligent people. But, when it came down to walking away from jobs and salaries, there were only four left: Jason, Richard, Andy, and Tony.

They split the equity of the company equally. Since I joined later, Jason promised that he would give me half of what he had, wherever we ended up.

Richard and Andy were our technically minded people—brilliant and motivated, they built the entire product from scratch. Jason came from a finance background and used his numbers-oriented brain to find the best deals and make sure we had money in the bank. He can also hype anything. After all, he recruited me to work for him for free. Tony, also on the business side, knew how to connect with the person in front of him and mix a sales pitch with personal flair.

From Jason and Tony, I really learned how to hustle. To be extremely confident in myself, even though I was hearing no left and right. We were working to convince just *one* person. Up until then, I'd never been rejected so much in my life. Though utterly discouraged, I learned to have a short-term memory and move on to the next person.

FORGED THROUGH FAILURE

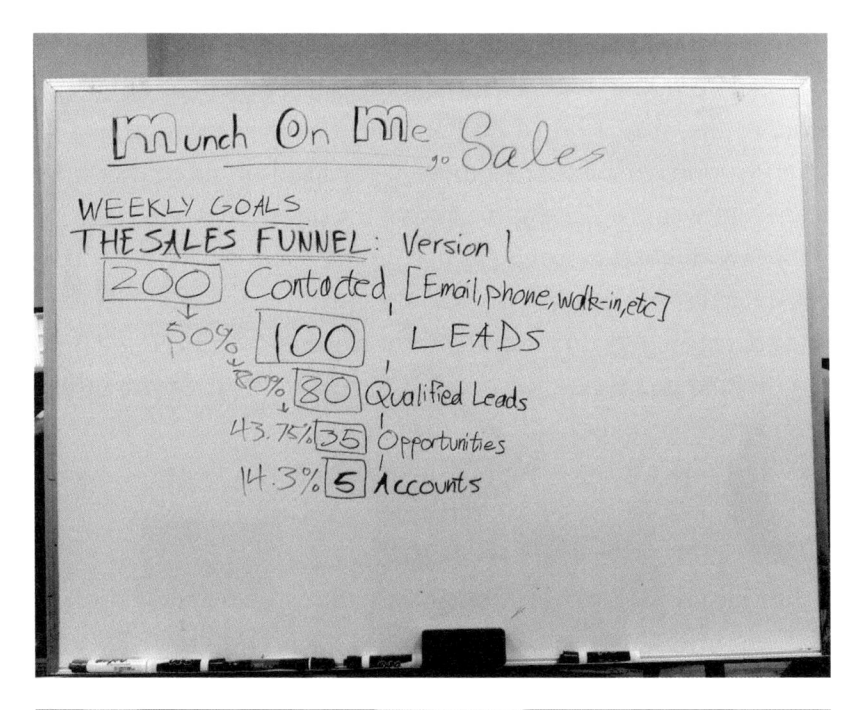

Top: We had 1 whiteboard in the office and we used it for tracking our sales goals.

Bottom: Our first marketing brochure. We printed thousands of these and went door to door pitching Caviar at offices in downtown SF.

After graduation, I went from doing sales here and there in Berkeley to taking over all the sales in San Francisco. From one store to the next, I heard no hundreds of times a day, trying to sign just one person. I tried to keep my head up no matter how bad I felt, went to sleep at the end of the day, and woke up to do it all over again. I enjoyed the hostile environment we were in, a constant day in, day out of pushing ourselves to get more sales and sign more restaurants. Whatever it took.

My first go at sales was weak. I would walk into a restaurant and say, "Hey, may I talk to a manager? I would like to bring in new customers for you guys. Would that interest you?"

"Oh, no. Manager isn't here. We're not interested," employees said.

Eventually, I learned how to track down managers by reading Yelp reviews. If I read one that said "Bob was great!!" then I would call and ask, "Hey, is Bob in?"

Employees, thinking I knew him, would pass me through.

"Who the hell are you?" the actual manager would say.

"I wanted to contact you because we're looking for great restaurants like yours to potentially bring you more customers. I was wondering if I could get a meeting with you. Just a quick ten minutes?"

Then I would set up a meeting and pitch to them in person. Once I got in front of a manager, the chances were fifty-fifty.

. . .

The Munch on Me website showed different restaurant dishes, like ice cream sandwiches, burritos, and Thai salads, all with a discount price of "free." When people claimed the deal on the Munch on Me app, they could use their phones to show the deal to the restaurants, who would cross names off their list. The idea was that if you had a deal for just one dish at a restaurant, the restaurant could upsell its other dishes in the future. We also thought that the hype would help restaurants get new customers. For instance, when we partnered with CREAM to give free ice cream sandwiches to Berkeley students, the line was three blocks long.

Still, I have to admit that the product was shaky at best. We weren't even using it ourselves, which is usually a bad sign. And at the end of the day, we couldn't raise any funding. People who couldn't keep working without pay dropped off, including Tony, who needed to work for a company that could sponsor his visa. That was a significant loss for me because he had been instrumental in convincing me to join.

We knew we were dead in the water if we didn't pivot, so we started shutting down Munch on Me and conceiving of a new company. One time, one of our restaurants mentioned that they wanted to get into food delivery. We took that idea and thought, *What if we did it for them?* Around the same time, I had wanted to get a sandwich from Ike's Place, one of the most legendary sandwich shops in the Bay Area. Because Ike's didn't deliver, I tried using a TaskRabbit to get it—a terrible experience that took three hours and cost twenty bucks.

Jason's wheels were turning at this point. I loved Ike's, and I had really wanted it. Some restaurants wanted to do food delivery, and we, their customers, wanted their foods delivered. Why not try to do it ourselves?

With Uber and Lyft starting to hire independent contractors as drivers, we asked one of our previous investors what he thought about hiring contractors as delivery drivers.

"You know, I know a company whose independent contract delivery people might be able to do your deliveries," he said.

That didn't work out, so Jason and I hired our own delivery courier crew. Richard and Andy developed entirely new apps in two or three months, including a courier-tracking service for customers. And Jason and I continued to call restaurants left and right. This time, unlike when we went after restaurants that needed to attract customers with freebies, we wanted only the best restaurants that customers already loved.

Restaurants hated deliveries back then. Getting grouped with "delivery available" restaurants, which were mostly associated with low-end restaurants, brought down their brands. That's why we called ourselves Caviar—to repackage delivery as high-end in every touchpoint of our sales pitch.

Jason and I were like a call center, trying to pitch restaurants on the delivery idea and getting rejected constantly. I would call the same restaurant twenty times to reach the manager. I even stalked the owner of Ike's Place for a month on Twitter. One day, when he tweeted that he was in Santa Rosa, we grabbed a car and made the hour-long drive, arriving right as he was walking out of the shop.

"Hey, Ike!" I blurted as we caught up to him. "I've been looking to pitch you our startup for a while. Do you have a second? I would love to get five minutes of your time."

"Okay. Let's talk," he said simply, to our surprise.

We sat down with him. Abel pitched Caviar, Jason explained the partnership terms, and I described how our operations worked.

"Okay, let's do a trial run," he said. He signed on the spot, less because of our sales pitch and more because he was an entrepreneur himself.

Once we signed Ike, I name-dropped Ike's Place everywhere else and signed more and more restaurants because everyone in the Bay knew his sandwich shop. The first few restaurants took a long time to sign, but after a year, restaurants began knocking on our door.

One of the best parts once we'd signed a restaurant was the setup process. We knew that people like to eat with their eyes, so we prioritized taking high-quality photos of every single dish—something that other food delivery apps skipped over. When we set up photoshoots, we ordered everything on the menu and shot our own photos. Then, I would take that food home—Ike's or tacos or whatever else we signed—and eat it for a whole week. It was fantastic.

> **"I dreamed about doing food deliveries; I dreamed about doing sales. I woke up and did both."**

. . .

As we built Caviar, we incorporated what we learned from our time in Y Combinator. Y Combinator consisted of weekly dinners with the other founders in our batch, plus a guest speaker. For me, some of the most memorable lessons came from hearing the Airbnb founders speak. They are truly hustlers with a legendary story, making cereal to fund themselves and selling their apartment listings on the streets for *years* before even raising a seed.

We learned a lot of lessons about design from YC companies' design philosophy, which largely came from Airbnb: large photos, in-your-face product, very little print, and a simple layout. If you want people to purchase something, make it really easy for them to do it—a simple idea, but it was executed poorly at the time. We decided that customers would check out with two clicks at most. Within the startup community, having a frictionless process was *delightful* for customers, hailing from Steve Jobs's vocabulary. I used to say we were *delectable*, because it felt more relevant to us.

The entire experience, including the customer service, also had to be on point. I was responsible for growing our customer support team, so I made sure that any customers who had problems could reach us immediately. They could text us through the Caviar app, call us, or email us, and they'd reach an actual human on our team within minutes. This gave customers a sense of ease, and they trusted that we were taking care of them.

Every day for the first year of building Caviar, Jason, Abel, and I would switch off who was "operating"—managing the couriers, customer support, and order assignments, all at the same time. When too many orders came in for our couriers to handle, we ran to the garage near our office and delivered them ourselves with Zipcars. Driving with stacks of poke bowls in the trunk and back seat, I would call a courier about a forgotten order while a customer service call came in at the same time asking for a refund. "Fuck—yeah—sure," I'd say with the steering wheel in one hand. I'm pretty sure Jason and I almost died multiple times.

I dreamed about doing food deliveries; I dreamed about doing sales. I woke up and did both. We were 100 percent focused on the company. The "life" part of "work-life balance" involved sleeping and then getting on the train back to work. Every day, we made mistakes and put out fires, never knowing when it would end.

Still, we really believed in ourselves.

With Munch on Me, I'd been more optimistic about the team than the product, but Caviar was a product I actually wanted to use every day—and we did. Munch on Me had users, but not enough repeat customers or strong advocates. With Caviar, we heard customers say things like, "Oh shit, you can get this delivered by Caviar. They're fucking awesome!" That gave me confidence that Caviar would work.

Caviar's 2014 Holiday Party. Also our last couple of weeks at the 220 Montgomery St location before moving into Square.

. . .

Two years later, we were beating our revenue goals every other week, and there was an 80 percent chance that a first-time customer would use us again—one of the best retention metrics out there. Our goal was to become just as big as our competitors, which were billion-dollar companies at the time. It was that simple.

So when we got an acquisition offer two months after raising our Series A, we were all surprised. Jason and I were in Miami, looking to potentially expand there. Square's business development guy called and offered us a nine-figure deal.

Holy shit. They valued us at that much? It was more than double our Series A valuation from only two months ago.

We talked it over with our cofounders and held off on making a decision immediately. . . but that night, Jason and I went to a Miami club, got a table, and just celebrated. It was fantastic.

We were nervous during the entire process from March to August, because the offer was still only verbal. They needed to do their due diligence, which meant they had to go into our code. We knew this was the riskiest part of acquisition because the acquirer can take your code and copy it. But luckily, that didn't happen.

We also needed signatures of approval from all of our investors. Two of them didn't like the acquisition and cussed us out for thirty minutes on a call.

"You fucking morons," they said. "You guys are worth way more than what you're getting offered. Maybe if it was an all-cash deal it would make sense. Fuck Square, they're worth nothing." Oh man, it was brutal.

After the call we were like, "...Should we still sell?"

Ultimately, Jack Dorsey met with the last two investors and convinced them to sign. The day we were supposed to sign the final papers, we rode to Square together.

"This is our last chance to back out," I said to everyone.

"If you guys back out, we will back out," Andy and Richard said.

Then we decided.

"You know what? Let's do this. Let's get acquired."

. . .

The day we signed our papers, Square invited us to an over-the-top party at their office and served actual caviar. When we announced the acquisition to the company, our staff wasn't sure if their jobs were safe, though Square ended up taking care of them. Many got massive equity from Square or had their salaries doubled. For some, it worked out, while others went from being leads to middle managers. The politics weren't easy, to say the least. But for me, it was a relief and also somewhat of a shock that we got acquired in two years.

We agreed on a deal where we would work at Square for two years as our shares vested. In the beginning, we got six figures in cash, which was a hundred times more than I'd ever had in my bank account—I already felt rich then. When our shares were fully vested two years later, Jason honored his original agreement with me. I finally got an apartment in San Francisco, because I could actually afford to. I could travel and eat at restaurants I'd always wanted to go to. I bought a new car because mine had $4,000 in repair bills.

Other than that, I didn't change much. Andy didn't even change his lifestyle at all. He still lives in a house with several roommates, drives a Subaru, and barely spends on anything. You would never know that he's a multimillionaire.

. . .

At the end of the day, all the success stories are the same. Yeah, you struggle, and something happens that makes everything great. But you never hear about the ones that get pummeled all the way to the ground.

People don't always talk about these struggles when you're doing a startup. You pay yourself nothing. Your friends party it

Our last day at Caviar in 2016—a bittersweet end to a journey that started in the summer of 2010.

up, travel, and eat at awesome restaurants, but you can't go with them for lack of money or time because you have to build your company. Every day for years, you face the temptation to stop what you're doing and go back to a nine-to-five. And when you fail, you'll know that you gave up years building relationships to create a failed startup.

We were extremely fortunate to exit well, but there are a hundred times more founders who have failed and are going through deep depression as a result. Yet, that also drives them to succeed, or the years they spent mean nothing. Today, Jason and I invest in other entrepreneurs. The thought of doing another startup in my lifetime makes me feel physically exhausted—though I do have a list of over a hundred ideas, or problems that I think should be fixed one day. If there was something I was really passionate about, then of course, I would do it. But right now, I'm just happy to support other people's dreams.

For further information, visit the following websites:

- Caviar: *TryCaviar.com*
- Omakase Capital Group: *OmakaseCapitalGroup.com*

CHAPTER 05
BUILDING NGUYEN COFFEE SUPPLY

The story of *Sahra Nguyen*, the activist entrepreneur rewriting the narrative and the actual landscape of Vietnamese coffee beans through *Nguyen Coffee Supply*

INTRO Vietnam is the second-largest coffee exporting country in the world, and the US is the second largest importer of Vietnam's coffee beans. Chances are that if you've bought coffee in the US, you have consumed Vietnamese coffee. But despite that, Vietnam is rarely, if ever, named as the source—nor included in the "specialty coffee" industry.

Why, though? Given that Vietnamese iced coffee, or cà phê sũa đá, has gained popularity alongside matcha and chai in the US, why is it that we never hear about the farmers of Vietnamese coffee beans and the producers of Vietnamese coffee culture?

While transitioning from a nearly decade-long career in filmmaking, storytelling, and poetry, Sahra Nguyen set her sights on uncovering the suppressed answers to those questions. Through her journey, she would rewrite the narrative of Vietnamese coffee in the US on a national stage by building her now iconic company, Nguyen Coffee Supply.

On our dead-end street in Boston called Colgate Road, in that rare city space without speeding cars, all the neighborhood kids came out to play. My older sister and I grew up in bustling communities of color among immigrant families hailing from the Dominican Republic, Haiti, Puerto Rico, and the Caribbean. The one other Southeast Asian family that my parents had befriended, a Cambodian family that had escaped the Khmer Rouge a few years earlier, lived a few blocks away. Every day when my mom went to work at her laundromat down the street, she dropped me and my sister off with our Cambodian mom, whom I also called Mom.

Our whole world was nestled in that familiar and neighborly quadrangle: my house, my Cambodian mom's house, my mom's laundromat, and the Roslindale Public Library, where I flipped through every book I could find on drawing, painting, folding origami, or doing arts and crafts. Within our little world, I felt safe. Playing with Heineken beer bottle caps on the ground,

Me with my dad, in our Colgate road home, Boston.

roaches running around—all the layers of poverty, scarcity, and hard work were just the normal textures of our lives.

But when my mom put me in preschool, my insecurities were born. Not only was I Vietnamese among a tiny group of East Asians and one of only three Asians among non-Asians, but I also had a bowl haircut, sideburns, and this rotation of boyish collared shirts and sweatsuits that made me look nothing like the other girls in the class. I had never interacted with white adults until I met my teachers. And it was my first time seeing my parents as outsiders, when contrasted with the parents of my classmates—how out of place my parents looked, how different their English sounded.

One week, my preschool teacher created the biggest hype around Pajama Day. All week, in her singsong voice, she announced, "Friday's puh-JAM-ma day! All right, everyone, make sure you come prepared!"

Me (left) with my older sister (right), Jennifer.

I asked my parents what Pajama Day was. They didn't know. My older sister didn't know. This was in the late '80s, so we didn't have the internet, nor did we have a dictionary or anyone to ask. My teacher slipped my mom a flyer that reminded the parents about Pajama Day, but my mom paid no attention to it.

At a loss, I decided to dress up for it because it sounded like a special celebration. Wearing my favorite denim overalls with sneakers, I showed up at preschool, where everyone else was holding their blankies and animals while wearing pajamas and slippers. My heart sank. *That* was what it meant—I knew what pajamas were, I just didn't know the word.

My teacher's eyes widened when she saw me. "Oh. Did you forget it was Pajama Day?"

"Yeah . . . I just forgot," I said. My cheeks grew hot, and my entire body became heavy with the weight of shame, embarrassment, and discomfort. I stood out like a sore thumb, again.

"It wasn't until high school when I started to understand my identity and my ethnic identity in a social and political context: *Asian American.*"

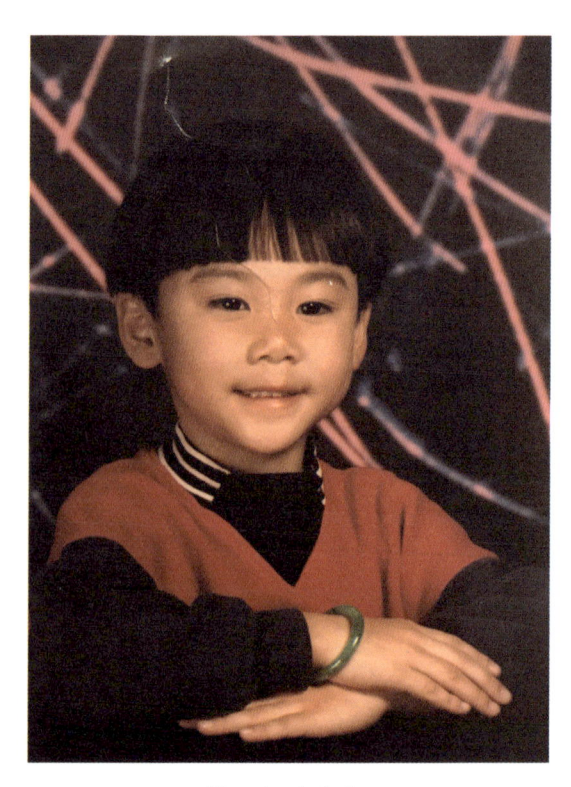

My school photo.

My parents hadn't protected me. *How come they don't know anything?* I thought, stewing. My culture always made me feel like I didn't know enough. Like *I* wasn't enough.

In the '90s, being Asian wasn't cool at all. We were still decades from the 2010s, when Vietnamese food would become trendy. Like many other first-gen kids, I stopped eating lunch at school for fear of letting the aromas of cá kho and curry waft out of my lunchbox amid everyone else's scentless bologna sandwiches and Lunchables.

These early experiences in preschool made me realize I was Asian. But in those moments, it was just *Asian*, based on external perceptions of me: Asian or, often mistakenly, Chinese. It wasn't until high school when I started to understand my identity and my ethnic identity in a social and political context: *Asian American*. Asian Americanness rooted me in America, whereas my earlier Asian identity uprooted me and made me feel alienated, like I didn't belong.

Then, as I dove deeper into Asian American history, I found the words to understand my Vietnamese American identity as well.

. . .

When I look back at my life, there's my life before CAPAY and my life after CAPAY. CAPAY stands for the Coalition for Asian Pacific American Youth, which is a youth-run, youth-led social justice organization sponsored by and housed in the Asian American Studies program on UMass Boston's campus. CAPAY is where I became woke, but we didn't use that term in the '90s. Instead, we used "conscious": Are you politically conscious? Are you critically conscious? What is your consciousness?

Every week at CAPAY, I joined a cohort of high schoolers at UMass Boston to unpack systems of oppression and absorb the histories we never learned in school, from Asian American Studies to Ethnic Studies to the Black Power movement and the civil rights movement.

" I was young, angry, and super fuckin' woke—and all I knew was that after high school, I wanted to be the baddest revolutionary."

After a year, we became youth organizers. Youth violence, state budget cuts for public schools, and the deportation of Cambodians were some of the biggest issues facing our community at the time. Around each of these issues, we organized rallies, demonstrations, and guerrilla actions. We built solidarity with other youth organizations in Boston. We wheatpasted posters in the subway and in the streets, organized workshops, and circulated student petitions.

It was the awakening of my consciousness. It shaped my sense of self and everything I did thereafter. I had finally learned about the US's role in Vietnam and the context for my family's refugee history. I was young, angry, and super fuckin' woke—and all I knew was that after high school, I wanted to be the baddest revolutionary. I wanted the world to know about Asian American history and Ethnic Studies and systems of oppression. This pursuit of personal and collective liberation was all I cared about.

In high school, I applied to the colleges with the top Asian American Studies programs on the West Coast, where Ethnic Studies originated. UCLA's program was the best in the country—my first choice. They rejected me at first, but I wrote an impassioned letter of appeal and was accepted after that.

After graduating from UCLA, I continued developing my own poetry, press kits, and art on the side while I worked at the youth arts organization that I'd loved as a high schooler, Artists for Humanity. While helping students improve their writing skills, I ran their video studio with my mentor, Jason (but everyone called him Swat), and learned video production. That kicked off a seven-year career in freelance documentary filmmaking, writing, and media correspondence in New York.

In New York, I developed my own documentaries, then would pitch, pitch, pitch until my projects got funded and greenlit. First, I directed and produced *Self-Starters*, a five-part series to highlight Asian American entrepreneurs' innovation, creativity, and leadership. At the time, we often associated Asian Americans with submissiveness, invisibility, and unoriginality, so I wanted to subvert those stereotypes. I was intentional about focusing on entrepreneurs who represented different industries (solar energy, street art, social impact, and food) and about highlighting ethnic and generational diversity. In one series of five episodes, I wanted to show how rich and diverse and nuanced and brilliant our community is. *Self-Starters* was the first series to launch the video platform for NBC Asian America in 2016.

Around the same time, the inspiration for Nguyen Coffee Supply hit me. As a full-time creative freelancer, I spent countless hours at cafés and drank loads of coffee every day. I started noticing that Vietnamese food and culture were having their moment in the mainstream. Restaurant-goers were venturing beyond phở and bánh mì to explore bánh xèo and bánh bèo. Pop-up and specialty cafés also began putting Vietnamese iced coffee on their menus, in addition to their regular espresso drinks, matcha, and chai.

> "Sweetened condensed milk doesn't make a coffee drink Vietnamese; Vietnamese coffee beans do."

Whenever I tried one of the Vietnamese iced coffees, I would ask the barista what coffee they used for it, and they'd tell me it was their house Ethiopian or house Colombian, and they'd added sweetened condensed milk.

That felt wrong on so many levels. It's miseducation to consumers. It's unfair to the farmers in Ethiopia and Colombia, who are rendered invisible, even though they produced the bean. And it's dishonorable to Vietnamese farmers and producers, who don't benefit from this transaction *at all*. Sweetened condensed milk doesn't make a coffee drink Vietnamese; Vietnamese coffee beans do.

In the specialty coffee industry, I was seeing so much excitement around transparency. Blue Bottle Coffee, Stumptown Coffee, La Colombe, Intelligentsia—everyone seemed to be talking about who the farmer was and where the bean came from, except when it came to Vietnamese coffee.

Vietnam is the second-largest coffee exporting country in the world after Brazil, but you probably wouldn't be able to find a single-origin Vietnamese blend in any Whole Foods aisle. Anytime I would ask roasters and baristas in the specialty coffee industry about Vietnam, they would dismiss it. I heard excuses like "They're not a part of the specialty community" or "Vietnamese coffee is cheap, instant coffee." But how did Vietnamese coffee get pushed into the cheap, instant coffee market?

Then when it came to conversations about robusta beans, of which Vietnam is the number one producer in the world, people told me even more impassioned opinions: "Arabica beans are superior, robusta is inferior. Robusta tastes bitter, like burnt car tires and your grandma's socks."

Yes, robusta beans have two times the caffeine content of arabica, so they do have a bolder flavor. But we are talking about a *bean*. Where was the aggression and meanness coming from? As a Vietnamese American, not only were these comments offensive and shocking, but they weren't true—because I love Vietnamese coffee, and I'm not the only one who does.

At the end of the day, this was just another instance of certain people controlling a single narrative, and they would never benefit from changing it. Otherwise, everyone who'd built their brands on "100% arabica" and "arabica's good, robusta's bad" would suddenly lose their prestige . . . and so would the people who wanted to capitalize on cheap, exploitative labor.

Robusta isn't bad; people and systems that create poor production are bad. I always say that specialty coffee as it exists today—in Ethiopia, Colombia, Brazil—did not grow out of the fuckin' ground. Specialty coffee is a collective investment from people all along the supply chain to improve lives and build a more sustainable, equitable coffee trade.

An agriculturist or scientist had to say: "Hey, Producer, Farmer, did you know that if we work together to improve your crop by using organic practices, all-natural bio fertilizers, and hand-picking the ripe ones, which takes more time and labor than grabbing all the beans at once, then you'll get a better harvest and sell it for a higher price to the buyer, who will sell it at a higher price to the roaster, who will educate the barista on the specialty qualities of the bean, and that barista will then educate consumer why "this specialty coffee is $6 instead of $2"? It is a collective investment, yet no one was willing to invest in Vietnam.

Well, I need to change this, I thought in 2016. *I'm not saying that I'm the only one who's gonna change it, but I'm gonna change it.* Looking back, working on *Self-Starters* that year did influence me to be an entrepreneur. More than anything, what inspired me about entrepreneurship was just the idea of creating my own lane, carving my own path, and manifesting my own destiny.

Growing up, I had felt boxed in—by stereotypes, what others thought of me, and how they projected their biases on me, whether it was the assumption that Asian women are passive, quiet, and submissive or whether it was the model minority myth. I constantly wanted to surprise people, which meant I was always leveling up and trying to do something unexpected.

That was a motivator for most of my twenties: "Fuck what you think about me, fuck what you think you know about me. I'm tired of it, and I'm *never* gonna let you pin me down."

And in a similar vein, if all these other coffee companies were going to write Vietnam off, then we would step in and change the conversation. We would create a channel to start importing specialty coffee from Vietnam, and we would roast it in the US. We would become part of the conversation.

. . .

When I first started thinking about Nguyen Coffee Supply in 2016, I visited my family in Vietnam while on my way to Cambodia to film my next documentary for NBC, *Deported*.

"Does anyone know someone with a farm?" I asked my relatives.

As it turns out, my aunt did. From Hanoi, we took a plane to Da Lat together and met my future coffee producing partner. We established a partnership, although I didn't place my first order until two years after the fact. At that time, I was still focused on my freelance filmmaking career.

Deported followed the grassroots fight to end deportation of Cambodian Americans after the signing of the 2002 Repatriation Act. The documentary series was filmed across four US cities and abroad in Phnom Penh, Cambodia. After its release in 2018, *Deported* won a national award in the same category as CNN's Lisa Ling.

By then, my films were getting better, bigger brands wanted to work with me, my impact was felt, and I had received some of the greatest accolades of my career—yet my financial security never got better.

Hold up, I thought. *My accolades and financial security aren't correlated?*

That's when I decided to get serious about building Nguyen Coffee Supply. The choice to step away from filmmaking left me sad and frustrated because, up to that point, my identity as a filmmaker, artist, and creative had shaped my whole career.

Little did I know, coffee entrepreneurship would become one more outlet for storytelling.

> "That was a motivator for most of my twenties: 'Fuck what you think about me, fuck what you think you know about me. I'm tired of it, and I'm *never* gonna let you pin me down.'"

. . .

When I was first deciding on a name for the company in late 2017, it came down to a toss-up between Nguyen Coffee Supply and Tiger Coffee: A Vietnamese Coffee Brand.

Worries filled my head. Would people understand Nguyen Coffee Supply? Would they be tripped up by how to pronounce

With my very first pallet of green coffee beans, 2018.

Roasting single origin Vietnamese coffee beans, 2020.

it? Would it backfire on me because of that? Was it too foreign? Too weird? The name "Tiger Coffee" seemed more digestible. I'm the Year of the Tiger, and tigers are strong and bold like Vietnamese coffee. And there would still be some heritage in there!

Ultimately, I decided to name it Nguyen Coffee Supply because I realized that it shouldn't matter whether or not mainstream Americans were ready for it. I would fully lean in with my family name—a name I grew up feeling embarrassed about because no one knew how to say it. This was an opportunity to get everyone more comfortable with *Nguyen*, even if it merely served as a talking point about how to pronounce it.

This would be the catalyst to start the conversation, which would then lead to another conversation about diacritics and how Vietnamese is a tonal language.

> "I can't tell you how many messages people have written us to say that they feel seen, and that they didn't know they could feel so seen by a *coffee brand*."

Like piecing together a jigsaw puzzle, I researched how to build every part of the business one by one—from incorporating to designing the packaging to importing my first pallet to roasting the beans. It took me nearly six months to learn enough about the complex world of logistics, importing, and exporting in order to receive my first pallet of beans from my producing partner in Da Lat in 2018. In a shared roastery in Brooklyn, I roasted the batch, bagged the beans, and threw a launch party in New York City. From there, we launched as an e-commerce brand.

I didn't pay myself for nearly two years, since I was bootstrapping the whole company from my savings and a credit card. Every dollar we made went back into inventory. With no budget for advertising or marketing in the first year, we focused our efforts on storytelling, brand identity, and voice. We brought awareness to Nguyen Coffee Supply purely through social media and word of mouth. Then, once one or two writers featured us, our PR efforts snowballed. The *Wall Street Journal* printed about us in June 2019, resulting in a celebratory moment that drove more interest. In 2021, all the articles and press about us, including our appearances on the *Drew Barrymore Show* and "See Us Unite for Change," came from writers reaching out to us proactively. What we're doing is clearly resonating.

Our affinity groups of Vietnamese Americans and Asian Americans ride for us. I can't tell you how many messages people have written us to say that they feel seen, and that they didn't know they could feel so seen by a *coffee brand*. The fact that a product like coffee can have that type of effect illustrates that our community is deprived of representation, which has the power to make people feel more human.

Outside of the Asian American community, our supporters are diverse, and we feel incredibly blessed about that. We're keen to break down elitist coffee culture, where there's a right way and a wrong way to drink coffee. You're not using a scale? You're not measuring out your grinds? You're asking for four shots instead of two? Those are elitist judgments, and that attitude is rooted in the idea of mastery. For us, if you want to use a scale, it's 14 grams. If you don't want to use a scale, you can eyeball it. Personally, I love using a pho spoon. There's no right or wrong.

Since we launched, customer feedback has been so affirming that we've never made changes to the product. If you scan our website reviews, countless people have changed their minds about robusta coffee. We have three main blends: one 100% arabica, one 100% robusta, and one blend of both. Our most popular ones are the robusta coffees. We're not trying to say that one is better than the other, but that we should allow variation in offerings, ideas, narratives, and ways of being. We should offer consumers a choice in coffee that's as diverse as the global community of coffee drinkers.

Today, we no longer import pallets—we import twenty-foot containers, or the size of a half truckload, with over forty thousand pounds of beans in each. Five people work on our team full time, including me. I'm not doing the things I did in 2018 and 2019, like packing the beans, but I have to hustle harder to create opportunities for myself, my team, and my producing partners in Vietnam. If anything, it's tougher because the stakes are higher. Now, I'm accountable to everyone on my team and responsible for making sure they can be in a healthy place financially. I'm accountable to my producing partner, who expects to sell me most of his crop, and if I back out because something goes wrong, then he might lose on his crop. I'm accountable to our investors, who have entrusted me with their dollars. I'm still hustling hard.

We're changing perceptions about Vietnamese coffee and robusta coffee, and we're bringing more diversity to brewing culture by elevating the phin filter. But what many people don't see is that we're also literally changing the landscape of Vietnam. Helping more farmers convert from cheap coffee production to premium coffee production leads to economic advancement for their lives and to long-term agricultural sustainability for the land.

This mission to uplift the Vietnamese coffee movement also extends to robusta growers around the world. Robusta beans are named such because they grow more robustly and create higher yields. They require less advanced irrigation systems than arabica beans, their higher caffeine content serves as a natural pesticide, and they can be grown at different altitudes. With less volatility and smaller chances of crop failure, growing robusta is more accessible for many farmers around the world.

There's an abundance of Asian American entrepreneurs right now who are entering positions of decision-making and influence as a collective. With many of us being first generation, it's an exciting opportunity to build intergenerational wealth, support, and resilience. It's on us to change our industries, by bringing in a level of cultural integrity that we can't expect from anyone else, and a care for our stories that only we have the unique perspectives to tell.

I firmly believe that the next wave of global coffee culture lies in Vietnamese robusta coffee. By creating this culture shift and building this reality, we will help farmers everywhere enter specialty coffee, increase opportunities for economic advancement, and sustain their coffee businesses in the future.

This summer, Sahra Nguyen graced the cover of the July 2021 issue of *Food & Wine*, a magazine that has defined the American epicurean experience for over forty years. *Food & Wine* told Sahra that it was the first time since 2014 that they've featured a person (let alone a Vietnamese American woman!) on their cover rather than food, and the first time in its history that they've featured an entrepreneur. We could not agree more with the title splashed across the image of Sahra holding Vietnamese coffee beans in her hand *(Game Changers)* and look forward to many more milestones in her mission to change the narrative around Vietnamese coffee and representation.

Further information and resources:

- Follow Nguyen Coffee Supply's journey at *NguyenCoffeeSupply.com* and *@nguyencoffeesupply* on social.
- Check out Sahra's two documentary series, *Self-Starters* and *Deported*, on NBC Asian America.

CHAPTER 06

QUEENLY

The story of *Trisha Bantigue*, the founder and CEO of *Queenly*—a dress resale platform powering a $13 billion formalwear industry that has long been underserved by the tech sector

CONTENT WARNING
Emotional abuse, gambling addiction, physical abuse

INTRO

The women's formalwear industry is a $650 billion market worldwide, and it's traditionally been monopolized by big brands that set dress prices high enough to be unaffordable to girls from families like Trisha's or her cofounder Kathy's. That's exactly what motivated Trisha to build Queenly, a resale platform that allows women to buy and sell new or preloved formal dresses. Today, Queenly is on a roll, graduating Y Combinator, raising a seed round, and breaking its sales targets even amid a pandemic that has shut down formal events across the globe.

For Trisha, the story of Queenly and the events leading up to its creation started in the Philippines.

PUH-TOWWW!

Uh-oh. The boy I'd just pushed had fallen onto a table and smashed a vase in the classroom. By this point, I'd lost track of how many times my teacher had ushered me to the principal's office. Same day, different boy making fun of me for something or other: my braids, my tomboy clothes, or my dark skin from long days of playing in the sun.

My grandparents were furious with me, but what could they do? I did whatever I wanted as a rebellious and rowdy kid, because I always knew I'd leave the Philippines one day—I just didn't know when. I kept dreaming of the day when my mom, this mythical motherly figure that I'd looked up to all my life, would come back to our little village in the province of Pampanga, take me in her arms, and bring me to the US with her.

My parents divorced when I was two years old and became Overseas Filipino Workers. My dad went to Japan while my mom went to the US, and I hadn't seen either of them since. Meanwhile, my grandparents raised me in their little yellow house attached to a bodega in our village, or barangay, two hours north of Manila. Lined with narrow streets and unique, colorful homes that looked as if they'd been built by hand a few generations ago, our town was so small that neighbors spoke as if they'd grown up in the same household. Everyone had something loving to say about my grandma, who was known to always go out of her way to help others, even when she didn't have much time or money herself. Subconsciously, I was learning to be like her too, even though no one who knew my misbehaved self back then would have guessed it.

I spent my life in a rush to reunite with my mom. When I turned ten and learned that she was finally coming for me, I realized that I should've appreciated my home and what I had around me growing up.

My mother was nothing like the angelic idol I'd daydreamed of my whole life. At the airport in Manila, her hug was cold and aloof. After a long flight, we stepped into the hundred-degree

"I kept dreaming of the day when my mom, this mythical motherly figure that I'd looked up to all my life, would come back to our little village in the province of Pampanga, take me in her arms, and bring me to the US with her."

Me at 5 years old in the Philippines.

Attending a wedding with my grandpa who raised me at 6 years old.

desert of Las Vegas and began the drive home. I took in the seven-lane roads, flashy casino hotels, and rows upon rows of identical suburban homes. Later that night when my mom and I slept in her bed, it felt like sleeping next to a complete stranger. I thought there could be no way we were biologically related, but maybe we just needed more time to warm up to each other.

From the moment my mom reentered my life, her gambling addiction soured our entire relationship. Right before she came to get me in the Philippines, she had gambled away her and my stepdad's life savings of nearly $100,000. But despite the trauma of losing everything, she couldn't curb her addiction.

She would tell my stepdad she was taking me to the mall—then take me straight to the casino. After handing me a twenty-dollar bill for the arcade, she would disappear from the lobby. When I ran out of money, I would text or call her, only to be ignored. I would sit in a bathroom stall for hours until she came to find me. Every time my stepdad caught her, she would apologize and promise to change, but a few months later, she would be back in the casino as if nothing had happened.

Me and my younger half brother, Justin, at Chuck E. Cheese in Las Vegas, when I first got to the US at 10 years old.

With so little I could actually control in our household, I focused my energy on excelling at school. Every generation of my family had lived paycheck to paycheck in service jobs, so I set my sights on being the first one to earn a college degree, get a good job, and build wealth. I brought my schoolwork to the casino, made honor roll, and even tried to support my mom by working at McDonald's and Best Buy. If I showed her that I was a good daughter, then maybe she'd be a better mom.

One day, we had a really bad fight that turned physical—the first time I was truly scared for my safety. I locked the door to my bedroom and called 911. But when the cops came, my mom told them lies as they talked to her first. Then, to my shocking dismay, they handcuffed me instead of my mom.

"What are you doing?" I shouted. "I called you guys here for help, you're not helping me!" They proceeded to pull on the handcuffs tighter and ignore everything I had to say.

As I rode down the freeway in the police car, one of them explained, "You know, if you were in California, then we would be handcuffing your mom. But here in Nevada, the law always sides with the parents—as long as they don't leave any lasting marks."

Livid didn't even begin to describe how I felt. "What the heck is a lasting mark? You're gonna wait till a kid is literally bleeding and bruised until you do something?"

"Yeah," they said. "The law is the law. Our job is to go by the book."

After crying and shivering in a cold white cell for twelve hours, I lost all sense of time. Kids that came in after me and got picked up before me. I felt like I was going insane waiting inside, as I had no control whatsoever. I felt hopeless, defeated, and disappointed in our justice system. The cops told me I would be placed straight into foster care if my mom didn't pick me up by the end of the day.

That incident was the last straw. A few weeks later, I left home. To support myself, I took on modeling gigs and sold phone cases from Alibaba to my high school classmates. I also applied and got accepted to UC Berkeley as a political science major. My dream was to become a politician and rewrite unjust, archaic laws like the ones I'd seen the cops in Nevada follow senselessly.

The summer before I started school at Berkeley, I received an email invitation from Miss Global, inviting me to participate in their pageant. They said that I only needed to pay for my plane ticket to LA and an evening gown, and the hair product company Paul Mitchell would sponsor me to compete in their pageant. After looking up Miss Global to make sure it wasn't a scam, I figured that it would at least be a free week at the Hilton with food included. I booked my tickets and bought a sixty-dollar evening gown from Alibaba.

The second I arrived at orientation, I regretted my decision. At eighteen years old, I was the youngest amid a group of intimidating women who were between the ages of twenty-three and twenty-six, and I looked like a total nerd in my glasses and the clothes I'd worn on the plane. I barely knew how to do any makeup besides simple eyeliner and lip gloss, while the other women looked glammed up like Victoria's Secret models, in full faces of makeup for the orientation photoshoot that nobody had told me about.

Yet, as the week went on, everyone was incredibly nice to me, especially my roommate, who became like a big sister. Since it was an international pageant, I met women from Australia, the UK, South Korea, Egypt, and Brazil. They were PhDs, scientists, lawyers, entrepreneurs, and doctors—the opposite of the ditzy, privileged, and disengaged stereotypes that *Miss Congeniality* had led me to believe participated in pageants.

I learned that in the contestants' eyes, pageants are a competition like any sport. Typically, there's an evening gown segment and the infamous swimsuit segment, which is increasingly being changed to a fitness one. Sometimes, in international pageants, they also feature a national costume segment. Contestants give a closed-door interview that's similar to a job interview, as well as a public Q&A on stage, where they answer questions on contemporary social issues in thirty seconds impromptu. Furthermore, plenty of pageants reward the winners with scholarship money and cash prizes.

I competed and lost, as expected, but I loved the experience so much that I knew I'd be back for more. I resolved to learn how to do my makeup, improve my posture, and speak more confidently, and I promised to stay in touch with all the incredible women I'd met.

> "I booked my tickets and bought a sixty-dollar evening gown from Alibaba.
>
> The second I arrived at orientation, I regretted my decision."

...

By the end of summer, I had $2,000 saved in my bank account. When I finally arrived at UC Berkeley, I had no idea that I was living in the most expensive area in the US, nor did I know anything about financing college. I thought that financial aid would cover everything, including dorms—and that in those dorms, I would meet my lifelong best friends and do typical US college things like attend frat parties together.

Instead, by the end of my first week, I sat in the financial aid office and stared down a $10,000 bill for out-of-state student costs that I'd never known about before. With my financial aid already maxed out, my three options were to take out a Parent PLUS loan (but I had no legal parents), take out a private loan (but I didn't have a credit score), or pay for it out of pocket (but I didn't have $10,000). Hearing all this, the officer advised me to drop out and go to community college instead. There was nothing they could do for me.

I'd worked my butt off in high school to get accepted to Berkeley, and there was no way I could give up right as I was getting started. I knew housing was my biggest cost, so I showed up at the housing office every day to beg them to let me out of my one-year contract. They gave in on the fifth day, and I moved into the cheapest room I could find on Craigslist, which cost $400 a month and was an hour and a half from campus. From then on, I was strict about only signing up for classes that knocked out two graduation requirements at a time, and I borrowed the textbooks for each one. For extra cash, I bought eyelashes on AliExpress and sold them on campus. Then I started scraping Craigslist for every part-time job I could find: receptionist jobs, modeling gigs for tech commercials and real estate photo shoots, and all kinds of paid medical or mobile phone research studies.

By the end, I'd paid off $4,000 for my fall semester, but it wasn't enough for the whole year. During spring semester, I took a leave of absence to work full time and pay for the next fall. As I walked down San Francisco's Market Street, I saw a small sign over a door that said "MOBILE PHONE RESEARCH STUDY $100."

I wasn't doing anything right then, so I walked into the tiny office and was greeted by six male engineers sitting at their computers. The CEO of this small tech startup interviewed me for the research study and gave me the hundred dollars—then asked if I'd like to work for them.

His team was trying to build an app to sell to the corporate office of Starbucks, but they were having no luck getting insider information or user research when they spoke with the Starbucks baristas at nearby cafés.

"You have experience working at McDonald's," he said. "Would you get a job at Starbucks and become an undercover spy for us?"

I didn't think it would be hard to get a job at Starbucks, even without McDonald's experience, but I accepted the offer for the promise of two paychecks. For three months, the startup paid me $500 a week to ask a list of questions to my coworkers at Starbucks and email the answers back.

By the time the assignment ended, the CEO helped me land an interview with the CEO of InfoScout, another small startup in San Francisco. When he offered me the position, I asked him what time I had to clock in, since I was used to working service jobs.

"Oh, you don't," he said. "You just come around eight, nine, ten o'clock, or whenever you want."

"What do I wear to work?" I'd never had a job without a uniform.

"Uhh . . . you could come in your pajamas, if you wanted to?" he answered.

It was my first exposure to the tech world, and I realized I loved my collaborative coworkers, the chill working environment, and the snacks and drinks all over the office. But most importantly, that was where I met my future cofounder, Kathy Zhou, who was interning as a software engineer. Because Kathy was a Chinese American computer science student at UPenn who also came from a low-income, unstable family, we bonded immediately and resolved to stay in touch.

. . .

The next year, I repeated the cycle of attending fall semester at Berkeley and working full time to replenish my funds during spring semester—this time, as an interview candidate host at Google. By the end of that second year, I became eligible for California residency. With my tuition reduced to in-state levels, my financial aid would finally cover it.

I took a class on the politics of Southeast Asia, and when we began covering the Philippines, I was all ears. Up to that point, I'd tried so hard to assimilate to the US that I'd never looked back at where I came from.

"Did you know that the first successful computer virus in the world came from the Philippines?" my professor asked.

No one did. Our collective reaction was, "There are engineers in the Philippines?" All I knew was that there were call

My graduation photo from UC Berkeley.

centers in the Philippines, but not people who could code. The virus, which traveled through email and later became known as the ILOVEYOU virus, was so successful that it shut down over 10 percent of the world's computers, including the CIA's. Because no cybersecurity laws existed to incriminate the Filipino creator overseas, the CIA ended up hiring him. The next sentence my professor said stuck with me: "The Philippines has the potential to be the next Silicon Valley of Southeast Asia—if only someone would connect the dots."

I wanted to connect the dots and help revitalize the Philippine economy through tech. But in order to do that, I had to be in tech as well. I needed to see the industry firsthand.

Once I graduated, I applied and got rejected from countless tech companies. Recruiters were quick to point out that my poli-sci degree was a huge factor in passing on me. No matter how hard I tried, I wasn't landing jobs that promised over $30,000 a year—and after fighting so hard for my education at Berkeley, I was determined to do better than that.

Job searching is brutal for many people, but for me, those six months were the closest I'd ever come to giving up on my life completely. What could I do after I felt like I'd already depleted myself in getting this degree that was holding me back? In the midst of countless rejections, the one thought that comforted me was that I could create my own job if I couldn't land one. Even though I didn't know anything about how to start a business or raise money, it was that backup option that kept me going.

Finally, I got a job in recruiting at Facebook. Recruiting was far from my first choice, but I knew it was a chance to get my foot in the door. Meanwhile, I started seriously looking into an idea for an app that I'd been stewing on for a while: making pageant gowns affordable.

Pageants had given me self-esteem, self-love, better communication skills, and a community of lifelong friends to rely on. But one of the biggest inhibitors to participating has always been the cost of an evening gown—easily hundreds to thousands of dollars, and typically only worn once. Whether for a prom, quinceañera, gala, or any other formal event, the typical $500 to $700 price tags on gowns at department stores simply aren't affordable for many women. When I looked at resale solutions like Poshmark, eBay, and even Craigslist, there was something wrong with each

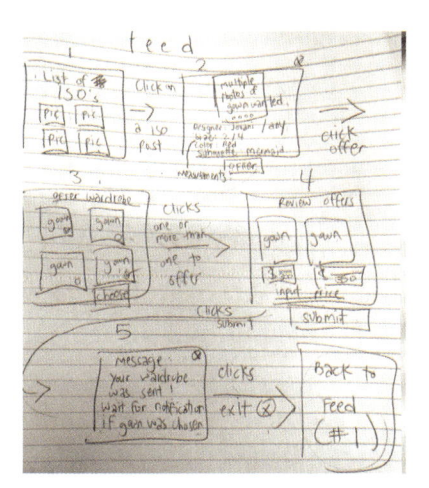

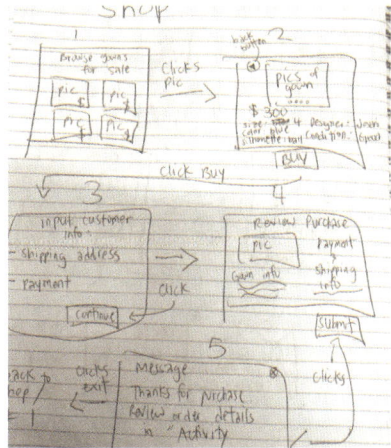

The first sketch of the app that I had in mind when I was first brainstorming in 2018.

of them. They weren't safe enough or convenient enough, or the platforms were too hard to navigate.

Four years after Kathy and I first met as interns at InfoScout, I started bugging her. She had started working as a software engineer at Pinterest.

"I have this amazing idea for an app," I told her, explaining my idea of a formalwear resale platform.

"You don't need an app for that," she said. "You just need a Shopify store."

I knew that the best way to change Kathy's mind would be for her to experience a pageant herself, so I tried to convince her to compete in one. But as a software engineer who didn't dress up or glam up, she said no to me eight times before finally agreeing.

Over the next few months, I coached her on walking in heels, working out, and overcoming her fear of public speaking. Meanwhile, I started drafting wireframes for Queenly and incorporating the business. By the time Kathy had finished competing and won a title at Miss Asian Global, I had started a new job at Uber, and she was finally down to build Queenly with me.

...

The concept behind Queenly is simple: sellers can upload their formal dresses like they would to any other online marketplace, and buyers can browse and purchase these dresses directly. For every transaction that takes place on the platform, Queenly collects 20 percent while the seller pockets 80 percent. In Christmas week of 2018, we launched Queenly's private beta app to one hundred users on the App Store.

Thus began what we now call the Dark Ages of Queenly: we had launched, but until enough people listed dresses to create a substantial pool of options, we wouldn't get any transactions.

I joined every possible dress resale Facebook group and commented on every post to suggest listing the dresses on Queenly instead, until Facebook banned my account. Luckily, a friend of

"We were screaming. Someone had bought from us— we were a legit company!"

Kathy and I sneaked into Miss USA 2019 when it was being held in Reno, NV, and we pretended to be press so that we could save money as we were broke startup founders with no funding.

a friend higher up at the company helped reinstate it, but I'm still banned from Poshmark for doing the same thing.

We wanted to find our first users for free, and in early 2019, we even drove a rental car to Reno to sneak into a Miss USA competition. Because we didn't want to pay $350 for tickets, we pretended to be part of the press. But once we arrived at the venue, we found out that press and media were allowed only in the press room and not the actual theater, which defeated our purpose. We had come with five hundred postcards with Queenly discount codes to hand out to the contestants themselves.

"We'll just have to sneak into the theater," I said.

Kathy and I each took a tequila shot at the bar and toasted to Queenly for extra confidence. Then, when people started flocking toward the theater for the start of the show, I tried convincing four different ushers before one of them escorted us in.

Giddy, we found empty seats and watched the show. At intermission, we plastered the ladies' restroom with our Queenly postcards. Then, when the show ended, we flanked the exit doors and handed out all of our postcards, as if we were staff.

Each effort helped us gain users incrementally, and we completed our first transaction nearly four months after launching the app. We were screaming. Someone had bought from us—we were a legit company!

In June 2019, half a year after launch, we got accepted to a startup workaway retreat in Hawaii hosted by Wefunder. There, we met other founders and mentors who gave us that final push to quit our corporate jobs, pursue Queenly full time, and start fundraising.

. . .

Pageants go from the local level (Miss San Francisco, Miss Contra Costa County) to the state level (Miss California, Miss Nevada) to the national level (Miss USA, Miss Philippines) to the international level. Then, across each of those levels, there are independently operated pageant systems, such as Miss Universe, Miss World, Miss Earth, Miss Globe, or Miss Any-Other-Synonym-For-World. This means that the Miss USA under the Miss Universe, Miss World, and Miss Earth competitions are all different.

Add to that the different age groups—ranging from juniors to older adults—and the cross sections of pageants for plus-size women, women of specific ethnicities, and trans women, and you get about one hundred thousand independently operated pageant events in the US every year. But pageants are also done all over the world, so every year, approximately 2.5 million active contestants compete globally.

When we started Queenly, we went after pageant participants specifically because we could easily ask our pageant friends to sign up. Since then, we've branched into formalwear for any occasion. At least 100 million women in the US will need a dress for a special occasion every year, and some of our users will pay hundreds to thousands of dollars for dresses multiple times a year, even during a pandemic.

Still, not everyone grasps the significance of a dress, especially the mostly male venture capitalists and angel investors that we pitched for our first funding. Girls and women often wear dresses to life-changing events. A dress can give them the inner confidence to shine and overcome fear. A dress can be part of a moment that turns into a memory, which will last a lifetime.

We've had a mom book a last-minute flight to San Francisco to pick up her dress from Queenly because she needed it by a certain date and didn't want any shipping snafus during Christmas to delay her dress. When she arrived, she said, "Thank you girls so much. My daughter and I have been looking for this exact

> "We went from just one transaction every week in the Dark Ages of Queenly to over one hundred thousand users making plenty of transactions every day."

Our first company trip to Napa, CA.

A cofounder photo that we took for our first TechCrunch article!

dress for the past year, and we couldn't find it anywhere until we saw it on Queenly."

Through user feedback, we learned that we differentiated ourselves by offering search functionality up to size 32, whereas most department stores and brands stop stocking dresses at size 18 or 20. Furthermore, when a plus-size woman shops for a dress online, the model in the photos is usually a size 2, even if the shopper has selected a size 20 dress. On Queenly, everyone can see each dress worn by a real person in their real size, per our listing requirements, which allows shoppers to imagine themselves wearing it.

We also learned to design around the fact that women with darker skin tones who shop for dresses with a nude mesh need to find a nude color that matches their skin tone—otherwise, it's not a nude mesh. No other platform allows women to indicate what skin tone their dress needs to match with. These are a few of the differentiators we've been pleased to implement in our first few years.

We went from just one transaction every week in the Dark Ages of Queenly to over one hundred thousand users making plenty of transactions every day.

We've had people tell us that a dress that took them five months to sell on Poshmark sold within two weeks on Queenly. We've learned that for some of our users, making money back from selling their dresses sometimes meant the difference between being able to pay their bills or not.

The most recent win that I'm proud of is that we went through Y Combinator, which is the number one startup accelerator in the world, and raised our seed round. I had set an original goal of raising $1.5 million, but we ended up raising $6.3 million led by a16z. Our first, preseed round was hellish and terrible, and we heard no many times. This round, we were still turned down plenty, but my skin had grown much tougher.

Female founders received 2 percent of all venture funding in 2020, which is a huge factor in why startups fail. I believe the best way to help female founders and entrepreneurs is to fund them—many startups fail because they can't fundraise their first round.

Our next step is to hire more people, and this part is nerve-racking to me. Not only can the first people you hire make or break a company, but I'm worried whether I'll be a good enough leader and manager for our employees. Of course, I want them to help me grow Queenly, but I also want to impact their lives in such a way that they're going to love this job, be inspired by it, and feel motivated to grow as people—and maybe even start their own businesses one day.

Ultimately, my vision is for Queenly to be the first thing that pops into a woman's mind when she needs a dress for a special event. Kathy and I want to shake up the formalwear industry, which big brands have always monopolized and set ridiculously high prices on. We want to create a circular economy with these dresses and make them more accessible to all—so that girls and women who have felt hopeless and small, like I once did, can have at least one reason to look inside themselves to find their inner strength, beauty, and confidence and feel like a queen.

Even in the midst of a pandemic that sent loungewear and sweatsuit sales soaring, Queenly made half a million in sales in 2020, with over one hundred thousand visitors to their website every month. Instead of making their appearances at in-person events, these dresses restored a sense of normalcy and celebration to Zoom weddings, Twitch pageants, socially distanced proms, and graduation car parades. Content creators on TikTok and YouTube bought dresses for their videos, and some women played dress-up at home to ground themselves with a sense of stability. And what about Trisha's casual side hobby of being a beauty queen, you ask? Since her first pageant the summer before college, she's now competed in ten total pageants and won three of them. More recently, ever since she realized that Asian Americans are barely represented in US pageants, she's been competing in Miss USA, which is considered the most prestigious pageant system.

Even though Asian women perform incredibly well on the international pageant level, Asian American women have traditionally been perceived as too foreign to be crowned in a US-level pageant. Trisha aims to change that on the stage of Miss USA in her hometown of Las Vegas this year—all while rocking a dress from Queenly, of course.

Further information and resources:

- Explore Queenly's dresses on *Queenly.com* or from the Queenly app.

- Check out Trisha and Kathy's episode on the Asian Hustle Network Podcast (episode 54) at *AsianHustleNetwork.com/podcast* and on Asian Hustle Network's YouTube channel.

- TechCrunch named Queenly as one of their favorite startups from the most recent Y Combinator batch in their April 2021 article, "Queenly Raises $2.3M for Its Dress Marketplace."

- Follow Queenly *@queenlyapp* on Instagram, Facebook, Twitter, TikTok, and Pinterest.

CHAPTER 07

LOSING EVERYTHING— TWICE

The story of twin brothers *David Nguyen* and *Jack Nguyen*, founders of semiconductor company *Ram Exchange*, multi-unit *Denny's* franchisees, and investors and board members of beloved boba chain *Teaspoon*.

INTRO Business and entrepreneurship content balloons every day, with more success stories, tips and tricks, and evolving business models to learn about all the time. So, it can sometimes feel counterintuitive to go back to some of the most basic tenets of hustling—buying low and selling high, spotting opportunities in plain sight, and getting lucky. For those who are overwhelmed with where to even start in building their business, Arthur Ashe— American tennis champion and first Black winner of a major men's singles championship—put it best: "Start where you are. Use what you have. Do what you can."

Identical twin brothers David Nguyen and Jack Nguyen exemplified this mentality completely. As twenty-one-year-olds, they started their entrepreneurship journey at the intersection of two typically invisible markets: the random-access memory (RAM) that powers modern computers, and recycling. With zero background in either industry, David and Jack acted on the clues in front of them at their warehousing jobs, and over the next fifteen years, they built a company that restores and sells over $40 million of used RAM in a year.

David: My name is David. I'm thirty-five years old. I'm an American-born Vietnamese. My wife's name is Debbie. I have two kids, a three-year-old and a one-year-old.

Jack: I'm Jack, and I'm also thirty-five. We're twins! Identical twin brothers. My wife is Julie. I have two beautiful daughters, Jolene and Jaycie, so we're JJ and JJ. David and Debbie are DD, and their kids are also DD. We're neighbors. We share the same backyard, the same investments, the same businesses—we do everything together. We worked at all the same jobs together. We went to the same school, UC Riverside, and studied the same major.

David: We're one. Kind of....

Jack: We have two different personalities, though. David's more serious, more laid-back, more of a tough guy. I like to talk more—that's the major difference. But we talk about everything together!

David: From when we were born until we were twelve years old, we wore all the same clothes.

Jack: The day we went to school wearing different-colored shirts, everybody thought we'd gotten in a fight. "What happened?" they asked. "Were you guys in a big fight?" But we had just decided it was time to be our own people.

David: We always had each other. We didn't need many friends because we had each other.

Jack: We also had the exact same health issues. If he had some condition, then I would get the same condition a month later: anxiety attacks, skin conditions . . .

David: Back in high school, we were bullied. Depression set in. We thought we would never get girlfriends, get married, or be happy with our lives. People used to always make fun of us because we have bigger lips.

"David's more serious, more laid-back, more of a tough guy. I like to talk more—that's the major difference. But we talk about everything together!"

We grew up wearing the same clothes like many twins do. This is us getting our medals for having 4.0 GPAs in middle school.

Jack: Bullies . . . They were so mean to us! I was so stressed that I wouldn't eat. I was 5'9" and 110 pounds in high school.

David: Doctors prescribed us antidepressants throughout high school.

Jack: But we had each other to lean on. When we hit our teenage years and started liking girls, we recognized, "Okay, I cannot be the same as my brother." It gets embarrassing.

David: You can't dress the same when you want to talk to a girl. They'll think we're kids! We realized that we could be similar but still be our own person. We even thought that we might not go to the same college, but then we ended up going to the same one.

Jack: I thought, *If he goes to UC Riverside and I go to San Jose State, I'll live at home and he'll live far away? No, forget it!* So we both went to Riverside and lived together. But then we had a phase where we lived separately. Because of the girlfriends.

. . .

David: We grew up in Section 8 housing in San Jose. My mom cut people's hair from our garage. My dad helped her, but he's older and can't really speak English. How much money can you really make cutting hair from your garage? At that time, it was four or five dollars a haircut. We couldn't afford toys, but we had piano lessons, Taekwondo lessons, Boy Scouts, and food on the table. My mom always told me, "I shopped at Goodwill so I could save money for you to take those extra classes." That's one sacrifice our parents made.

Jack: They dressed us alike because they wanted us to be close. We were also close with our parents because they were always working in our garage. We realized that family is all you need.

David: If you're raised in the hood like us, it's rare for parents to work at home. Normally, they're never around because they need to work odd jobs, and it's easy for their kids to get in with the wrong crowd. We only got into the wrong crowd when we went to college six hours away in Riverside—the gambling crowd. We used to go to the casino and play poker, blackjack, or pai gow. One day, we gambled away every single dollar of our money and another $10,000 of our school loans. We had zero dollars in the bank.

Jack: Then, we took out another $10,000 in student loans and gambled that away too! We were $20,000 in debt. I had to live off my girlfriend, who was working at the time.

David: We survived those months by setting up a poker table, buying nice casino poker cards, and hosting private games for other people to play Texas Hold'em on a regular basis. Jack and I would then act as a dealer and collect tips, our way to hustle and get some income to pay our living expenses. We did that for a couple of months until summer, when the poker players went home because it was a college town. We were like, "Oh shit. How are we going to live and pay for stuff?" I went online and applied for a warehouse job that paid eight dollars an hour. The boss hired both of us.

Jack: We worked all summer. Then, toward the end of summer, we lost everything. Again.

David: Everything! The first time had been in a casino, and this time was in online blackjack and poker, which is illegal now. After losing everything, we decided to overdraft my bank account using Neteller. Neteller is similar to PayPal, and it overdrew our bank account to –$2,000. I worked all summer, gambled that all away, and had –$2,000 in the bank. What the hell, man?

. . .

Jack: Toward the end of summer, our boss called me to ask if I could pick up his client from a hotel. In the car, the client told me about his life in India. He was a multimillionaire, and his wife was a surgeon. As a twenty-year-old who had never known money, I really looked up to this rich guy in his forties.

At the end of the workday, David and I drove him home, but he asked us if we wanted to have dinner and told us to bring our girlfriends too. We were happy about getting a free dinner! We talked with him for three hours at Applebee's, asking all kinds of questions.

"When people buy computers, they buy new, but there's a lot of money in used parts," he said. "I sell used RAM, used CPUs, all the components of a computer."

Our warehouse job was actually at a computer recycling company, so I started searching the prices of different computer components on eBay. I realized that one stick of RAM the length of my palm was worth twenty dollars if I sold it individually, but I could buy a pack of fifty for ten dollars total. We started buying packs of fifty and selling them one at a time on eBay—mostly to people who were building their own desktops and laptops, and big companies that were refurbishing their equipment.

We started with both RAM and CPUs, but then we saw that you could sell a lot more RAM than CPUs. One computer would have one CPU, while it might have two or four or eight pieces of RAM. When summer was

"We knew we needed to make RAM Exchange work. We moved back home in 2009 and made a warehouse out of our garage, and my parents stood on the sidelines and watched, just as we had watched them when we were young."

Our messy apartment when we first started Ram Exchange.

over, we quit our jobs. We were just buying and selling on eBay, making around $3,000 to $4,000 a month.

David: That's baller status!

Jack: If you're in college making that much money, you can go to Denny's every night! For the first year, we went to school and sold RAM as our side hustle. The second year, we dropped out. We decided that if we'd been side-hustling for two hours a day and were each making $2,000 a month, then we should focus on that. We called our new company RAM Exchange.

Before starting RAM Exchange, my goal was to make a $50,000 salary within three years of graduating college by working for the county in water testing. Our family never had money, so a $50,000 job was a dream. But when RAM Exchange took off, we told our mom, "Okay, we know you want us to go to school and become pharmacists, but we think we can scale and make good money. With your blessing, we want to put school on hold."

Around then, our parents had both started having health problems and couldn't work anymore. My dad still has bullets in his back from the war. After being a POW for many years because he had been a captain in the army, he started over in his forties: got married while speaking no English and having no money, and he has PTSD to this day. Both of my parents never had the opportunity to succeed in life, and their hair salon was out of business. We knew we needed to make RAM Exchange work. We moved back home in 2009 and made a warehouse out of our garage, and my parents stood on the sidelines and watched, just as we had watched them when we were young.

. . .

Jack: We were fortunate when we started in 2006. Computers were still relatively expensive, and not many people competed in the industry. The first five years were no joke—it was really hard. We put all our money in one basket. We had customers who didn't pay us. We almost went out of business a couple of times.

We spent all our time meeting buyers on eBay, cold calling, and cold emailing to find customers and vendors. We were doing a thousand cold calls a month, and businesses kept hanging up on us. But as soon as we got lucky and hit that one customer or that one vendor, that would blow it all up. When we got some of these big customers like Lockheed Martin, we went from making up to $4,000 of profit a month to making $25,000 in some months—and that was net profit in our pockets!

David: After moving back home in 2009, we became Denny's franchisees.

Jack: We used our life savings to buy our first restaurant, Lyon's, and worked there for six months to get experience. Then we converted it into our first Denny's. That became the number one Denny's on the West Coast, outside Las Vegas. There are four hundred Denny's in California. Four hundred! But we were number one.

We got into Denny's because, even though you can outsource manufacturing and a lot of other things, you can't outsource restaurants. Americans will always eat. We looked at other casual dining restaurant concepts but did not like them.

David: Our first Denny's is next to the San Francisco International Airport. From there, we got all the way up to nine restaurants. Luckily, we sold four of them right before COVID, which saved us. Casual dining restaurants suffered the most during this pandemic. Quick-service restaurants are doing a lot better. We run a boba franchise called Teaspoon. We consider ourselves an American boba company, and we want to bring it to mainstream America. To us, Teaspoon is a lifestyle brand where people think of happy moments when they drink boba. You are usually in a good mood when you and your friends or family go out to get dessert, and boba is basically a dessert drink. Our motto is "Enjoy life one teaspoon at a time." We feel like we are the Starbucks of boba!

Jack: Many entrepreneurs want to get into the food industry and have a dream of owning their own business. But it's not that easy. The food industry is probably the most difficult business to be in. Teaspoon is a beverage business that brews loose-leaf tea and uses the freshest ingredients. We pride ourselves on having baristas who serve artisan boba drinks. We have built a model that works for business owners with a strong customer following. Customers are coming back and telling us that they want more Teaspoon drinks!

David: We haven't always been successful, though. One of our biggest failures happened when we bought a full casual restaurant called Flames Restaurant with our business partner. We saw that their food cost was too high, so we lowered the food quality to have bigger margins and to make money. Instead of fresh eggs, we used liquid eggs. Imagine trying to cook an omelet, and it looks like steamed eggs.

Jack: Instead of thick, quality bacon, we used paper-thin bacon because it was cheaper.

David: Customers left.

Jack: And then IHOP opened next door.

David: Yeah, what the hell. People want high-quality food for the price they pay. We lowered our quality of food, but we kept the price the same. We wanted a low cost of goods. Make money, man.

Jack: We made money at the beginning and then we lost our customers.

David: When sales dropped to a point where we were losing more money than rent, we closed. The landlord sued us because we got in on a personal guarantee. We didn't know what to do and even thought about paying him off. We converted the restaurant to one called Red Rocket Cafe, and that failed too.

Jack: We hired a consultant and used a good chef. We opened, we were busy, and the food was excellent, but our food cost was 45 percent. At diners, the food cost should usually be around 25 percent. Again, we were losing money, and we closed. All in all, we ended up losing

" We've failed at three restaurants and screwed up in a couple of real estate deals, but you need at least one big hit, in either a business or an investment, to succeed. Because if you don't succeed in at least one venture, how are you going to grow even more? Our first venture was the lucky one that started us off."

This is the Teaspoon team in front of one of our stores. Amy (CEO) is in the middle. The three of us run the show at Teaspoon.

over a million dollars between buying Flames and closing Red Rocket.

David: After changing the name, our problem was that we didn't consider garnishes, condiments, and food waste. It pushed up the actual food cost so much.

Jack: You're going to need ketchup, mustard, onions, napkins. We didn't calculate all that. We weren't experienced at opening our own restaurant. We were used to franchising, just paying bills and making money.

David: That was one of our failures, but we don't regret it. Why? It was a learning experience, and we came to understand the importance of leases and operations. We realized what we did wrong and how it would make us better. We also learned not to be so money-hungry and greedy, trying to make every penny possible. If you want a business to thrive, to last long, you've got to do it the right way.

. . .

Jack: I'm very fortunate. In life and in business, people say it's always hard work that shows results. But do you know what the number one thing is? Luck! It's meeting the right people at the right time, making the right decision at the right time, and being lucky.

We've failed at three restaurants and screwed up in a couple of real estate deals, but you need at least one big hit, in either a business or an investment, to succeed. Because if you don't succeed in at least one venture, how are you going to grow even more? Our first venture was the lucky one that started us off.

David: Really, we got lucky with our first two. RAM Exchange and our first Denny's made us a lot of money. RAM

Exchange is by far the better of the two. Starting early at twenty-one years old gave us a head start.

Jack: We're lucky we focused on RAM. If we'd focused on anything else, we would not be as big as we are today. RAM goes in TVs, tablets, self-driving cars, and many technological applications—everything electronic. It's a very niche market.

David: The semiconductor industry is a multi-billion-dollar industry.

Jack: When we started RAM Exchange, we mostly sold to businesses that build desktops and laptops. We started struggling because people were buying fewer laptops and fewer computers as they started using smartphones and tablets! Phones use a different type of memory. We decided to pivot from computers and laptops to the server side, so we started selling RAM to server companies who were getting into cloud computing. Cloud became the future of technology. Then came Bitcoin and the cryptocurrency craze. Many big companies opened data centers, or crypto farms, to mine bitcoins and other digital currencies, and that blew us up. We went from $15 million revenue to over $40 million within one or two years.

Now that I reflect on our lives, I realize that we gambled everything away twice. It was frustrating to lose our money like that, but gambling also helps desensitize you to the value of money—losing it and making it, losing it and making it. It actually helped us in RAM Exchange, because we buy and sell all day. If we had only $100,000, and that was all of our money? I'd put it in. I'd take that risk. We are not afraid. It all started from gambling, anyway.

David: Nowadays, the most important thing we use our money for is supporting our parents. If it weren't for us, they'd

	be working until they're eighty. We came from the hood and grew up with nothing. We now pay for everything in their house and take care of them. They don't have a single worry right now when it comes to money.
Jack:	The thing that makes me happiest is making our parents proud. My mom and dad have had such a hard life.
David:	My parents never had the opportunity to succeed. Our goal now is to give them the best possible life. To us, family is the most important.
Jack:	The most important.

Further information and resources:

- In California? Check out Teaspoon at *TeaspoonLife.com*.

CHAPTER 08

A VOICE FOR THE AAPI COMMUNITY

The story of *Dion Lim*, an Emmy Award–winning TV journalist who tirelessly advocates for the AAPI community through her news coverage

INTRO If you've been following the rising tide of reported hate incidents against the AAPI community throughout 2020 and 2021, then chances are you've heard of Dion Lim, an Emmy Award–winning TV anchor with a sunny personality and a tireless dedication to the community. Not only did Dion break some of the first stories connecting the dots between early COVID cases in the US and increasingly overt anti-Asian sentiment, but she also does much more. She broadcasts stories on her personal Instagram that don't get mainstream airtime, organizes speedy financial support for victims of incidents and the first responders who arrive, and serves as a trusted leader in the AAPI community who cares deeply for others and advocates for policy change.

Anti-Asian hate is not an uplifting topic on its own, but we celebrate the hustle of Dion and hundreds of other community leaders who are doing their part to build power and solidarity, both within our diverse community and with other communities of color. We spoke with Dion for this piece in August 2020, with a focus on her journey through a dynamic TV and writing career that has allowed her to develop her voice and ultimately lend it to others.

It was early in my career at ABC7. I had been on the station for just three months, and as such, I wanted to be on my A game—not that I'm not on my A game every day, but I really wanted to show everyone that I deserved to be there and was great at what I do. After a very long day, I was anchoring the eleven o'clock newscast, filling in for the main person, and all eyes were on me.

Later that night, I got home, all my Spanx came off, and I breathed a sigh of relief.

Clink.

I looked at the ground to figure out where that noise had come from. Illuminated by the moonlight radiating through my window was a nub of bone from a chicken wing.

Earlier, I had gone to a friend's house on my dinner break to eat some delicious San Tung chicken wings before hurrying back to the station. Unknowingly, I had left one chicken bone, with its little cartilage bits, in the cowl neckline of my dress. Mortified, I ran the TV—it was midnight by now—and rewound the show. *Oh my God, please don't let there be a greasy stain on my dress for everyone to see*, I prayed.

Hallelujah, there was nothing! This oily secret covered in sticky sauce had been hidden in the folds of my dress in front of the hundreds of thousands of people in the Bay Area who had watched the newscast and seen only a put-together woman with her Crest Whitestrips smile, eyelashes on, and hair all nice and done. Part of me felt relief, and part of me felt satisfaction: *that really happened*. It was glorious.

The look on my face is discomfort.

I was not only wearing thrift store fashions and pants made by my mom, but I was bigger than all the other kids in my grade. What made it worse was being only one of the only Asian kids at my all-white elementary school in Cleveland and then later again in Connecticut.

My dad worked extremely long hours as a chemist.

As a scientist he wasn't big into talking about emotions. It was all about facts. It took me a long time to understand that it wasn't that he didn't want to learn more about me and my brother, but that he just didn't know how to communicate with his Americanized kids. I wish I had known that all of his hard work was for us.

> "I was twenty-three years old when I landed my first anchoring job in Kansas City, a medium-to-large market at a legacy station. With all my coworkers being one to four decades older than me, I was fully consumed by trying to be perfect.
>
> > I deepened my voice on air, cut my hair like Dora the Explorer, and copied everyone else's outfits—oversized jackets with shoulder pads over turtlenecks with shoulder pads."

. . .

I am the daughter of immigrants from Taiwan and Hong Kong, who wished for me to assimilate the best I could to the environment around me. Growing up in Michigan, Ohio, and Connecticut, I was always the odd kid out. In the Connecticut town we called home, Asian Americans made up 1 percent of the population, and my whole family was likely the majority of that demographic. As a kid, I hated speaking in front of groups because I thought people were going to look at me strangely—even more than they already did, since I brought pork buns and pork floss on steamed bread to school.

My parents had me sit in front of the TV every day to watch ABC's *20/20* with Hugh Downs and Barbara Walters so I would learn to speak English without an accent and become a better communicator. As a first-year student in high school, I also wanted to get into TV journalism because there was a guy I secretly liked in the program. That class was only for upper-level students, which required a special waiver to get in. I asked the journalism teacher to make an exception for me, and I effectively became the youngest TV anchor at my high school station.

Thus began my TV career: every morning, my classmates would see me standing at a table, wearing not-anchor attire, welcoming everyone to school during the Good Morning announcement, relaying school-related news and whether there was a cancellation somewhere, I mean—wink wink nudge nudge—really hard-hitting stuff. Do you remember the brand French Connection UK, abbreviated "FCUK"? Yeah, I was one of those high school students who thought it was cool. I saved up all this money to buy one of their FCUK t-shirts, took a purple grocery store sticker that said "Fresh Tuesday," and stuck it over the middle letters so it looked like I was blurring out the F word. I wore that on "Good Morning HK" (Haddam Killingworth, the name of my school) and promptly got in trouble for it.

I didn't take the idea of journalism seriously back then. To me, it was an excuse to be on TV and do stupid high schooler stuff. Still, I had a knack for it, and it was much better than learning about chemistry and history and the other things I was bad at remembering. Eventually, I realized that every day is different, and when you're on TV, you get to have a voice—or at least give it to someone else.

I learned about a partnership between our high school and FOX 61, a FOX affiliate called Student News. Students could submit news stories, and the best ones would be broadcast on the air while earning the students scholarships. They aired my stories, and I received a significant amount of scholarship money from them. I interned there for multiple summers, allowing me to get my foot in the door.

I was twenty-three years old when I landed my first anchoring job in Kansas City, a medium-to-large market at a legacy station. With all my coworkers being one to four decades older than me, I was fully consumed by trying to be perfect. I deepened my voice on air, cut my hair like Dora the Explorer, and copied everyone else's outfits—oversized jackets with shoulder pads over turtlenecks with shoulder pads. Most nights, I lay awake while staring at the ceiling, not only because I had to wake up at two or three in the morning for work anyway, but because my mind gorged itself on worries about what I was going to say the next day.

I focused so much on being perfect that the opposite happened. Every day, I stumbled over my words on air, to the point that my boss warned, "You've got to clean up your act, or else you are going to look like a total disaster." On a particularly bad anchoring day, while reading a story about the Speaker of the House at the time, John Boehner (pronounced "Bainer"), I called him John "Boner" multiple times. I'd been too preoccupied with how I looked on TV and whether I would make that exact mispronunciation.

One day, the vice president of News called me to his office. *This is it*, I thought. *I'm fired. My anchoring career is over before it started.*

"Dion, do you know why I hired you?" he asked as I entered the room.

"Because I was cheap?"

"No."

"Because I'm Asian, and you had to fill some kind of Asian quota."

"No," he said. "I hired you, because of you. When you came in for this interview, you were effervescent. You dressed like a twenty-three-year-old professional person should. You did not have"—he gestured toward me—"this turtleneck."

I took his words to heart. At home that day, I threw away all my boring black, gray, and brown suits with shoulder pads. The next morning, I put on a dress in a bright color, and everything changed for me in an instant. I could move my arms, I could express myself, and I was not afraid to smile. I realized I was onto something: maybe "me" is enough. Even today, color is correlated with how I feel, and I don't own any clothing in black.

. . .

The day of an anchor can go one of two ways. Get to work, shoot a promo, sit, read, repeat. Same for reporters. Attend the editorial meeting, do whatever story someone hands you, go live in

A VOICE FOR THE AAPI COMMUNITY

Get ready for some funky mis-matched thrift shop fashions! If only as a kid I knew this would one day be cool.

Bundled up before school on one of those cold Cleveland winters. Again, plaid jacket, pink boots, red hat. I was a Salvation Army fashion poster child!

the field and go home. There are many journalists who think this is fine, but actually, it's not fine—it makes me mad. Because we have voices that are powerful and can change the world around us for the better. Especially now, during this time where race and social justice are at the forefront of many people's minds. To me, the idea of sitting back and doing nothing while Asian Americans are under attack and communities of color are suffering is a disservice—these groups need a voice more than ever.

There are still anchors who make a ton of money by just sitting in front of the camera and reading off a script. Their value comes from being the face of a news program for forty years. But today, in a difficult economic climate where people get their news from social media and more newscasts than ever before, we have to make a name for ourselves in the community. To me, anchors are better communicators if they can tell the stories of the people

Reconnecting with my parents many years after I graduated and left home for my TV journey. Family meals by mom with a pinch of MSG, I realized, were a part of my own story.

around them and actually be invested in them. This means going beyond emceeing galas and being at events that we get invited to, but actually showing up, having conversations, and caring about the people around us.

I will be honest in saying that there were days I felt burned out before, chasing down fires, going to car accidents, going to boring city council meetings, and wondering why I was wasting my life. But I've always been passionate about certain issues, and my purpose has been renewed through reporting on the xenophobia and hate that the Asian American community is experiencing in the wake of COVID.

When the Gilroy Garlic Festival shooting happened in 2019, I was on the anchor desk by myself for five hours. I started tearing up, especially after hearing from a young boy who watched his sister get shot. That was hard enough, but when I covered the story of a grandma who was beaten in Visitacion Valley and left to die, that was the first instance I recalled thinking, *My God, she looks like she could be my grandma.* I went home in tears. The news can be too much sometimes.

Earlier in 2020, I broke the story of the older Asian man who was attacked and humiliated while collecting cans in San Francisco's Bayview neighborhood. That was a turning point for me. I had uncovered crimes in the Asian American community before, but the videos had always been blurred, so this experience resonated that much more. It made its rounds on social media, not only in the US but around the globe. News outlets from Asia and the UK reached out to me and asked if I had more information. That story put me on the map as someone dedicated to raising awareness of Asian hate. Not only had it reached a tremendous number of people, but it also showed me that we were onto something. Then COVID happened, and the stories snowballed out of control.

We never know when the news will break. For example, I am technically not working today, but I got tipped off to a story. As such, I feel responsible for working on it and helping those affect-

"The ultimate goal of covering these stories is to change public policy, urge our elected leaders to listen, and change laws."

Going live with the ABC News crew for a nationwide special to Stop AAPI Hate. Never in a million years did I think I'd have this opportunity and that the world would be listening.

ed by it. The other day, I received a tip from a viewer at eleven o'clock at night, so I spent the subsequent hours following up on leads. That way, at seven in the morning, I could pitch it to my team and make sure it saw the light of day. Because if I don't fight for it, nobody's going to.

The ultimate goal of covering these stories is to change public policy, urge our elected leaders to listen, and change laws. Whether or not that has happened is yet to be seen. One example comes from a story I'm proud of, which was about a Laney College student who received an email from her teacher asking her to anglicize her name. The teacher said that the student's name, Phuc Bui Diem Nguyen, sounded too much like "fuck boy." An anonymous Laney College professor later emailed me about the aftermath of that incident: *After your story, we had an ESL professor train us on how to pronounce challenging names and how to be more sensitive about it.* Even though it's not a grand, sweeping law, the fact that a school changed and acknowledged that this cannot happen again was significant.

These stories are meaningful to me, and for the longest time, I second-guessed what I thought would be good content every day. Pitching stories basically means learning how to ask for things, because you're making a case for someone to embark on this crusade of seeking answers. I remind myself that if an issue elicits a certain feeling or emotion within me, then there is something to it and deserves to be pursued. To what degree that is and how I go about it will change based on the subject, but I will push. It's like asking for forgiveness instead of permission.

A manager recently said to me, "You must like it when people like you."

"Of course," I replied. "If people can relate to my own story and they like me, then they'll be more willing to open up and share theirs. On the other hand, I also do not have a problem with holding you accountable and pelting rapid-fire, hardball questions at you to make sure you tell the truth."

We've got to sass people back and call them out. If we're in this job and have a platform, then when we see something wrong, we've got to ask why it happened and why we didn't do something about it. I may be nice, honest, and personable, but nobody walks all over me. I saw my mother and father constantly avoid ruffling feathers, keep their noses clean and their heads down, and do what they were told—but I've always been invested in justice.

Speaking out is hard enough as it is. We've been taught to keep our heads down and our noses clean and to not cause trouble. Speaking out would cause trouble. . . right?

Not anymore.

Because of the power of social media, speaking out can be as non-invasive as sending a DM or making a comment. When one person shares their story of an injustice, a snowball effect takes shape. Others begin to realize they're not alone and feel empowered to share their own stories. It used to be that about 90 percent of Asian American victims would *not* want to speak out and go on camera for an interview with me. Today, that number has gone down tremendously, and I thank the younger generation who understand the importance of speaking out and encouraging their elders to be bold and brave.

Since Dion pivoted her news coverage to give greater visibility to the increasingly overt hate incidents the AAPI community is facing, it's as if the floodgates have opened. Asians from across the world have asked for guidance or help with amplifying their stories. For every naysayer or critic of sharing these stories, there are a thousand who want to scream about the mission from the mountaintops and make their voices heard. Asian Americans are bucking the model minority myth, taking a stand, and coming out in droves. Seeing the change is inspiring and starts a snowball effect that empowers more people to act.

Further information and resources:

  • Dion published her first book, *Make Your Moment: The Savvy Woman's Communication Playbook for Getting the Success You Want*, in 2019. Her book is a labor of love that documents the career battlefield she navigated in her rise from local reporting to a national stage, and it focuses on practical tips for better workplace communication that women who are also seeking to "make their moment" can implement.

  • You can stay in touch with Dion *@dionlimtv* on Instagram, Twitter, and Facebook.

CHAPTER 09

MY FIRST AMERICAN DOLLAR

The story of *Mony Nop*, a community leader, advocate, and entrepreneur who will never forget where he came from

CONTENT WARNING

Alcohol abuse, death, gambling addiction, intimate partner violence, war

INTRO   Mony Nop's childhood took him from the Killing Fields of Cambodia to refugee camps in Thailand and the Philippines, then finally to Stockton, California. Along the way, he had no choice but to develop his creativity, ingenuity, and perseverance—all key to hustling—to outlast seemingly endless hardships. The only thing he lacked was leadership skills. He had no role models of responsibility and accountability, no mentors to ask questions, and no understanding of how to effect real change.

> At age seventeen, Mony decided to take his life into his own hands, and he resolved to become a person who would serve others. After twenty years of working in service jobs, he started his own businesses, nonprofits, and foundations to build greater community power in his current home city of Livermore, California. In 2020, he even ran for Mayor for his city. But his journey began on the other side of the world, in war-torn Cambodia . . .

For the first six years of my life, my family lived in a shack that stood on stilts in the Killing Fields of Cambodia—labor camps set up during the Cambodian Genocide for Pol Pot's communist regime, the Khmer Rouge, which killed over two million Cambodian people between 1975 to 1979.

We had no running water, no electricity, and no food. My parents worked from six in the morning until six at night, wearing all-black clothing to dig ditches and plant rice. I wouldn't see them until the evening, when we would sit in a small circle on a dirt floor, clenching our bowls and spoons as we waited for someone to put food into the center of the circle. Once, when I was five, I sat with children my age and waited. As the food was running out, I dumped the last of the group's food into my bowl. One boy was so mad that he jumped up, latched on to me, and bit me on my chest. I still bear a two-inch bite mark on the right side of my chest as a reminder of my childhood and where I came from.

In 1979, the Vietnamese army fought the Khmer Rouge and liberated our country, creating the perfect opportunity for my family to leave the communist rule. We left everything behind and followed thousands of refugees to somewhere unknown. As a child who was hungry and scared, all I could think about was stepping on a land mine and blowing myself to pieces.

Amid bombs going off, people getting shot and maimed, and dead bodies littering the place, we walked all the way to the border of Thailand. We snuck into the country in the middle of the night and somehow found our way into a camp called Khao-I-Dang, run by the United Nations High Commissioner for Refugees. The tent city, constructed from bamboo in the middle of the woods, spilled over as thousands of us overcrowded it. Robbers would make their rounds through the camp and threaten people with hand grenades if they didn't give up their possessions. The sounds of complete chaos rang throughout the night, along with the banging of aluminum cans, which people used to alert all nearby refugees that the robbers were coming to collect.

Because rats scurried all around the camp, the United Nations offered one dollar for every five rats that anyone caught, killed, and turned in. Shuffling through the dilapidated buildings in my thin slippers, I stalked each room with a wooden stick in my hand and killed rodents with it. Then, holding them by their tails, I would wait in an endless line in the hot, sizzling summer to turn them in. Sweaty and exhausted, I exchanged my first five for my first American dollar, which has also been one of the greatest ironies in my life: turning rats into money instead of eating them as food.

The UN workers would give our family a chicken to ration over four days. More than anything else about the camps, I remember going to bed hungry every night. Sometimes we would fall asleep crying out of hunger. Rats were one way to supplement our rations, or else we would use a slingshot to shoot birds for food. My father would skin them, season them with salt, and put them on a roof to dry them up. Once, in Cambodia, my brother

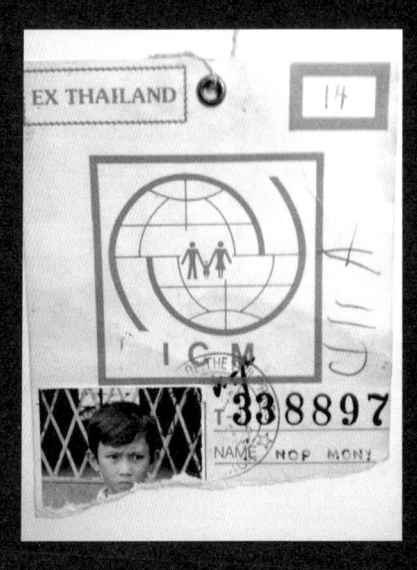

My only childhood photo
Entering into the United Nations Refugee Camps (Khao-I-Dang) in Thailand, 1979.

" Sweaty and exhausted, I exchanged my first five [rats] for my first American dollar, which has also been one of the greatest ironies in my life: turning rats into money instead of eating them as food."

My family, including my mom's only surviving siblings, in the United Nations Refugee Camps in Thailand, 1979/1980.

ate the rest of the dried up rats raw because he was so hungry. My dad spanked him for that because the rats were supposed to have fed the rest of our family. Another time, my sister and I were so desperate that we ate the poisonous skin of jicama. We became sick enough that blood seeped out of our pores, and we were certain that death was imminent.

After four years in Thailand, we were given permission to come to the United States. However, before we were able to do so, we were transported to another refugee camp in the Philippines, located in a tropical forest of Morong, Bataan. This way, we could spend the next nine months learning English and understanding more about life in the US.

This island was where I learned how to hunt and fish for the family at the age of nine. My father and I used an umbrella spoke, a rubber band, and a carved piece of wood to make our own gun. We would spend four to six hours each day in a stream, starting knee-deep and then swimming to twenty-foot depths. Armed with homemade goggles and wooden guns, we swam through the streams and spotted shrimp, eels, and fish throughout the crystal-clear water. For intervals as long as our breath would allow, we shot the shrimp, bagged them, came up for air, and went back down into the cold stream. When we became too cold, we would lie on boulders to soak up the sun and get warm. Once we filled our bags with enough to feed our family, we were done for the day. On our way home, we would pick the tropical fruit dotting the forest, from rambutan to milk fruit, find the firewood, carry them back to our camp and cook our catch for the family. Looking back now, it was one of the most amazing childhoods anyone could have experienced, one that taught me how to survive and be independent and resilient.

On July 7, 1983, our family was given permission to come to the United States of America. From our refugee camp in Morong, Bataan, we traveled to Manila on narrow roads. People got sick from never having been on a rickety bus before, and threw up all over the bus. The stench of vomit in a hot, humid bus will forever be seared into my memory.

Once we arrived in Manila, we were placed in a former prison camp, to rest and prepare for our flight the next morning. Our first stop was Japan, where our airplane refueled. We tried to leave Tokyo on one of those huge Pan Am planes with four hundred people, but two hours into our flight, we had to return to Tokyo because of bad weather. The airline put all the passengers on a luxury bus and transported us to a hotel.

> "On our way home, we would pick the tropical fruit dotting the forest, from rambutan to milk fruit, find the fire wood, carry them back to our camp and cook our catch for the family.
>
> Looking back now, it was one of the most amazing childhoods anyone could have experienced, one that taught me how to survive and be independent and resilient."

In the Tokyo hotel, people ran to the mirrors to look at themselves, because most of us had never seen a mirror before, or an escalator or a food buffet or a phone or a TV, which we couldn't figure out how to turn on in our room. This was the first time I could eat all I wanted, and I went to bed with a full stomach. When the phone rang in our hotel room later, we ran and hid because we didn't know what the sound was. Meanwhile, my aunt turned on the tap water and burned herself right away, since it was the first time we had running water. We'd also never seen toothpaste or toothbrushes, because we'd been brushing our teeth with rock salt.

The next day, we landed in San Francisco to be processed by the immigration center. It was summer, the coldest time of year there. This was when I received my first few gifts from America. The immigration officer gave each of us a jacket, the kind with fake fur around the collar and sleeve. I had never owned anything new before, so it felt like heaven. Then, about four hours later, we arrived in Tempe, Arizona. We all wore our jackets proudly, only to step off the plane into the 118-degree heat.

Our sponsors were friends of my grandfather, a Cambodian family that had come to the United States a few years earlier. They drove us to their home and cooked us a full chicken. For the first time, we had a whole chicken for ourselves as a family. We slept in a home with running water, electricity, toilets, and carpet. I had my own spoon and fork, my own blanket, and my own pillow. When they took us on our first grocery shopping trip, I wanted to cry—I'd never seen so much food in my life. During our first picnic, my siblings and I ate so much that we had to walk away, sit on a bench, and breathe slowly with our mouths open to hold it all down.

A week later, we moved into our first apartment, where my sister and I would wake up at six every morning and dumpster dive outside the complex. We'd find plates, canned food, and aluminum cans to turn in for cash. I would make my siblings line the uncrushed cans outside and fill them with red clay from our backyard, and then I would spray water into the cans. This way, the cans would be heavier when we recycled them, earning us more money from the recycling center.

When I started school, I was ten and a half years old, but I was seven on my official immigration paperwork. They put me in second grade, where I was the same size as the younger kids because of malnutrition. The first word I learned in my ESL class was "apple." Right before our first lunch, I followed the girls to the wrong bathroom because I didn't know what the teacher had said. I quickly ran out of the bathroom in embarrassment, all because I didn't speak a word of English and didn't know that the teacher had told us to wash our hands before we ate.

CHAPTER 09

"Survival was all they'd ever known. In our family, there was no love, no affection, no sweetness, no traditions."

With my family in our first
week in the US, 1983

Me and my brothers
in Stockton, 1984

My first day at Thew Elementary School, I wore baggy clothes and felt like an alien, just as we were described on our resident alien ID cards. I had to eat the fruit cups with my hands because I didn't know how to ask for a fork or spoon. Other students gawked at me in disgrace, or at least that was what it seemed like.

. . .

My father had gambled in the refugee camps of Thailand, but once he started gambling in the US, he made enough money to buy a Ford Fairmont, our first four-door car. One year into our stay in our new country, my father got into beef with someone while gambling, so we had to move to Stockton, California, before trouble brewed.

My father started drinking vodka like water. As soon as he woke up in the morning, he would down half a bottle. He and my mother bickered all the time, but they still went everywhere together—both of them absent from my childhood and from my life.

How would they have known how to be good parents? When my father was five, the French secret police in Cambodia snatched his father away and shot him in the head down the street from their home, leaving my father an orphan in the care of monks at a nearby monastery. Meanwhile, my mother only received six months of education in her whole life before the Killing Fields, where six of her nine siblings were slaughtered. Then they came to the US, not knowing the language or culture of this country. Survival was all they'd ever known. In our family, there was no love, no affection, no sweetness, no traditions.

In order to survive, I had to learn how to forge my father's signature beginning in third grade. I signed all of my own paperwork for school until adulthood. Because of that, I decided to skip fifth grade and registered myself into sixth grade, where I met my teacher, Mrs. Debbie Cardoza. Two months into my sixth-grade year, I convinced her that I was older and asked that my birthday be changed to make me four years older. Amazingly enough, the principal listened.

With this new record and at the age of seventeen years old, I convinced the US Immigration Office to change my birthday by four years on my green card, just by showing them my report card. I went on to accumulate more than enough credit for high school and was able to graduate early so I could begin working to support myself.

Over the summers, I worked on farms as a child laborer with migrant workers, sometimes all the way in Oregon. During the school year, I started working at McDonald's for $4.25 an hour. On my first day, I didn't know what a cheeseburger was, but six months later I became employee of the month, because I wanted to learn and be great at everything I did. Those early immigrant work ethics are still with me today, allowing me to excel no matter what I decide to do.

Meanwhile, my father's gambling and alcoholism reached a climax. One day, when I was seventeen, my father tried to kill my mother with an ax during their heated argument. I had to jump over a sofa, tackle my father to the ground, tie him up with a lamp cord I ripped from the wall, choke him out, and hold him down until the police arrived. Shortly after that, I moved out of my parents' home.

I rented my own place and bought a car at the age of seventeen. One afternoon, as I sat at the red light on March Lane and Pacific Avenue, I told myself that I was going to do something with my life and would never be like my father. Thinking about the last moment I'd seen him before I left home, I decided to become a police officer.

...

It took me four long years to pass the police written exam because I was not proficient with the English language at that time. I didn't know I could prepare for the test by studying books, so I sat through every test I could, committed the questions to memory, and scribbled down everything I could remember on a pad of paper afterward. After four years of struggling, I finally passed the police exam at the age of twenty-one.

When I graduated from the police academy a year later in 1995, I was twenty-two with my first son. I kept testing to become a police officer. I became a full-time police officer on December 4, 1995, the day that changed the trajectory of my life. Then, in 2003, while working, volunteering, raising two boys, and going through a divorce and custody battle, I decided that

> "My life is no longer about money—it's about effecting change so that young people like me, who have gone through so many trials and tribulations, can at least have a fighting chance in life, too."

I wanted to continue my education. I attended night school at Saint Mary's College in the East Bay. Up to that point, I had read only six books in my entire life, but I graduated at the top of my class with a degree in business management. I'd always been street-smart, but getting that degree made me book-smart and developed me into an avid reader.

Twelve years into my career as a police officer, my back locked up with terrible spasms, enough that I had to be transported to a local hospital. I realized it was time for a backup plan. At the suggestion of some friends, and because of my love for people and homes, I decided to get my real estate liccnse. Every morning when my policing shift ended, I would drive an hour to Sunnyvale for my seven-hour real estate class. Those were long days with little sleep, but no amount of pain can stop me once I've decided to do something.

On March 2, 2012, I decided to quit my job as a police officer and transition into a full-time real estate agent. During that first year in business, with a lot of hustling, I sold twenty-seven homes. Since then, I've sold between twenty-five and forty homes every year. That's more than enough for me, where I can pay my bills and afford the lifestyle I want.

My life is no longer about money—it's about effecting change so that young people like me, who have gone through so many trials and tribulations, can at least have a fighting chance in life, too. Today, I'm the co-founder of the Tri-Valley Nonprofit Alliance, which brings together over four hundred nonprofits in the Tri-Valley area of the East Bay, and I'm also the founder of Rising Young Leaders, an organization focused on youth leadership.

I met my co-founder for the Tri-Valley Nonprofit Alliance in the elevator of the building where my real estate office was located—we literally pitched elevator pitches in the elevator. Six weeks after we met, the Tri-Valley Nonprofit Alliance was born. Thank goodness that elevator is so slow, allowing me to meet so many people in it! As a result of meeting people in that elevator, I've sold three homes and connected with an attorney that helped me form the two nonprofits.

At the Tri-Valley Nonprofit Alliance, we bring like-minded nonprofit leaders into the same room and ask them to share their best practices for running their nonprofits and stories about their growth. This allows people who've never done it before to learn from the community. The organization recently added a ten-week fundraising program, teaching nonprofit leaders to raise money and become certified professional fundraisers. We also share resources, a job board, and an equipment exchange. This revolving door of giving makes an alliance unique.

I left the Tri-Valley Nonprofit Alliance after serving seven years on their board. However, I still talk to my co-founder on the phone weekly, trying to find ways to help. Now, between the real estate business and the nonprofits, I talk to anywhere from fifty to a hundred people on the phone daily.

These conversations give me energy, and I'm most at peace with myself when I help others be successful. That's my own way of healing. My phone contains over 6,800 contacts, and the number continues to grow. Every day, I get five to ten texts a day: *Mony, who would I talk with for this or that?* It took years to build these foundations, but these types of connections can be life changing.

Behind the scenes, my goal is to give everybody in the community more access to opportunities. In Livermore, where I now live, none of the minority groups have ever been asked to participate in the political process. The city is about 11 percent Asian American, 21 percent Hispanic, and less than 2 percent Black, and no one in the existing administration has ever tried to educate the population on how to be involved in politics or decision-making. So that was why I decided to run for Mayor in November of 2020—to sit down with young folks and members of our diverse community and teach them how to be advocates, too.

What does advocacy look like? One example is that Livermore is about to choose our next chief of police. The current one is retiring, and in the interim, the city has assigned another white person to this position. It doesn't have to be this way. If we would like to see change, we need to organize so we can say that, collectively, we want to choose the next one. We should be writing letters to the editor weekly, organizing a rally, speaking up at community meetings and finding influential people in the community who can write those letters. We also need to speak at city council meetings, to tell them that we want the community to be involved in the process and have a say in the process, too. If diverse leaders were part of the hiring process, the next chief of police could be a person of color or a woman. As advocates, we have to fight to make that change.

Another example is that the Mayor of Livermore makes only $18,000 a year. To me, that's discriminatory because it means that only the wealthy and only the older generations can govern our city. I truly believe that someone in their thirties or forties could do the job just as well. Michael Tubbs, the former mayor of Stockton and a Stanford grad, was elected at twenty-four years old. But because no one can make a living with that miniscule salary, only wealthy people or retirees in their sixties or seventies with great wealth and benefits can do the job. If someone is older or has always had wealth, how would they understand what a person living below the poverty line goes through? What about people who don't speak the same language? How would they be included in the process and lifted up, too?

Even if I'm not always vocal about these issues, I help organize others to speak about them. Advocacy doesn't only have to come from us—a big part of it is inspiring and organizing others to rally and to create a canon of voices with greater longevity. I'll never forget where I came from. After the hardships I went through and the thousands of mistakes I made along the way, nothing is difficult anymore. Today, I no longer have any fears of anything. When I reflect on my life, I think of one of my favorite authors, John Maxwell. John says that the first forty years of your life are about collection, and the second forty are about giving away. Now, I want to pass the lessons on so that the young leaders in my community can do the same.

At 22 years old, on December 4, 1995, I was hired as a Livermore police officer. The national dialogue around policing has been charged, but personally, in retrospect, that day changed the trajectory of my life and the life of my family. I consider this photo to represent one of the most pivotal moments of my life.

"I'll never forget where I came from. After the hardships I went through and the thousands of mistakes I made along the way, nothing is difficult anymore. Today, I no longer have any fears of anything."

My oldest son Andrew, my grandson Kaiden, and me.

In the November 2020 mayoral elections, Mony received 35 percent of Livermore's votes for a total of 15,870 votes. He raised $45,000 for his campaign, in great part because of individual donations of $5 and $10, which meant the most to him because they showed the support of everyday people in the community. While he ultimately placed second in the election and lost, he brought bold and outspoken ideas to his campaign while representing the possibility of becoming the first Cambodian American mayor in US history and the first person of color elected in Livermore's 143-year history.

Further information and resources:

- Support Mony's work at *TVNPA.org* and *RisingYoungLeaders.org*.
- Learn more about Mony at *MonyNop.com*.

CHAPTER 10

RISING ABOVE ABUSE

The story of *Urooj Alam*, who started a photography business that gave her the financial power to leave her emotionally abusive marriage

CONTENT WARNING

Emotional abuse, intimate partner violence, suicidal ideation

INTRO   In 2017, a global Gallup poll revealed that only 15 percent of the world's one billion full-time workers felt engaged at work, with the number rising to 30 percent in the United States. Phrased another way in the poll, 85 percent of the world's workers and 70 percent of workers in the US report hating their jobs. While disengagement at work is far from the only reason that nearly 50 percent of surveyed millennials in the US report having a side hustle (staying afloat financially is a top reason), "escaping" the nine-to-five is a common motive shaping the hustle culture of today.

Not the case for Urooj Alam, though. She had taken a straight shot at her earliest dream of being a public school teacher, achieved it, and loved it. But a few years into teaching, she became a stay-at-home mom to raise her two kids—and became further entrenched in an emotionally abusive relationship. Without a way to return to her career and have the financial freedom and flexibility she desired, she searched for something she could do to earn money. She never expected that it would lead her to find a self-taught career that would replace her full-time teaching income in less than a year, and would also give her the power and confidence to leave her marriage.

I wanted to be a teacher ever since I visited my grandma's classroom in Pakistan. In her concrete room on the second floor of a dusty building, kids sat against the walls barefoot. She used the few resources at her disposal to leave such a positive imprint on these kids' lives that they would come back to her classroom twenty years later to thank her. When I went home, I taught an imaginary classroom full of eager students, with made-up words, nonsensical ideas, and my younger brother as my first—reluctant—participant.

Decades later, when I actually became a fourth-grade teacher, I sat on the rug in the front of my first classroom on the first day of school. The kids who encircled me couldn't have known that, in my head, I was flapping my arms and screaming on loop, "Holy crap! I'm actually a teacher right now! This is what I've wanted to do my whole entire life, and I'm doing it right now!" I was a teacher at last, and it was truly a dream come true.

Warsaw, Poland, 1988.

As a child I grew up around the world since my dad was an accountant for the Pakistani government working in foreign embassies.

I taught in Texas at Title I schools, where the majority of students came from families with lower income. What I loved most was forming bonds with the kids who were the hardest to reach, labeled "bad" for whatever reason. Several of them called me "Mom" by accident—they knew I would be there for them and that I cared about them. I spent ten to twelve hours at school every day, and on weekends, I graded papers, wrote lessons, and prepared for another demanding week ahead.

As a teacher, you always have to be the best version of yourself. For me, that became extremely hard over time. If I had been up all night crying and arguing with my then-husband, I had to leave all of it at the door when I entered my classroom. Teaching, getting my paychecks, saving, and being able to get myself a car and contribute to our mortgage all gave me a deep sense of fulfillment. Yet, despite the joy I felt in my career, my ex was beginning to wear away at my independence and self-worth, until I barely knew who I was anymore.

CHAPTER 10

> "Anyone who saw our photos would think we were a beautiful, happy couple."

. . .

My ex and I were married less than a year after we started dating. In my culture, and in many South Asian families, daughters marry and start families soon after graduating college. I always assumed I would, too. He was attractive, educated, and generous, and part of me couldn't wait to have an excuse to escape my obligations to help at my parents' multiple failing gift and toy stores around the Dallas–Fort Worth area in Texas.

Even though my ex was of a different faith—I'm Pakistani and Muslim, while he is white and raised Catholic—he converted so he could marry me. We got along well and had similar values and morals, yet I overlooked red flags from the beginning. On our honeymoon, he started cussing at the top of his lungs in our cruise ship cabin over a stain on his shorts. I'd never seen an adult so furious over a bit of berry juice. What was happening?

From there, we started our life together. Sprinkled in the fabric of our days, he made comments that were never so horrible in isolation, but always meant to put me down: "If I wanted your opinion, I'd ask for it." "What did you even do all day?" "Why is this towel over here? Why are the dishes that way?" The sound of me eating cereal or sipping coffee made him so furious that I ate in a different room than him—and even then, he would yell from two rooms over, "I can still hear you!" Never mind that he woke me up with the clank of his spoon against his cereal bowl all the time. "You're imagining things," he would say in response to me pointing out his own loud eating.

Maybe I really am crazy, I started to think. Not having the words to identify my ex's narcissism and emotional abuse was the hardest part of what I went through. I googled "What is verbal abuse?" and "What is emotional abuse?" early on in the marriage, but there wasn't much information about either in 2009.

After a certain point, I gave up searching. My ex had me close my personal bank accounts and cancel all but one of my credit cards, and he instead put me on an allowance. He said it was to help us keep better track of our expenses. After almost every visit to my friends or family, he would criticize them for anything he saw fit. He would make me feel guilty for spending time away from him. Going out with my friends was not approved. I'd always rush home after work, rarely joining my colleagues for post-work dinners or outings. They eventually stopped asking me to hang out with them because I'd always say no. I had become isolated. No one knew what was really going on—not even me.

My mom would comment that I had changed, that I was way too serious all the time. I'd snap at her and blame her or whoever else for something they said or did. To avoid confrontation, she stopped mentioning it, and I kept the isolation and pain to myself. When my ex and I struggled over a year to have kids, he said, "How do you feel as a woman that you can't even get pregnant? If I were you, I'd get a divorce so you can be free to have children with someone else."

We traveled together and would get along so well, and then my life would turn upside down again. Many times, I look back and wonder why I stayed. That roller-coaster illusion lulled me into thinking that things were getting better, that on our upcoming vacation, we'd have a good time. We just needed to work on our communication.

Once I returned to teaching after our first child was born, my ex often complained that I worked too much and that my job wasn't even important. He would say, "When are you going to stop this playing teacher bullshit?" Five years into my teaching career, I quit and became a full-time stay-at-home mom to my two kids. In that time, I set up a mini homeschool for my daughter. I had loved painting my whole life, so I sold a couple of paintings on Etsy. I wrote, illustrated, and self-published a children's book called "How Will You Leave the World Better Than You Found

It?" That gave me a much-needed sense of accomplishment, and I even visited different schools in the area to read it to students.

"You got this. This is great!" my ex encouraged—then immediately criticized me for spending too much time on it and neglecting the kids. He criticized painting for wasting time and money.

I let it all go. I was back at square one.

A burning need filled me, to find something for me. Yes, I was a mom, but my sadness came from a sense of feeling completely useless. I hated myself to the point that I cried when I looked at my reflection. I have no talents. I'm not smart. I'm not good at anything. I wish I could figure out how to make some money and be independent.

Many days, I thought it would be better to be dead than to experience the agony that I felt, and a few times, I came close to wanting to end it all. When my mom found out, she broke down in tears as she hugged me. "Don't ever do anything to yourself, because I won't be able to take it."

In this moment of comfort and vulnerability, my ex took out his phone and started to record us in each other's arms while he laughed. "You guys are so weird," he said.

He's inhuman, I thought. *He has no heart.*

. . .

Still, a small part of me wouldn't give up on myself. And I'm proud that I didn't.

I discovered photography when I started to see people sharing pictures of their families on Facebook. *I think I could do that,* I thought. I always liked taking pictures with my old, cheap digital cameras, and we had a six-year-old mom-and-dad camera. I watched YouTube videos, learned to shoot in manual mode, and bought a cheap 50 mm lens.

After getting that lens, I began taking pictures and posting them in a Facebook garage sale group in my community. I wrote that I needed to take pictures to build my portfolio, and I would take five photos for free. Any more than five would cost twenty dollars. Dozens of people responded.

At my first experimental photo shoot with complete strangers, kids were running around all over the place at the park—a totally uncontrolled environment. That day, two out of the three families I photographed paid me twenty dollars for those pictures.

"Twenty bucks? I just made twenty bucks. This family paid me twenty—oh my gosh, I just made forty. This is great!" I had tried so many different things and never made forty dollars.

I registered myself as a business right away and posted in the garage sale group again with a call for newborns, families, and events to photograph. With a price tag of twenty dollars, who wouldn't want pictures done? My calendar filled up. From twenty dollars, I raised my prices to thirty, then forty, then fifty, and then sixty.

People were paying me sixty dollars for a photo shoot? It was wild. I couldn't believe it. My ex encouraged me to invest in the best camera body I could get. In classic roller-coaster fashion, he went ahead and bought me a $3,000 camera. He even helped me transform the formal dining room into a studio space and set up the flex room as a client waiting room.

I started to gain momentum, charge more for my sessions, and build a reputation among moms who would recommend me to their friends. I found ways to make clients laugh, even those who were notoriously camera shy. I took a toy Elmo to photo shoots with children and did impressions that made both the kids and grown-ups crack up. I learned how to make a website, maximize exposure through SEO, and invest in myself through better lenses and classes from mentor photographers on every aspect of photography as a craft and as a business. I stood out even more for the price I was offering and for the value people were getting.

But as my successes grew, so did my ex's accusations. "You must be having an affair," he said. "You're neglecting the kids. Why don't you put photography aside? I wish I could put my job on hold, but I can't. You can put your photography on hold whenever you want. Why don't you do that and pick it back up later?"

But I finally felt like I was actually good at something, and for once, I wasn't going to stop. I was earning income and gaining a sense of fulfillment that I couldn't let go of. My ex's tactics of trying to make me feel stupid and worthless weren't working anymore. I started to feel strong again.

Just over a year after my first photo shoot with strangers, I left my ex. Since then, it's been a long healing journey, with plenty of help along the way—counseling at a women's shelter, self-help books, more counseling. I spent nine months meeting a counselor on BetterHelp.com once a week, working on boundaries, and learning what I want out of life. I made it out of that mucky, nasty, emotionally abusive situation with plenty of tears and internal conflict, but it doesn't stop there. Now that I've

"Still, a small part of me wouldn't give up on myself. And I'm proud that I didn't."

In 2014, I took this photo of myself after a long night of arguing. My ex would make hurtful comments then say I needed mental help if I got upset.

My first professional photo shoot in 2019. It was like I "leveled up" when I paid a professional to take my business photos.

entered into a new world of regenerative freedom and independence, I know I need to continue working on myself, but I've taken significant steps.

Since my divorce and rediscovering myself, I started traveling, purchased furniture I liked so I could upgrade my home aesthetics, and even bought a pickup truck to help me be more autonomous as a single mom and homeowner. These may seem like ordinary or normal things to many, but to me it's been a source of pride to be able to take care of myself in ways big and small. I'm in control of my life like never before, and that is a priceless feeling.

. . .

When I was a teacher, I constantly read or thought about how to be a better one, how to have better classroom management, how to handle difficult parents, how to be more creative, how to reach more students that were hard to reach . . . Whatever it was, I wanted to be the best at it.

I know I'm passionate about photography because I'm constantly thinking, *How can I get better? How can I take better pictures? How can I become a better businessperson? How can I improve my image? How can I gain a bigger following? How do I find my target audience?* I'm always learning. I have to figure out how to get better at it all the time.

I enjoy each day so much that I'm willing to fight for myself and my business. It feels like an addiction or obsession, but without the detrimental side of both of those words. I want it so badly that I constantly think about it, dream about it, and want to get my hands in it. It builds my self-worth, makes me happy, and gives me a fulfillment that I couldn't feel otherwise.

When I first started photography, my goal was to make as much as I made as a teacher, and I've reached and exceeded that goal. One of the factors that helped me early on was that I didn't try to start off charging hundreds of dollars for photography just

Photography gradually built up my self-esteem, which then opened my eyes to my own worth, which I had never seen before. In all honesty, I don't believe it's healthy for me to base my self-worth on my success as a photographer, but finding photography gave me enough self respect and self love back that I could finally see that I'm way more badass—talented, intelligent, capable—than I ever gave myself credit for!

because others in my area were doing that. I charged less because I lacked experience. I felt it was better to charge less and be more easily forgiven if I made mistakes. People are less likely to get upset about spending $30 than $300 on a bad photo shoot. Thankfully, most of the sessions were successful, and my clients were thrilled with the great deal.

> "I enjoy each day so much that I'm willing to fight for myself and my business... I want it so badly that I constantly think about it, dream about it, and want to get my hands in it. It builds my self-worth, makes me happy, and gives me a fulfillment that I couldn't feel otherwise."

Word of mouth spread quickly from clients. I kept raising my prices in small increments frequently. Despite how often I increased my rates, my calendar often stayed full. I offered incentives to past clients for referring their friends and family: a ten-dollar credit for every successful referral for them, and a few free pictures for their friends. This referral program helped, but I realized that it wasn't the discount or credit that made people want to spread the word. The reason they were excited to tell their friends about me was because they had such a great experience working with me. That kind of support has been invaluable!

Another significant factor was that I found something I'm truly passionate about. I don't think I'd work so hard at something I didn't truly enjoy. My mom has commented that I could be a data analyst because they make good money, but I'd rather not, thank you very much, because it would be soul-crushing for me. I want freedom. I want room to express myself. I want to create art, not spreadsheets. Someone else might get enough fulfillment from programming or doing technical work that they're willing to work hard at it, and I think the key is finding something you're passionate about so it doesn't feel like work. Then you feel motivated.

I frequently reflect on where I started, from $20 photo shoots then to $600 photo shoots now. I used to substitute teach in high schools for $90 a day, and now I make $900 at a newborn session that I truly enjoy. Reflecting reminds me how far I've come and motivates me when I look at my sales over the years and see the growth and patterns.

My business has expanded every year, despite the pandemic, and I continue to inch closer to my goal of making six figures. At one point, I charged sixty dollars for a nearly three-hour newborn session and provided plenty of digital images. I now charge ten times that and still book sessions. Seeing my own worth and valuing my time have been instrumental in this change. I also don't feel guilty charging more than I used to because I have the experience and know-how to back up my pricing. That and the trust I've built over the years have been big factors.

Some newborns I photographed a few years ago have been promoted to big sister or big brother, and I've had the honor of photographing two newborns for several families now. The same has been true with high school seniors, where I've later photographed their younger siblings. I recently photographed the firstborn of a couple whose wedding I documented in 2019. This was especially meaningful, as it felt like things were coming full circle.

Photography can visually capture the essence of who or what something is—not just the outward appearance of an instant, but all the emotions and power that go into it. For the first time in my life, I can enjoy the precious moments in my own life, the ones with my kids that I was numb to before: the three of us sitting together on the couch, watching a movie together, and eating popcorn. Soon they're not going to want to hang out with Mom anymore, so I have to soak it in. For my clients and for me, these moments are never coming back again. Every day, I'm thankful that I get to make my living by preserving the moments in photographs forever.

"I want freedom. I want room to express myself. I want to create art, not spreadsheets... I think the key is finding something you're passionate about so it doesn't feel like work. Then you feel motivated."

November 2018

First portrait with my children post-divorce.

From her home studio in the Dallas–Fort Worth Metro Area, Urooj continues to photograph some of a family's most precious milestones, with a specialization in newborns, children, families, and graduating high school seniors.

Further information and resources:

- Visit Urooj's business website at *UroojPhotography.com*.
- If you're seeking support for your mental health, we recommend checking out the Asian Mental Health Collective's Asian, Pacific Islander, and South Asian American Therapist Directory. You can also visit *BetterHelp.com*, as Urooj mentions in her story.

CHAPTER 11

ROCKING THE BOAT

The story of *Lucia Liu* and the zigzag career path that led her to start *Rock the Boat*, a podcast about unconventional Asian Americans challenging the status quo

INTRO In 2021, Asian American narratives have surged on a national stage. But as recently as 2018, the prevalence of Asian American stories in the mainstream was so low. After all, that was the year that *Crazy Rich Asians* became the first Hollywood film with an all-Asian cast and Asian director in twenty-five years since The Joy Luck Club in 1993.

It was on the tails of that momentum that Lucia Liu and her friend Lynne Guey launched their podcast, Rock the Boat, to highlight unconventional Asian Americans who challenge the status quo. Rock the Boat was one of the early podcasts that inspired this reaction from listeners: "Wait—that company was founded by Asian Americans?!"

Today, thanks to the efforts of Lucia and countless more creators, it's easier than ever to learn about the stories of extraordinary Asian American leaders, beyond just a handful of household names.

Starting *Rock the Boat* felt like birthing an elephant, except it took twice as long—four years—to actually do it. When my friend Lynne and I first conceptualized it in 2016, we sat in a coffee shop, talking about our zigzag career paths. I was running my solopreneur chocolate business, Lululosophy, while my husband and all of my friends were in corporate or finance or medicine or law. I questioned whether I was cut out to be a small business owner, while Lynne was questioning her job at a government agency.

We had always felt that there were no helpful resources out there for Asian Americans to guide us on figuring out our career paths. Since we are children of immigrants—parents with a survivorship mentality and very specific expectations for us—the follow-your-heart type of advice that we'd always heard in school simply didn't feel practical for us. Lynne and I brainstormed different ideas for resources through the years, such as a coworking space for Asian entrepreneurs in New York and a college career center workshop series.

Two years before we started the podcast, we put together a focus group consisting of eight of our entrepreneurial friends. Some had been running their own businesses for close to a decade, and some were working nine-to-fives but searching for more. We asked each of them, "What are you struggling with in terms of your career? Where are you finding mentorship? How are you hearing stories? What are some of the things you need?"

Lynne and I concluded the session thinking that we should create a career handbook. But at the same time, I had begun listening to podcasts as I tapped my chocolate molds late at night, preparing for the next morning's catering runs. The podcast that stuck with me most was *StartUp*, where I would listen to Alex Blumberg talk about his trials and tribulations setting up Gimlet Media. I realized that audio could be an interesting outlet for us. Asian Americans weren't represented in the media in general, and there weren't many female or Asian voices in podcasting.

"I realized that audio could be an interesting outlet for us.

Asian Americans weren't represented in the media in general, and there weren't many female or Asian voices in podcasting."

While Lynne and I were thinking about whether to create a career handbook or start a podcast, I sent her an article from Asia Society that discussed why Asians represent less than 0.01 percent of all board members in Fortune 500 companies: they aren't breaking the bamboo ceiling because they're considered timid, they don't want to put themselves out there, and they're afraid to rock the boat.

"Why don't we call our podcast *Rock the Boat*?" Lynne said. "That's what we're trying to do, right? We're trying to get more people to rock the boat, start their own things, build their own destinies, and create their own happiness."

We were seeing Asian stars in the new media landscape recognizing their talent and marketability, and they were telling those who weren't offering them contracts that they'd take their skills elsewhere and show the world what they were capable of.

So we decided that *Rock the Boat* would be the perfect name for our podcast.

"I'm on the boat," my husband still jokes.

All my friends are. They had always made fun of me because they're on these "steamships" in their solid careers as doctors, lawyers, and consultants. I had my hodgepodge entrepreneur friends, but overall, I felt alone navigating my entrepreneurship journey. I was making chocolates in a commissary kitchen in Manhattan for eighteen hours a day and lugging them around in suitcases to sell at food festivals, hotel lobbies, and coffee shops, all while wondering if I'd made the right choice in walking away from my corporate career years earlier.

In 2016, across texts, phone calls, and many more meetups, Lynne and I agreed to start *Rock the Boat* and to put our all into making waves in how Asian Americans understood themselves, their community, and their possibilities. As we stayed in touch over those next two years, our lives continued to expand in dif-

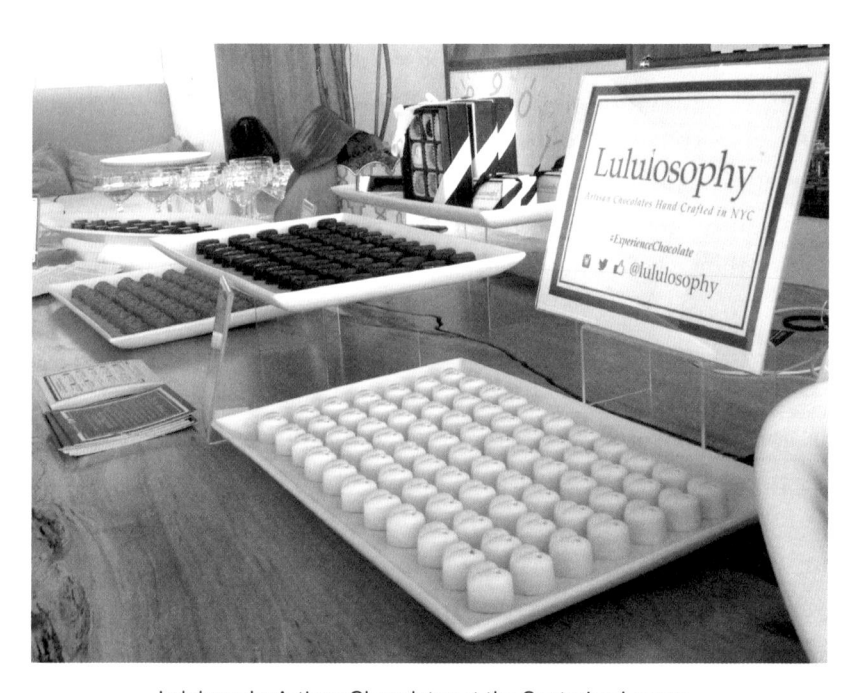

Lululosophy Artisan Chocolates at the Centurion Lounge.

ferent directions: she earned her yoga teacher training certificate and left her government job, while I shut down Lululosophy, obtained my real estate license, cycled through jobs at two early-stage startups, and got married.

...

Six months before we released the first podcast episode, we hosted a mini storytelling event as a soft launch. We each asked a few friends, and then thirty-five of us crammed into a little room at a coworking space in downtown Manhattan.

Roni told the story of how he and his father started their three restaurants. Monica talked about how her father's death had impacted her. This was a roomful of thirty-five Asians, and the feeling of camaraderie and belonging was palpable—so rarely had we created spaces to center ourselves and our stories. We recorded the session to feature in our early episodes, and from there, Lynne and I began reaching out to all the founders we could think of in our networks.

"You know, Andrew Yang is running for president," Lynne said. She worked for him at Venture for America, before he had announced his presidential campaign or gone on Joe Rogan.

I knew we had to have him on the show. I felt like nothing epitomized rocking the boat more than an Asian person running for president. After some deliberation, we tweeted him. Surprisingly, three days later, we visited his campaign office in a small Midtown walkup for the interview that would become episode 9 of season 1.

For our launch, we booked a beautiful coworking space in the Meatpacking District in Manhattan. Despite it being the coldest day of the year and quite out of the way, we sold out and filled the room with two hundred attendees, much in part because of Andrew.

The sheer number of people present made us realize that Asian Americans craved this space. We launched three prerecord-

Our Rock the Boat Launch event on January 15, 2019.

ed episodes to iTunes on the first day and had two hundred downloads right out the gate. Those first episodes were stitched together using recordings from our iPhones, then rerecorded, picked apart, and recorded again too many times to count. But we'd finally landed on a storyline that we loved for the first episode, an interview with our parents called "Standing on the Shoulders of Giants." My parents listened to it from Shanghai and texted me: *We're so proud of you.*

. . .

Over the next few weeks, we brought on more guests by shamelessly emailing hundreds of former classmates, coworkers, and anyone else we could think of in our networks to ask for introductions. We wrapped up season 1 with a group of self-starters, including local Asian American leaders and restaurateurs in Manhattan. We featured Deepti Sharma; Roni Mazumdar; Ben Sun, who founded Asian Avenue in the '90s; and Charlotte Cho, who's credited with bringing Korean beauty and skin care products to the United States through her brands Soko Glam and Then I Met You.

For season 2, which launched during Asian American Pacific Islander Heritage Month, we focused on Asians in the media. Charlotte Cho came through with an intro to YouTuber Michelle Phan, whose publicist booked us a time to be in LA. With that interview set, we bought tickets to LA and built everyone else in season 2 around her, such as the Fung Brothers, Jason Y. Lee of Jubilee Media, and Bing Chen, who founded Gold House.

By that point in *Rock the Boat*, the episodes had started circulating enough that people started pitching their own stories to us. Jason Wang wrote in about being a second-time founder who was formerly incarcerated and part of a gang. To this day, his is one of the most memorable interviews on the podcast, and we built the rest of season 3 around Jason's story—a heavier series tackling the more taboo issues facing the Asian American community, like mental illness, incarceration, bankruptcy, and regret.

By then, I had started devoting all my time to the podcast, hell-bent on figuring out how I could make it work long term. We started hosting weekly mental health events and talks about allyship, while I was running a Slack group of two thousand community members and forming partnerships.

But after wrapping up season 3, Lynne told me that she would be dropping out of *Rock the Boat* to get her master's degree and work on the Pete Buttigieg campaign. Talk about rocking the boat! I was happy for her . . . and I also felt like we were going through a divorce where I would be keeping the kid.

Lynne and I had balanced each other out well. She's civically minded, while I'm business minded. Even when we had creative differences, we always ended each day agreeing that working together made everything better. When I have a partner, I feel like I can do anything—if someone's relying on me to do something, I'll always get it done.

Still, I prepared to produce season 4 on my own. Around that time, Patrick Lee, cofounder of Rotten Tomatoes, had emailed his whole network about hosting an event in San Francisco. Looking through his roster, I was shocked. I'd never known that

Crunchyroll, Airtable, Patreon, and many other platforms were founded by Asians.

On a whim, I pinged Patrick that I was considering attending. He offered to fly me from New York to San Francisco, so I booked my flight and showed up at his event a few days later. Just like with season 2, I booked the majority of my guests for season 4 over the course of a single trip to California. Back at home, I shortened the production process and continued hosting events on the side. Season 4 was the most successful season in terms of downloads and listenership, but it was by far the hardest.

Rock the Boat has absolutely been a labor of love. Even though we topped a record one hundred thousand downloads and had over five thousand people attend our events, I did consulting gigs on the side to keep the lights on—and then I took a break.

. . .

Within my experience of the Asian community in the US, there was always this interesting dichotomy between the Asian Americans who've been here for generations and the more international Asians, which is somewhat closer to my own background. When I had attended high school in Shanghai, I'd always felt overly American, but in the US, I sometimes feel too Chinese. From a community perspective, we need to be more inclusive. Whether you're born in the States or consider yourself a FOB, you're still part of this struggle. No matter what, we are racial minorities in this country. No matter what, we don't look like most of the people here. And no matter what, we're going to be treated differently. We can be upset or angry about it, but that's the reality. So how do we as a community get together to fight for the things we need, and how do we create the resources and products necessary to help each other out?

My way of rocking the boat is to challenge assumptions with the podcast, and even with my guests. When I came back from my break from *Rock the Boat*, I recorded season 5 to focus on

Asian Americans disrupting the status quo in government, politics, civic engagement, and advocacy, leading up to the November 2020 elections.

We need representation, because no one else is going to think about us until we raise our hands and say, "Excuse me, we have this problem in our community. Who's going to give me resources to do that?" If we get a seat at the table, we can't just sit back and wonder how we can keep our heads down and do a good job. Instead, we should be asking how we can give back to the community and elevate the people we represent.

I started *Rock the Boat* with ambition, thinking I was going to change the world or that the podcast would be a huge success. When I was a student at UPenn, people would always say, "I'm going to be the youngest MD at this bank, the biggest this, or the baddest that."

Reach, reach, reach. Be, be, be. Do, do, do.

That mentality is exhausting.

Now, I think there's beauty in simply being alive and present, and I don't place as much importance on outward recognition as I used to. Instead, I wonder if I can make one person feel less lonely, or if this is something I'm proud of producing. If season 5 makes just one person want to work in public policy, volunteer in their community, or run for office, that's a win.

I've started thinking that maybe it's not the worst thing in the world to carve out a small space that's my own, almost like a little garden, and be content with that. Maybe what my parents have wanted for me all along isn't so bad: having a stable career, running something on the side, having a happy family, helping where possible, and impacting the people I can. Maybe, that's enough.

"Maybe what my parents have wanted for me all along isn't so bad: having a stable career, running something on the side, having a happy family, helping where possible, and impacting the people I can.

Maybe, that's enough."

Since 2019, hundreds more podcasts and storytelling series have launched to showcase Asian American experiences across all kinds of interest areas and fields, many of which Lucia helped mentor or even inspire unknowingly. Today, Lucia is continuing to work on *Rock the Boat* and other initiatives to support the AAPI community. She has spoken out against violence toward Asian Americans at various panels and with different corporations.

Further information and resources:

- Listen to the *Rock the Boat* podcast at *GoRockTheBoat.com*.
- Check out Lucia's favorite episodes of *Rock the Boat*:
  - Episode 12: Michelle Phan
  - Episode 22: Jason Wang
  - Episode 55: Adele Lim
- Follow @*rocktheboatnyc* on Instagram.
- The "bamboo ceiling" is a term first coined by author and consultant Jane Hyun in her 2005 book, *Breaking the Bamboo Ceiling: Career Strategies for Asians*. Ten years later, authors Buck Gee, Denise Peck, and Janet Wong at the Ascend Foundation published the influential paper "Hidden in Plain Sight: Asian American Leaders in Silicon Valley," which dives deeper into the mechanics affecting career mobility for Asian professionals in Western workplaces.

CHAPTER 12

INVENTOR, REINVENTING

The story of *Seibo Shen*, a cannabis entrepreneur and life coach

---

INTRO If you've ever felt stereotyped, then playing into people's contrived expectations of you can feel maddening. Yet, sometimes trying so hard not to fulfill a stereotype feels like just another side of the same coin. In either case, did you really want to do that?

Seibo Shen knew this dilemma well from a young age. Having grown up within Asian American communities and a family of a hundred cousins, he internalized his own stereotype of the Asian American man early on. But through his journey to prove others wrong about it—spanning the world of Hollywood, boba, psychedelics, and cannabis entrepreneurship—he found a new freedom from the voices that had been governing his life from the outside.

Growing up, I wanted to defy every stereotype I'd ever heard about Asian men: *They don't speak up. They're spineless. They fold over easy.* Or even, *They're highly technical.* Consciously or not, I *made* myself bad at math and excellent at speaking and writing so that I could be an Asian person who actually scored near zero on the math section of the SAT but high on the verbal one. Every time a teacher asked a question, I raised my hand like a firecracker so others might think, *This Asian speaks up.* In my heart of hearts, I didn't want to be vocal—I would have rather doodled quietly in my notebook in the back of the classroom and listened to others. But against my deeper desires, intuition, and self-knowledge, I always felt like I had to prove myself.

I grew up in a predominantly Vietnamese and Chinese community in the Bay Area, with entrepreneurial parents who had started and shut down a string of failed businesses: pizzerias, small motels, rental properties, and a jewelry store in San Francisco Chinatown. Not only was I surrounded by all kinds of Asian people in the community, but I also had a huge family around me: my mom and dad each have six siblings, and each of them has between four and eight kids. Being the youngest and smallest of literally a hundred cousins gave me even more reason to fight the expectations of people who claimed authority, whether it was my cousins constantly forcing me to do their chores, adults at my Catholic school telling me what I knew to be half-truths, or even commercials saying that kids shouldn't smoke.

My response was always "Fuck that. Let me see for myself." I first smoked weed when I was nine, and I was constantly picking fights with others, even though I was clearly shorter and skinnier than everyone else. When I was in first grade and saw my older brother getting picked on by his peers—all sixth graders—I jumped in to fight them. Those scars are still visible on my face.

In college, I majored in Asian American studies and became immersed in the rave scene, exploring both the angry and charismatic side of me that excelled in speaking out for the movement, and the side of me that had found something worthwhile in ex-

My younger days with my three Cabbage Patch Kids.

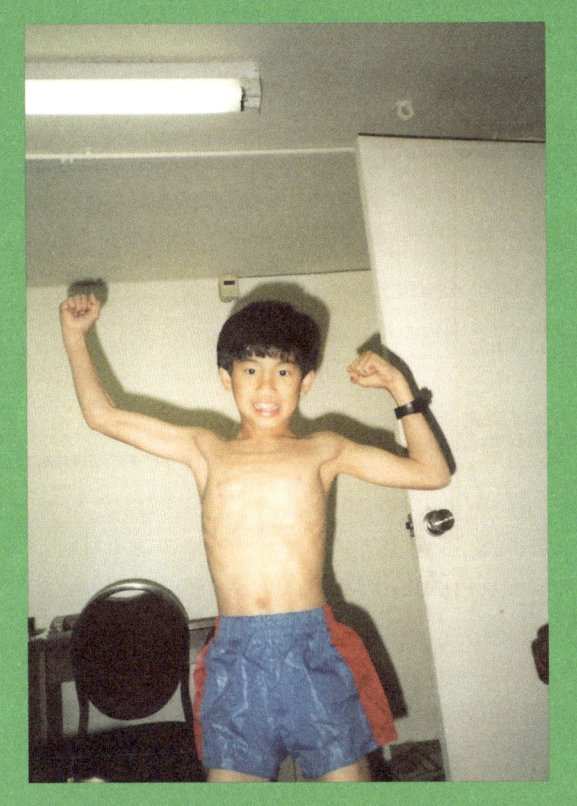

My obsession with muscle, age 10.

ogenous drugs: the empathy, the openness to ideas, and the connection with myself. After I graduated, I worked as a stuntman in Hollywood, which led to meeting Madonna, playing one of the "scrubs" in TLC's first music video for "No Scrubs," and enacting numerous Asian gangster roles in Bone Thugs-N-Harmony videos. Stunt performers earn anywhere from $200 to $300 a day, and with no insurance, an increasingly banged-up body, and a love of the martial arts but ultimately no desire to be an actor, I left the profession after two years.

I should probably get a real job, I thought. My sister had recently opened a boba shop and needed a manager, so for the next two years, I lived at home and worked for her.

One day, my friend stopped by and told me he was going to take the LSAT in a few weeks. "Do you want to go with me?" he asked, knowing I had nothing better to do as the manager of RAYS Tea Time.

"Yeah, sure," I said, even though I had no reason to take the LSAT.

I got high, tagged along with my friend, took the test, and did a double-take when I saw my score a few weeks later. I never knew I wanted to be an attorney, but I was really good at that shit! Maybe this was my calling.

Over the next few months, I applied to law schools and got accepted to Santa Clara University's program. Despite this unexpected twist in my journey, I had big dreams of making six figures as a lawyer. Leading up to the first week of school, I interned at a law firm for the summer.

"Based on your personality, you look like you're outgoing and like to have a lot of fun. I don't think you'll be happy as an attorney," one of my colleagues commented offhand one day. I ignored him—I had been accepted to law school, and I was determined to go down this path.

But as orientation week at Santa Clara neared its end, his words began to plant a seed of doubt in my mind. As one of the final activities of the week, we watched a presentation called "Five Reasons You Shouldn't Be an Attorney."

"Number one," the speaker said, "because of the dot-com burst. Number two, because you want to get rich."

These are my reasons, I thought. *If the third is also one of my reasons, I've got to quit.*

"Number three, you don't know what you really want to do with your life."

At that point, they said we could still get 90 percent of our tuition back in the first week. My decision to drop out of the program was met with significant resistance. Everyone in my family told me to just tough it out and that I'd be happy in three years. My sister Angela was the only one who told me to follow my gut, and luckily I did.

When we first immigrated to America in 1977 in Chicago.

My godmother and me in Taiwan.

Embarrassed and depressed, I started working as a video game tester at Sony. Instead of finding my professional calling and setting myself up for a six-figure career, I was making twelve dollars an hour playing video games and smoking weed all day. Every time I met up with my friends from college, who had all begun working at startups or investment firms, they talked about what they were going to buy next, while I was calculating how I would pay for my meal. I knew I had to make something of myself, fast.

At that time, one of my sister's friends was dating a guy named Glenn, who became my mentor. "I do software sales," he told me. "I make a quarter million a year, and I play golf three times a week. You like to talk. *You* could be a software sales guy."

My only work experience up to that point had been jumping out of windows or playing video games, so I offered to work for commissions only—no pay. At my first company, the salespeople had to make a hundred calls a day, all while standing. Then, at the end of each day, we had to interview another salesperson interested in working there, who could potentially take our job.

Trying to look like an office professional for the first time in my life, I wore a collared shirt that was wrinkled and khaki slacks that were five sizes too big. My voice went hoarse by the end of the first day, trying to charm the pants off everyone I called. Slowly, I realized I wasn't as charismatic or influential as I'd thought.

I finally closed my first deal on day ten. My rate was officially one out of a thousand, but it was enough for my body to learn its first evidence of success. The next deal took one hundred calls, and then twenty—which, at 5 percent, is considered a good rate for a sales rep.

Within three months, I became the number one sales rep at the company, and within two years, Salesforce acquired us for $175 million. While I didn't get a ton of stock options, I had experienced the Silicon Valley dream of going from a startup to a successful exit, and I suddenly had more money than ever before.

After the Salesforce acquisition, I went to a second startup called SuccessFactors, helping build revenue for a year and a half until SAP bought us for $3.4 billion. The same thing happened at a third company, then a fourth, then a fifth.

The happiness from each exit lasted for a week maximum, before I started thinking about the next thing. How many years of my life had I put into experiencing seven days of joy? I had just turned thirty-three, had my first daughter, and began to fall into a state of depression again. Even though I had accomplished my professional goals, I was still empty inside.

> "My voice went hoarse by the end of the first day, trying to charm the pants off everyone I called. Slowly, I realized I wasn't as charismatic or influential as I'd thought."

...

"Seibo, what have you been doing lately?" my former boss Chris asked as he got on a chairlift with me. We had run into each other while out snowboarding.

"Since the most recent exit, I've been helping my neighbor Mark sell vaporizers," I said.

Mark had created a janky vaporizer using a heat gun and glass. Since I was in between gigs at that time, I was helping him sell anywhere from $20,000 to $40,000 per month of his high-school-science-experiment-looking device that looked less healthy than plain smoking.

"Is he looking for investors?" Chris asked.

A few days later, I brought him to Mark's makeshift production garage.

"I didn't like him," Mark said as soon as Chris left.

But the prospect of my old boss's investment helped me see potential in my friend's product. After some discussion, he gave me his blessing to take over the business.

Given my outright rejection of math prowess early in life, I was far from an engineer—but I was a cannabis connoisseur. I understood the plant on the physiological and biological level, knew the boiling points of the active ingredients of the different cannabinoids, and had bought and disassembled over 150 vaporizers in my lifetime to evaluate what worked well within each of them.

I went online to Fuck Combustion, one of the only vaporizer forums back in 2009, which had twenty thousand active members who were all hard-core vaporizer nerds. I posted, *I want to start a new company and create the world's best vaporizer. If you guys help me with it, I'm more than happy to give this forum credit.*

As a result of responses to my post, I created a blog called *I Want to Build the World's Best Vaporizer*, where I would document the vape product development I was doing that day, post photos of my process, respond to comments, and actually try out people's suggestions. That blog received over a million hits in our first year and logged feedback from hundreds of enthusiasts in the vaping community.

There was no SEO optimization, Google Analytics, A/B testing, or heavy lifting to get the branding, messaging, positioning, and marketing on point. I was just authentic about what I wanted to do. So, my first vaporizer was essentially crowdsourced: I took the best ideas from people all over the world, brought them to a mechanical engineer in the Bay Area, and asked him to build a new prototype for me.

With my old boss's seed capital, I created that prototype and won the Cannabis Cup in 2013. The Cannabis Cup is the world's largest annual cannabis competition, where farmers from around the world submit their varieties and products to a panel of judges. The festival draws a crowd of tens of thousands per year in Amsterdam. We had hoped to win Best Vaporizer but won Best Overall Product instead—even better. Our device was the first and only vaporizer, to this day, to use an all-glass heater

INVENTOR, REINVENTING

The original concept for the Vapexhale EVO.

"There was no SEO optimization, Google Analytics, A/B testing, or heavy lifting to get the branding, messaging, positioning, and marketing on point. I was just authentic about what I wanted to do."

The current model the Vapexhale EVO, released in 2014.

core. This was a game changer because glass is inert and nonreactive, so not only was our prototype a safe material to use, but it also allowed the full flavor of the cannabis to shine through. In addition, the Vapexhale EVO produced some of the largest vapor clouds that could resemble the opacity of smoke (most vaporizers put out wispy vapor), which was unheard of from a vaporizer during that time. Once we won the Cannabis Cup, I was able to raise legitimate money by saying, *"This ugly design here* actually won the Cannabis Cup. If you invest in me, I will make it look production ready."

Back in 2013, the legal cannabis industry was still gaining traction. Finding investors for a cannabis company was next to impossible, so instead, we crowdfunded on Indiegogo. We surpassed our $100,000 goal, reaching $350,000 in the end, and we finally had the capital to launch Vapexhale. We designed an $800 vaporizer for high-end cannabis users. My first thousand orders were from my former colleagues. Over the next eight years, our team grew to thirty members, and Vapexhale became a preeminent brand for over ten thousand customers. Given the price of the vaporizer, this was quite the healthy revenue stream for a premium product.

Five years later in 2018, the market was going mainstream, with over 50 percent of states allowing either medical or recreational cannabis. We created a new company called Hanu Labs and launched a product with aesthetics we thought women would like. Then COVID started in 2020, and I knew we would be in a recession. People wouldn't want to buy $800 vaporizers anymore. We created our third brand, BRNR Lab, in which we took all of the Vapexhale technology and sold products for twenty to thirty dollars, based on Zara's fast-fashion model or affordable luxury brands.

Once I started realizing that our fast-fashion model generated more waste, my conscience started nagging me, which led me to start a sustainable hemp initiative at our company. Now, my partners handle everything related to vape, while I oversee the sustainable hemp and bio plastics for manufacturing.

In the last three years, our umbrella company, Hanu Labs, went from low seven figures to mid-eight figures. And this year, I'm going to walk away from all of it.

...

I interviewed every CEO I worked for and asked them how fulfilled they were with their exits. Every one of them thought that adding another zero to the exit would have made them happier.

"We just exited at one point four billion dollars. What would fourteen billion change?" I asked.

"I don't know."

Dude, you're the drug addicts here! I thought.

If a billion dollars doesn't make them happy, will going from one million to ten million make me happy? Probably not. I'm a T-shirt and jeans guy who drives a Prius. Why would having more money change anything in my life? I would just be able to buy more bongs that I think are cool.

I find that my mind is wandering during investor calls and updates. I'm not excited to show them the $40 million. They've already asked when the $80 million is coming. Realistically, if we could make that jump next year, we *could* have a billion-dollar exit. A 10x multiple isn't out of the realm of possibilities. But these questions deject me even further.

Do I want to stick around just so I can brag about how big one of my exits was? More recently, my intuition has been telling me that my calling is to teach fellow Asians how to rewire their central nervous system and their thinking frameworks so that they, like me, can start understanding whether there is true congruence between what they're wanting and what they're doing. To say "This is what *I* want" versus always thinking about their next promotion, their next home, or their next vacation. And being able to step away from my own businesses is proof for my clients that I can actually do what I teach.

I believe I've always followed my intuition, but I didn't know it at the time. I used to ask other people for their opinions, but in actuality, I was ignoring all the input I didn't want to hear until I found the people who validated what my subconscious already knew. A good example of this was that I listened to my sister even though every other friend and family member told me to stick with law school. But in the last year, I stopped asking people what they thought and started listening to my intuition. This change has allowed me to create a coaching side hustle that started making $15,000 a month within six months.

In every one of my journeys, the darkest moment and the brightest moment have converged into one: waking up and realizing that what I'd once loved is no longer what I love. The lowest low and the highest high are the same.

I've experienced this several times in my career. In the past, I would try to hold on to the status quo for as long as possible—for instance, sticking around for two more exits even though I was emotionally done after the third—but I know now that there's never an easy way around it.

I just have to reinvent myself. Again.

Speaking at New West Summit.

Since interviewing Seibo for this piece in December 2020, he stepped down as the CEO of Hanu Labs, which operates Vapexhale. For the open CEO position, Seibo appointed one of his former strategic advisors, Ricardo Willis, the first African American CEO of a cannabis vaporizer company.

Today, Seibo is solely focused on serving others through his coaching. True to his own journey, he specializes in working with C-level clients who've amassed decades of achievement but are looking for greater inner harmony or reinvention. He also works with other groups: Asians who want more leadership skills, emotional intelligence, and joy in their lives but feel stuck because of societal or familial standards; those who want to raise their consciousness so that they are better able to tap into something greater than themselves and experience the fulfillment of helping others; and people who believe that life should be fun and abundant, not just a professional grind.

Further information and resources:

- To find out more about Seibo's companies, check out Vapexhale (*xhl3.com*), Hanu Labs (*HanuLabs.com*), and BRNR Lab (*BRNRLab.com*).

- Learn more about Seibo and his coaching business at *SeiboKnows.com*.

CHAPTER 13

DORM ROOM HEDGE FUND

The story of *Christina Qi*, who founded a hedge fund, *Domeyard LP*, from her dorm room at MIT

INTRO Hedge funds have headlined the news, with stories of epic standoffs between everyday retail traders and hedge funds over GameStop and other meme stocks that kicked off 2021. But what exactly are they?

A hedge fund is a private investment vehicle whose goal is to maximize return on investment that's pooled from wealthy individuals, or "accredited" investors. These individuals must have an annual income that has exceeded $200,000 for the past two years or a net worth above $1 million, excluding their primary residence. A hedge fund can invest in anything—land, real estate, stocks, derivatives, and currencies—whereas mutual funds have to stick to stocks or bonds. In exchange for maximizing returns for investors, hedge funds charge a fee structure known as a Two and Twenty, which is a 2 percent asset management fee and a 20 percent cut of any gains generated.

For the most part, they are out of the public eye. And Christina Qi started one in her dorm room as a senior at MIT. Born out of an impulse to prove herself, she never thought it would be one of the rare few that actually survived over the course of a decade, trading $7.1 billion on its busiest trading day.

Christina grew up in Utah, after her parents immigrated to the US from China when she was three years old. She spent her childhood hanging out in the one Chinese restaurant in town. While her parents waited tables, she entertained herself by playing with straws, pouring sugar from sugar packets into glasses of water, and getting lost in thought. Before she entered the world of finance and trading, though, there was her high school homecoming parade.

"Oh, crap."

I emerged on the catwalk in my white lab coat and goggles, holding a beaker in my hand. Everyone was staring at me, and the pageant moms in the audience actually gasped. Before facing the crowd, I had thought it would be fun to try something new as the chosen representative of the science club at my high school's homecoming parade. I'd always loved anime, and backstage, I'd felt like a cosplayer.

"That's so . . . *Asian*," people murmured, loud enough for me to hear. As one of the few Asians at my school, I hadn't realized how embarrassed I would actually feel to cater to people's stereotypes. As I walked and waved down the parade line among the other delegates, who all looked like princess debutantes, my face burned with shame.

After the event ended, I stood alone in the parking lot. *Well, at least all the emo kids were proud of me*, I thought. At that moment, an email pinged on my phone with the subject line "Have you heard of MIT?"

Duh, I'd heard of it. I had always planned to go to the local state school where my parents had gone, Utah State University, and major in music. I scrolled through MIT's email, which was littered with typical buzzwords like "innovation" and "disruption." Despite how uninspired it was, at the bottom of the email was a photo of a young woman wearing a lab coat and goggles—just like me at that very moment.

Maybe I would belong there, instead of here. So I applied—and to my surprise, I got in.

. . .

When I sat in the student center at MIT, students around me were not only eating Chinese food but also posting pictures of it on Instagram. *Are you effing kidding me?* Dumplings and shrimp were suddenly the coolest things ever, whereas in preschool and elementary school, kids had called my lunch boxes with dumplings and shrimp "gross" so often that I would toss them into the trash can or take them back home.

Before I even had time to finish the thought, my friend, who was white, introduced me to boba for the first time. "Are you really Asian?" he asked. "What kind of Asian doesn't know what this is?"

Interesting, acquired taste, these bubbles. In Utah, I'd never even seen a photo of this foreign drink.

My next culture shock came while I was in my first-year dorm: all the students on my floor spoke better Chinese than me! Up and down the hallway, all the Black, Hispanic, and white students were speaking Chinese with my parents. What was this alternate reality?

I really did go to a school full of geniuses, and whether or not it was actually true, I felt like I was at the bottom of the barrel in every way. I got a 21.5 percent on my first exam, which was in physics. One of my friends teased me for getting a 21 percent, but I countered, "It was a twenty-one *point five* percent!" Feeling like I was barely going to make it to graduation, I declared management science, which was known as the sell-out finance major—and the easiest.

The benefit of my major was that almost every company has a finance division, so internships were never in shortage. Leading up to the summer after junior year, I'd worked at five internships already, all of which had been amazing experiences. But during the last one, at a trading firm on Wall Street, everything changed.

On our floor of one thousand people, I was one of only two woman interns. Because I sat next to the front door, one of my tasks was to greet every person who walked in. People would sometimes respond by saying hi to my boss, who sat next to me, but not to me. The other woman and I had to grab coffee every day, which is never beneath anybody, but in our case, the men on our team would start a stopwatch. If we didn't return with coffee within five minutes, we had to do push-ups. On the first day, no one told me about the five-minute deadline, so I obeyed and did the push-ups like in a fraternity hazing.

I texted my friend after work: *Ha, I was paid to do push-ups today.*

My friend texted me back: *Christina. That's abuse.*

Oh . . . It is?

I was clueless.

Our team would always compare me and my sole woman colleague in front of us. Because she was white with light-colored hair and I was Asian with dark hair, they would characterize me as the devil and her as the angel. They called me "Qibola," like the Ebola virus but with my last name, and "the lazy coffee girl" because I had stopped doing coffee runs altogether.

Meanwhile, she knew I was sick of the task and had picked up my coffee shifts for me without even discussing it. We both knew better than to pit ourselves against each other. They were trying to make us enemies, but we decided to defy their expectations and be friends, even if they only chose one of us for a return offer at the end of the summer.

At the end of our internship, we each had to pitch a stock in a final presentation. Since I went to a technical school, I presented a mathematically based quantitative strategy. My team absolutely hated it and laughed in my face.

Afterward, I cried in the office bathroom stall. As my friend comforted me, she suggested, "Well, why don't you just go and prove them wrong?"

With piqued interest, I thought that I might as well use my strategy to trade on the side during the semester to see if it would actually work.

That's how I decided to start my own hedge fund.

. . .

At MIT, a survey on sleep once showed that three in the morning is when the most students are awake at the same time. I found that to be absolutely true. When I looked around the dorm in the middle of the night, I saw some people playing video games and some doing their homework. At that time of day, it felt like everyone was doing the thing they truly needed or wanted to do. For me, that was trading.

Back then, before Robinhood existed, it was much more difficult to get started trading. I started an account with Interactive Brokers, put in $1,000 from my internship, and started trading the German markets at three in the morning.

I had already done three months of research about this statistical arbitrage strategy during my internship. The company I'd interned at used a more traditional strategy called discretionary trading, which is based on the information you can gain from your network. The other interns I'd worked with, including one whose family owned loads of oil shares in the Middle East, also used their insider networks to contribute insights on stocks to buy and sell. I wasn't from an oil family, and my parents didn't even know what finance meant. But since I went to tech school, I did know some data science and some statistical techniques. Why not analyze historical data?

For example, I might notice a correlation where if Company A stock goes up and Company B stock goes down, I can predict that they're going to come back together at the end of the day at some point. If I bought Company B and sold Company A when they split apart, and then the stocks came back together—called mean reversion—there'd be a high chance of making money from that knowledge. This is known as a quantitative strategy, or quant trading, because it's based not on insider information but on trade data from the past ten years, which is public knowledge.

Early in the semester, I started entering trading competitions to learn more. In one of the competitions, I got third-to-last place, but I met one of the winners and my future cofounder, a guy from Harvard.

We messaged back and forth and realized that we had the same career goal: we both wanted to break out as independent traders and run our own business or hedge fund. We met our third cofounder the same way. We had different majors and were from different programs, and we had nothing else in common, but we had the same career aspirations.

We decided to create a startup and go from there.

Hedge funds are often named after their founders: J.P. Morgan, Goldman Sachs, Morgan Stanley—essentially the names of rich white dudes. Between our three cofounders, our last names were Qi, Lin, and Wang. Even though we were all Asian, the US was our common denominator. We hailed from China, Hong Kong, and Singapore, and our parents wouldn't have been able to understand each other's languages. Still, any way we stacked our names, it would sound like a Chinese joke that no one could pronounce. Also, it wasn't SEO friendly, so it would be tough for people to find us online. Instead, we named it Domeyard after symbols of our schools: the MIT Dome and Harvard Yard.

Not long after my initial $1,000 investment, I had made 100 percent returns. Over time, I kept reinvesting the profits, and as my cofounders came on, they put in money as well. Within the revenues that we ended up taking home, there was an additional $40,000 at the end of the year. That amount was more than my parents made waiting tables. By coincidence, I was $40,000 in debt from student loans, and I was ecstatic to have earned enough money to pay it off.

Yet, in the hedge fund world, wildly enough, anything less than $500 million is considered small. Between $500 million and $2 billion is medium-sized, and anything over $2 billion is large.

Could we really make this into a career and formalize an actual hedge fund? I didn't have enough money on my own to manage, so we decided to embark on a journey to find investors.

. . .

With hedge funds, it's difficult to raise funding as a first-time founder, especially if you're twenty years old with no experience whatsoever. I signed up for every single pitch contest in town, as well as remote pitch events. The experience can be embarrassing because you're putting yourself out there and letting everyone judge you—sometimes quite harshly—with the goal of eventually finding the right investor.

One day, Microsoft hosted a pitch competition that had only thirty competing startups. They offered a whopping twenty-five different prizes, so the chances of winning were substantial. We were definitely going to win something at this one.

But when the words "high-frequency trading" came out of my mouth, the judges' faces dropped. In the end, we didn't win a single thing. Out of thirty startups, we were in the bottom five. That day, I lost to a chocolate milk company and an Etsy shop that sold knitted mermaid tails for humans. What in the world was I doing with my life?

In hindsight, the results made perfect sense. Here I was, pitching next to startups driven by curing diseases and fighting poverty, with founders who made products to delight their customers and make the world a better place. In contrast, we were a "high-frequency trading, money-making machine," as one of the judges called us.

At the reception held after the event, everyone congratulated each other, since most of the people in the room had won. I tried to hurry out, but I remembered that I should thank the organizer.

"Oh, no problem," she told me. "Thanks for participating. By the way, have you met Gary?"

"No. Who's that?"

She brought me over to an older gentleman. "He's in your industry. You should meet."

Gary and I went to a quieter place to chat, and I told him my struggles. "I don't know what I'm doing, I don't have enough money, and I don't have a reputation to start this fund, but I really want to do this."

"Well, how much money do you need?" He reached into his pocket and pulled out a checkbook.

"Wait. Is this for real?" I was on the verge of tears.

"Believe it or not, I was in your shoes at one point," he said to me, "It's time to pass the baton to the next generation."

He explained that he had started his own hedge fund in the 1970s when he had just graduated from college. He was a kid in this industry as well, working from a garage, and someone was his angel. They wrote him his first check, and now his company manages $100 billion—one of the biggest asset managers in the world.

I sat there speechless and in tears. I had started off the day by losing the pitch contest and feeling totally defeated, and by the end of it, I'd won a jackpot. His $100,000 check was more money than I'd ever seen in my life. I didn't even know if a bank could hold that much money. And when I called to ask, they laughed in my face. "Of course we can deposit that for you, ma'am."

...

With Gary's funding, the first thing we did was celebrate. Everyone in our dorm was freaking out because getting funding as a student back then was a big deal. I was so ridiculously happy. I was still a senior in college at the time, and that moment solidified that I needed to do this as a career. It was too exciting and fun, despite—or maybe because of—the startup journey being a giant roller coaster.

The next morning, I met with my cofounders in my dorm room and googled "how to start a hedge fund." It just goes to show that most founders are clueless as crap, and that's okay. The top result of my Google search was a video of a dude saying, "It was really hard, guys." No advice at all. Then there was an article that said, "You want to start a hedge fund? I'll give you an answer right now: *don't do it*. It's not worth your time. Most hedge funds fail." I researched for four or five hours and felt more clueless than when I'd started.

We took three years to launch, which is forever in the hedge fund space, but it took time to build and test our technologies and substrategies. During those years, we paid ourselves the bare minimum to survive. We figured everything out over time, such as setting up the computer programs, raising venture capital for our operations, and getting contracts in place with lawyers, accountants, and auditors. One year in, we started raising funds to invest from limited partners.

I'm not that extroverted, but compared to my cofounders, I like talking to people, pitching, and learning sales and fundraising. Though we didn't do titles at our firm, I did the duties of CEO, CFO, CMO, and C-anything-O that wasn't CTO. My colleagues, who were more proficient on the technical side, did the coding and infrastructure.

Looking back, a mistake I made was thinking I was worth less than my technical team members, and therefore asking for only half of the equity that my cofounders did. In the startup world, there's a stereotype that the nontechnical cofounder is less important. Especially at tech schools like MIT, the tech person has even more dominance. I, too, thought that I must be worth less because I couldn't code.

But thinking back on it, we wouldn't have had any success, raised money, or had employees without me hustling my butt off in a nontechnical, noncoding way. We were three cofounders, so we should have split things equally. If only I'd known my worth back in the day!

...

In the hedge fund space, the hardest part is getting to launch. When we finally turned on the trading strategies, relief swept over me. Many nights, I thought we were never going to make it.

In the five years after we launched, we traded $7.1 billion in our largest trading day. Our single biggest external investor is SoftBank, but we also raised money from family offices, financial institutions, and individual investors. A few years in, we received a phone call from someone at the old company where I had interned at—the bank where I'd been required to greet every person who came through the door. After googling his name, I recognized him as one of the senior people who had ignored me every day when I said "good morning" to him. He wanted to invest in our fund, but years before, he'd ignored me every day and hadn't even bothered to learn my name.

Over the years, we also learned many lessons the hard way. When my cofounders and I first started, we wrote down a set of principles (inspired by Ray Dalio's book of the same name) that we felt set us apart from the status quo, that were edgy and cool and different. It turns out, a lot of them were wrong in the end.

We made expensive mistakes in choosing the wrong service providers. We had to go through many audits, where the stakes could have been shutting down or going to prison. One year alone, we went through six audits. I couldn't sleep and often wondered why I couldn't just run away. Golden handcuffs are a real phenomenon in this industry.

Another unique aspect of running a hedge fund was that I received more questions about the morality of my job than about the job itself. I thought I'd be at least fifty years old before I started reflecting on what difference I'd made in the world, but we hadn't even launched the fund yet when *Flash Boys* came out in 2014. The book brought high-frequency trading into the public eye, and suddenly every time we went to pitch, someone in the audience would say, "I hate everything you're doing. You're evil, and you're not making a difference."

When you first start a small business, you aspire to pursue your dream or help your family or pay off debt, or maybe make a difference. But we were a money-making machine that made billionaires richer. And over the years, the cognitive dissonance grew and grew.

My professors, parents, and peers had all spent their lives making a positive difference in the world. And there I was, wondering what had happened with me. Yes, our company employed people and allowed us to pay off our student loans and help our families substantially. But once we grew larger, I realized that it wasn't what I wanted to do for the rest of my life.

It doesn't matter if we're trading ESG or socially responsible products that divest from fossil fuels; at the end of the day, the business model is to take billionaires' money and give them a higher return. I think it's important for hedge funds to be upfront about that.

After almost a decade, I left Domeyard and started a new company called Databento. At Domeyard, we wasted millions of dollars on data. After talking to my trader friends, we realized that market data is overpriced and that we could decrease the barrier to data by offering it on a metered basis, so you only pay for what you use. We provide data for our customers in a matter of ten minutes rather than months, which was how long it took us to access data back in the day. I've enjoyed being back in the startup scene, and I'm proud to have created a company with a positive mission.

I've learned many lessons over the years, and if there's one I can impart on readers, it's to normalize rejection. I still remember the first time I was rejected from an internship. Despite the sting, the rejections hurt less and less over time. We still get rejected daily, by investors, job candidates, customers, and more. But I've learned to throw them onto my "mountain of rejections" and try again with another investor, another customer, another opportunity. When you finally get a yes, it means so much more because of what you have been through.

Outside of Christina's work at Databento, she advocates for women's financial literacy on multiple boards, including Invest for Girls. In 2021, she published a memoir, *The Finance Snake: A Memoir About My Billion Dollar Hedge Fund*, detailing her unique and at times unbelievable experiences building her hedge fund.

Further information and resources:

- Learn more about Christina at *ChristinaQi.com*.
- Check out Databento at *Databento.com*.

CHAPTER 14

A TASTE OF HOME OR A SOURCE OF DISCOVERY

The story of *Sandro Roco*, founder of the first Asian-inspired sparkling water brand, *Sanzo*

INTRO Calamansi, also known as calamondin or Philippine lime, is a citrus fruit that strikes a hybrid taste between a lime and an orange, and it's most widely cultivated year-round in the Philippines. Given that it's only sparsely grown in the US at certain Californian citrus farms, most people in the US haven't tasted it before. That is, until Sanzo came along.

Sanzo is an Asian-inspired sparkling water brand that celebrates the unadulterated flavors of Philippine calamansi, lychee from Thailand, and Indian Alphonso mango. The name Sanzo is a portmanteau of its founder's first name (Alessandro) and middle name (Lorenzo) and aims to bridge cultures through its fresh and trendy fizzy-water concoctions. And just two years after its founding, Sanzo is fast expanding and opening the door for its fans to enjoy the flavors of their heritage or to discover something entirely new.

My parents immigrated to the richly diverse borough of Queens from the Philippines in the mid-1980s with my two older brothers in tow. While I was born in Queens, I was raised my entire life in Sayreville, New Jersey—a historic brick manufacturing town whose main point of pride is that it's the hometown of Jon Bon Jovi. It's a point of pride for me too, and I don't even say that sarcastically! I didn't appreciate it enough at the time, but Sayreville was such a dynamic place to grow up, with its dual identity of having firm blue-collar roots in the construction and manufacturing industries, and being an exurb that houses the eclectic workers of New York City. Among predominantly Irish American, Polish American, and Italian American communities, my family was among the first wave of Asian families in the town.

I came to love the area for the food triangle we lived in the center of. We would drive to our neighboring town of South River to eat Portuguese food, which is still one of my favorite cuisines; New Brunswick and Perth Amboy for incredible Latin American food; Edison for foods from every possible Asian diaspora in the US; and back to Sayreville, which has pizzerias and red sauce restaurants in every nook and cranny in town. As much as I love Filipino food, chicken parmesan with spaghetti is my greatest comfort food to this day.

I was truly a fat kid growing up. Ever since I fried my first egg at five years old, I was always standing on a chair to cook snacks for myself outside of the meals my parents served. When my grandparents came to visit us from the Philippines, I used to order the best dish on the adult menu while my grandpa would order off the kids' menu—and I would eat from both. I've always been infatuated with food and the memories that food holds. And like many other people I know, I first began embracing my Asian American identity through the portal of food—though I'm embarrassed to say that I only really connected the two in my mid-twenties.

The two people who first showed me that Asian food was desirable were David Chang, the founder and restaurateur of

I'd just finished a really long day, was exhausted and wanted to just hang out. But we had 100+ orders to fill, and it was time to get to work.

"I've always been infatuated with food and the memories that food holds. And like many other people I know, I first began embracing my Asian American identity through the portal of food— though I'm embarrassed to say that I only really connected the two in my mid-twenties."

Momofuku in New York, and world-famous chef and travel documentarian Anthony Bourdain. Bourdain was most known for his travel and food show *Parts Unknown* on CNN and its predecessor *No Reservations*. Not only would he travel to the Philippines and other parts of Southeast Asia, eating cheap noodles and drinking Hanoi beer with dignitaries like President Barack Obama, but if you listened carefully to his words, watched his body language, and married them to his Asian love song chapter in his memoir *Kitchen Confidential*, you could see that the region deeply impacted him as a person.

A tall, lanky white dude who had credence as an actual trained chef, he talked about how his favorite foods and cultures were those of Southeast Asia. He loved the flavors, the communal aspect of the food culture, and the idea that anyone, rich or poor, should have access to great food.

Before *Parts Unknown* and *No Reservations*, Bourdain produced a show called *The Mind of a Chef*, where the first episode featured David Chang traveling to a ramen factory and exploring the effects of alkalinity on the chewiness of noodles. Chang had trained under French chefs but famously walked out on his career at Café Boulud, one of New York's most prestigious French restaurants, effectively saying "Screw it, I want to make noodles!" His first concept was Momofuku Noodle Bar. Within its first couple of years, Momofuku (and I'd also include Xi'an Famous Foods) completely shifted the landscape of fine Asian dining, from white-tablecloth pan-Asian or Asian fusion into a casual dining experience that still boasted great food and premium ingredients.

Before watching these two riff on food and culture in all its dynamism, I honestly didn't know I could bring my Asian American or Filipino American identities to the forefront of who I was. Even today, I think most of us don't want to be defined by just those things. I'd always internalized a set of instructions that told me to push aside where I came from. After all, what did I have to offer? I mean, corporations don't care where you come from;

they care about what you can produce for them today. It wasn't until after I graduated from Villanova University, worked for three years as an engineer at a nuclear power plant, and moved to New York to work on the trading floor of J.P. Morgan that I got in the headspace that maybe people *would* be more open to hearing about my background than I'd assumed.

. . .

The seeds of Sanzo were planted when I was twenty-nine, while rising in my career as the head of growth for a men's styling tech startup and preparing to move to San Francisco to join my long-distance girlfriend. But we broke up out of the blue, and at almost exactly the same time, my roommates got married to each other. It was time for me to move out.

The first thing I did after licking my wounds was decide to reinvest back into New York City, this place that I'd always loved so much yet held at arm's length in anticipation of relocating to California. I moved to Long Island City in Queens, partially so I could afford to live by myself while still having close access to the city, but also because I relished the opportunity to connect with the borough my parents had first immigrated to from the Philippines. Over my four years in that apartment, one of my go-to activities after work was taking the 7 train farther out, exploring new areas, and trying the food in Jackson Heights, Woodside, or Flushing.

The startup I worked for was starting to plateau, and I began thinking about what was next for me. I had several opportunities from recruiters who were offering me different roles as marketing lead at other venture-backed startups, but I knew I wouldn't enjoy a position where I already knew what to expect. Mulling over the next transitions in my life, I opened the door of our startup's fridge one day and noticed that, seemingly overnight, the Diet Cokes had been replaced by LaCroix and five other sparkling water brands. This was 2018, the year that a sparkling

sparkling water revival swept over the country to the tune of $2.2 billion in sales and a projected $24.5 billion in the next five years.

How many other fridges at startups across the country are starting to look like this? I wondered. Even before I learned the actual numbers driving the industry, I intuited that there was an opportunity here. There was enough space for the legacy brands—LaCroix, Perrier, and San Pellegrino—and then some. And with *Crazy Rich Asians* coming out in the same year and K-pop breaking cultural barriers and reviving a palpable hype around Asian representation, I started wondering why there wasn't an Asian Perrier or an Asian San Pellegrino. In trendy Asian restaurants like Momofuku Noodle Bar or Ssäm Bar, where their cocktail menus included lychee soju and jasmine-infused gins, why were Coke, Dr Pepper, and San Pellegrino the only nonalcoholic options? I felt that, in another world, David Chang and his team would love to have an Asian sparkling water offering. In my head, my initial go-to-market strategy involved getting on board with Asian restaurateurs of David's ilk, similar to Oatly's playbook in the US, which gained popularity with consumers by launching exclusively in third wave coffee shops.

> "It's almost embarrassing to say, because part of me expected trial and tribulation at this stage, but I got the formulations right on the first try. The first recipe I developed in my kitchen is the same drink in the can today."

With this rough plan hatched, I turned my attention to formulating the product itself. I started out by buying a couple of liters of Canada Dry sparkling water, ordering purées off Amazon, and setting up a kitchen scale and Google Sheet in my kitchen. The spreadsheet kept track of my formulations to answer two questions: Does this thing taste good? And what would it cost to produce?

My purées were calamansi, lychee, and mango—the same flavors you see today. Calamansi was number one for me, and in my mind, it's the best citrus fruit. Filipinos typically use it in its pure form as a garnish, or in a limeade-type drink with enough added sugar that the natural flavors no longer shine. A formulation with only sparkling water and calamansi would be a new way to properly celebrate the fruit.

It's almost embarrassing to say, because part of me expected trial and tribulation at this stage, but I got the formulations right on the first try. The first recipe I developed in my kitchen is the same drink in the can today. The only difference is that now we buy purées by the container load. When you buy in that kind of bulk, you get access to the freshest, highest-quality ingredients from wholesalers, which aren't available on Amazon. And I'm proud to say that we source all of our purées from producers in Asia.

Because I self-financed the business with my own savings at the start, I couldn't afford to make big mistakes, just small ones. I knew I could only succeed by shipping product quickly, getting feedback, and iterating on it even faster to catch up to legacy brands that had more money for up-front R&D and brand development.

My first mistake was trying to bottle the home mixture by hand in my apartment. I learned instantly that this was not a part of the process to save money on. With all the safety certifications and equipment needed to do it right, we ended up needing to dump the first batch, though fortunately it didn't cost us much.

The way production for most beverage inventions works is that you hand over your ingredients and recipe to a manufacturer called a co-packer, then supervise the first few production runs alongside them at the facility until everyone gets the hang of things. I realized immediately that it was worth investing in a co-packer and that, in general, the high manufacturing costs in the early stages of a brand are what makes beverage an expensive industry to get started in. We spent $2,000 for our first pro-

CHAPTER 14

The very first batch of Sanzo was hand-produced in my apartment. Most of the bottles weren't properly sealed, so I had to immediately throw this batch away.

My first sale was to Bernie Yoo, my boss at the time. I'm eternally grateful for his mentorship, empathetic leadership, and now friendship.

duction run of around two thousand glass-bottled drinks across three favors—approximately $1 a bottle. I created a janky website and emailed my friends, family, and friends of friends to ask if they'd like to buy some for $2 a bottle at a minimum of one case of twelve bottles.

Because the bottles were incredibly heavy, I didn't want to ship them all over the country. I restricted the delivery area to New York City and decided to hand-deliver every one of the initial two thousand bottles myself. As orders started coming in, I loaded cases into Ubers at six in the morning, before the early commuters made prices surge, and used a hand trolley to cart them onto subways.

Customers invited me into their homes to shoot the shit, exchange cash for the goods, and give me feedback on the spot. In the first stage, I kept hearing repeat feedback that the colors of the liquid through the glass made it look as if the drink contained sugar. We were already planning to move to aluminum cans, so those comments gave us further validation. Our first labels also stated the calorie count front and center, but we found that a much bigger draw for folks was that the product was made with real fruit and contained no added sugar. Now, the can prominently features those two specifics, while the calorie count is off to the side.

I did zero press and zero promotion, but thanks to my friends and family's word of mouth and because of random people discovering us, we finished selling our first batch in a month. For all the talk of how much negativity exists in the world on a global scale, I learned through this experience that at a local level, people want to be supportive and see others succeed, or at least be part of their journeys. Within my closest friend group, I was the crazy one who decided to do something like this from scratch, so people were stoked to forward our information to everyone they knew. I started with an email list of just fifty friends and family members off the top of my head, and they were somehow able to spread the word informally to my first set of customers.

DIRECTION 1

DIRECTION 2

DIRECTION 3

DIRECTION 4

DIRECTION 5

DIRECTION 6

Sanzo was brought to life by The Working Assembly, a New York City-based branding agency led by Korean-American creative director Jolene Delisle.

The variety pack was our most popular item for folks shopping for Sanzo online for the first time. So we wanted to make sure our packaging for the variety pack delivered a "wow" experience.

Once the first batch sold out, we went back to R&D and launched aluminum cans a few months later in the spring of 2019. We began selling to trendy casual restaurants like Momofuku and by CHLOE. I also continued hand-delivering to our direct-to-consumer customers. But after two months, it was clearly time to start shipping. With about three pallets' worth of product sitting in my 500-square-foot studio apartment, my fiancé and I packed hundreds of orders to be shipped around the country as we constantly ran out of printer paper, bubble wrap, masking tape, and boxes. In that time, we relaunched our website, started to put money into paid advertising, and landed features in Grub Street and Epicurious. About five months after those features, we moved into a fulfillment warehouse, what they call a 3PL or third-party logistics, and I haven't packed my own orders since.

In the beverage industry, once you get moving and find product-market fit, growing and scaling tends to follow a playbook. That playbook has been completely rewritten during COVID, because people never used to buy beverages online, and this has been a game changer for emerging brands like Sanzo. It means we don't need to immediately launch at every conventional grocery store possible just to have people discover us. But at the same time, beverage brands still need to win on retail shelves in the long term.

Even without a global pandemic, it can sometimes take a beverage brand upward of a year to get on a grocery shelf, so you have to reach out before you think you're ready. This serves as motivation because you have a goal to work toward, like making sure this brand is ready for Whole Foods. That requires you to have all the operations, labeling requirements, and data to support that your brand is going to make a splash. After operating in the direct-to-consumer market and the smaller, trendy grocery space for the first year, I got Sanzo into the fifty-one Whole Foods stores in the Northeast region by sending a cold email to the buyer for the region and offering to send samples. Fortunately, the task ended up being that simple, but the preparation we'd done to land that business was what resulted in such a smooth process.

Beverage is an expensive industry to get started in, as is any hustle that involves the sale of physical goods. I had the privilege of putting in close to $100,000 of my own savings to front the twelve to fourteen months of R&D and production, then raised another $100,000 from friends, family, and angel investors to fund bigger production runs in the second year. The younger version of me would think that these numbers sound ridiculously high, but they're considered extremely lean and are the minimal amounts you need in order to survive. Most beverage startups raise over $1 million in funding before having a proof of concept, and if they fail, they can throw it at a wall and start over with no consequences.

We raised our first big round of investment of $1.3 million in August 2020. It took six months to raise the first $200,000 from investors, and only six weeks to raise the remaining $1.1 million—which goes to show how perception can matter in fundraising dynamics. Now, eight months later, we're putting the finishing touches on our second fundraising round. Typically, if it's going well, early-stage beverage brands end up raising about once every eight to twelve months, because that shows you need to fund more growth.

Now that so many different debt products exist to fund operations—better credit cards, more competition among lenders, better payment terms with manufacturers who know there's a hard asset you're going to sell later on—we don't spend nearly as much on funding operations as we used to. As long as your unit economics are healthy, you want to fund sales in stores, since that's the tried-and-true way to get folks to try it out, and you also want to give away your product at events that reflect your customer. For us, that has meant giving away Sanzo at any Asian gathering we can be a part of during the pandemic, such as in a swag bag for a Zoom gathering or at wellness-related events.

Though starting as a solopreneur can be incredibly lonely, I found zen in packing orders late into the night. With all distractions having gone to bed, I used this time to think about the future and how else I could build my business.

But the best evenings were when my then-girlfriend (now soon-to-be wife) Ysa Yu would join in. She's been a never-ending fountain of support for my journey.

Our first batch at our first co-packer, Organic Food Incubator, in New Jersey was produced in glass bottles and still required quite a bit of manual labor. I'm eternally grateful for the ecosystem that exists in this country to incubate small brands.

As an early-stage operator, I cannot overstate the value of being physically in attendance when a co-packer produces your product. Learnings from our first several runs have already helped us save tens to even hundreds of thousands of dollars as we've scaled up to new manufacturing facilities.

Ultimately, our mission for Sanzo is to bridge cultures, whether as a taste of home or a source of discovery. I see this as a continuous process of relationship building as opposed to a final destination point. With my generation's constant need for immediate gratification, there's a trap in thinking that we'll wake up one day and all bridges will be built. Even if that's the case, those bridges need to be maintained for future generations. I'm overwhelmed with gratitude that both Asian American and non–Asian American communities have supported us. I'm also driven by the idea that bridging cultures can cross continents, where the conversation about the diasporic Asian experience can be brought back to our home countries. And lastly, there's bridging cultures in other parts of the US. Perhaps in the places where we grew up, we never saw products repping lychee or calamansi before, especially by an Asian American brand rather than an Asian brand relegated to the ethnic foods aisle. I'm going to be just as excited when we're selling Sanzo in Manila and Hong Kong as when we're selling it in my hometown of Sayreville, New Jersey.

> "Ultimately, our mission for Sanzo is to bridge cultures, whether as a taste of home or a source of discovery. I see this as a continuous process of relationship building as opposed to a final destination point."

I always say that if Sanzo does make it big one day, it's not about retiring on an island somewhere. We're putting money back into the community because I believe that everyone in the world just wants a shot. I don't even think people want a guarantee of success—I certainly don't. If my success was certain, the journey would be less exciting. It's why I founded Sanzo when I could have taken a more charted course. If I fail, I fail; that's it, and I can learn from it. But there are others who don't even get the opportunity, and that devastates me. For people who want to take a shot, I want to contribute to giving access to opportunity. It doesn't need to be with entrepreneurship, because I don't think entrepreneurship is right for many. Regardless of the opportunities people pursue to improve their livelihood and that of their families and communities, I want to be a part of that solution.

Sanzo just closed its second round of funding and expanded from New York to Texas, Los Angeles, and the Bay Area. Sandro plans to add more flavors to the line, continue distribution expansion, and evaluate exciting product-line extensions.

Further information and resources:

- Taste Sanzo for yourself by visiting DrinkSanzo.com, and follow @*drinksanzo* on Instagram, TikTok, Twitter, and Facebook.

CHAPTER 15

CELEBRATING DISABILITY PRIDE

The story of *Tiffany Yu*, a content creator and entrepreneur on a mission to increase disability representation, access, and visibility

---

INTRO The impetus for starting a business can sometimes be the same driving force behind the creation of so much of the world's most influential art: to heal the creator. Tiffany Yu hid her disability from the world for twelve years, after a tragic car crash left her with a paralyzed right arm and without a father. But today, she proudly leads Diversability, a for-profit social enterprise that connects disabled people with job opportunities, visibility, and a community to explore what it means to be disabled and to thrive.

CHAPTER 15

> The global community of people living with some form of disability makes up the largest minority group worldwide at 1.3 billion people, representing 17 percent of the world's population. That means that nearly one in every five people would consider themselves to have a physical or mental condition, including chronic illness and pain, that substantially impacts one or more major life activities that others may consider to be a daily function, as defined by the Americans with Disabilities Act (ADA). Yet many people and institutions still have a long way to go in understanding the diverse lived experiences and brilliance of disabled people, and Tiffany is on a mission to change that.

My disability origin story begins at age nine. Over Thanksgiving weekend, the day after my dad's birthday, we dropped my mom off at the airport for a business trip. On the way home, my dad lost control of the car. He, my siblings, and I drove off the road in a single-vehicle car accident. My dad had been forty-nine years old for only a day.

I woke up in an air ambulance with broken bones in my legs and a right arm that was paralyzed through a spinal cord injury known as a brachial plexus injury. As my mom stood in my hospital room, I saw her cry for the first time in my life.

When I was discharged from the hospital, Christmas had already snuck up on us. We had no time to prepare gifts, so we found whatever we could around the house—little bits of paper, stuffed animals, and other trinkets. We wrapped each object in newspaper, and on Christmas morning, we passed our gifts around to each other. Our world was broken, yet we tried to keep up whatever semblance of togetherness we still had.

But alongside the tender moments, a harsh expectation of invulnerability also ran through our family. Shaped in part by my mom's refugee identity from the Vietnam War and my dad's immigration from Taiwan, we were all hell-bent on maintaining a "normal" and acculturated family image—which meant we avoided bringing shame to the family at all costs. From the car accident in 1997 onward, the collective shame that we had to bury expanded to include a death, a disability, and all the mental health ramifications of that moment.

We didn't talk about the accident after it happened. I shed no tears at my dad's funeral. I saw my mom cry for the second time in my life at the funeral, and then never again. She would tell people who weren't familiar with the accident that my dad was away on a trip. And in the years to follow, I hid my disability by wearing long sleeves, no matter how hot the summers in Bethesda, Maryland. The trauma in my story turned out not to be the accident and the injury themselves—it came from hiding them for twelve whole years.

. . .

As a senior at Georgetown University in 2009, I had only shared my story a handful of times—usually on an intimate, need-to-know basis—though sometimes I omitted the fact that my dad had been the driver, and other times I hid a different part. I was always calculating which slice of the story I could tell, to minimize the shame I might bring to my family. By the time I told my story on a public stage for the first time that fall, I realized that my sharing of this story had been shrouded in shame. In my narratives, I was always a victim, and my disability was a reason for me to be excluded. But what if, instead, disability could be the reason to belong?

Tiffany as a toddler and her siblings in Barbados.

"The trauma in my story turned out not to be the accident and the injury themselves—it came from hiding them for twelve whole years."

Tiffany as a toddler and her dad in Barbados.

A newfound desire to find this sense of belonging made me want to create a disability-centered community. I applied for the ReImagine Georgetown grant because I wanted to reimagine Georgetown as a more inclusive place for disabled people—and won. In the grand scheme of organizing an event, the $500 prize was only enough to cover the cost of food. The grant committee had also asked whether a group like this was necessary, and that inquiry became one of my main drivers of self-doubt.

But the vote of confidence that winning the grant gave me was enough to keep me going, at a time when my self-confidence was in the negative. I desperately needed to do this for myself.

A Taiwanese friend helped me create a logo, the same one we used for twelve years. I pasted that logo on flyers that referred to us as the Diversability Committee Working Group, a planning committee for both disabled and nondisabled people to host events where we could explore the diverse lived experiences of disabled people. Underneath, I included the email *diversability@gmail.com* and left my own name out of it—partly to take my ego out of this work, but also, as I realized more recently, because I was ashamed to fail in public.

To my surprise, all kinds of people started emailing with interest, including some I knew but didn't expect would be interested in something like this. That year, we hosted two events: the Ability to Laugh, where we watched a documentary about comedians with disabilities and facilitated conversations afterward, and the Ability to Express, where we painted our visualizations of disability and partnered with a local coffee shop to hang the artwork.

After I graduated from Georgetown, I worked in investment banking at Goldman Sachs for three years, then pivoted to television journalism for Bloomberg, business development for P. Diddy's music network, and a venture-backed coliving startup. Diversability became a largely inactive side project.

At the end of 2014, I received an email and a tweet out of the blue from two people within three days, both asking how they could become involved with Diversability. I was surprised by the inquiries but viewed them as small signs. In a community of entrepreneurial women called Dreamers & Doers, I asked, *Could Diversability still become something, so many years out of college?*

Gesche Haas, the founder of Dreamers & Doers, suggested, *Why don't you try hosting one event? If people show up, then you're onto something. If not, you tried.*

I followed her advice and organized a launch event for Diversability, featuring a panel, silent auction, and gift bags from sponsors. In the event flyer, we described Diversability as a movement to reshape conceptions of ability by organizing events that get more people thinking and talking about disability. The event sold out. The commissioner for the New York City Mayor's Office for People with Disabilities attended, and afterward, people asked me when the next one would be held.

Shortly after, the New York Public Library asked if they could pay us to organize an event to help their librarians better understand how people with different disabilities navigate libraries. It was the first time anyone had ever sought us out and offered compensation. Disabled people are often used to doing things for free because we feel humbled that someone is even acknowledging us. I realized then that I needed to take Diversability more seriously, that there is value and worth in the disability community and in our lived experiences.

Today, we're a for-profit social enterprise with an entirely disabled team of seven working to support our network around the world. Many are surprised that we're not a nonprofit, but we want to signal that just because we are working toward disability inclusion does not mean that we can't find ways to be financially sustainable outside of a nonprofit status.

We've made our model work by splitting the operations into three arms. First, we run a speakers bureau, where Diversability negotiates speaking rates on behalf of our speakers and takes a 20 percent cut. This is what I call "valuing disability lived experience." Second, what I call "valuing disability expertise," entails organizations tapping into the Diversability community for user research, interviews, user testing, and branded partnerships, like a sponsored blog post for someone seeking to redesign a wheelchair wheel. The third is organizing ticketed events, where we will sometimes be supported by corporate sponsors. We've hosted and been a partner on over one hundred events, and our digital network has grown to over forty thousand members. We were also one of a few communities to win Demo Day as part of Facebook's 2020 Community Accelerator Program. But what I'm the proudest of is the impact we've made to elevate the disability community by helping members get speaking and press opportunities, be paid for their work, or find their own sense of pride in their disability identity and narrative.

"I realized then that I needed to take Diversability more seriously, that there is value and worth in the disability community and in our lived experiences."

Tiffany in San Francisco.

> "I feel liberated, and I'm finally able to be myself and tell all parts of my story—in my own way, in my own words.
>
> I don't need to hide the fact that someone died or that I have a mental health condition as a result of it. I feel free."

. . .

There's a saying that you need to fill your own cup before you can fill other people's cups. When I started Diversability, my cup was empty, and I had the lowest self-esteem of my life. But I showed up before I was ready, and growing Diversability created a community that helped my own healing journey.

Then, in 2017, I started going to therapy as a result of a traumatic event unrelated to the car accident. For the two years after that, I had emotional outbursts, paired with a level of crying I had never seen from myself. Random things triggered my emotions in very public ways, and I couldn't control them. A psychiatrist told me that it was nine-year-old Tiffany grieving, and twenty-nine-year-old Tiffany was allowing her to do so for the first time.

In September 2019, I was diagnosed with PTSD, or post-traumatic stress disorder. That diagnosis felt validating, to know that being unwell for so long was related to a mental health disorder. I started more intensive therapy, and now I am the most emotionally well that I have ever been. I feel liberated, and I'm finally able to be myself and tell all parts of my story—in my own way, in my own words. I don't need to hide the fact that someone died or that I have a mental health condition as a result of it. I feel free.

Vulnerability researcher Brené Brown has said that shame festers in spaces of secrecy, silence, and judgment. My lack of confidence was rooted in my insecurities, which were the source of my shame. I've challenged myself to give voice to the things I am ashamed of, even before I'm fully comfortable. For example, I still hold shame around the physical manifestation of my paralyzed arm on my body, so I've been intentionally posting pictures on Instagram that show my arm. This is one way that I step out of my comfort zone and continue to grow. We sometimes have to do things before we're ready.

As someone who has experienced childhood trauma, I know I engage in some negative self-talk. I still have an internal voice that's always asking, "Who do I think I am to do this?" For a long time, I kept trying to affirm myself with comments like "You got this!" or "You are enough!"—all this positivity porn. My therapist told me that it's fine to have negative thoughts, but it's the action associated with the thought that matters. So, even though I didn't think I was the right person to start Diversability, I still did it. Even though I wasn't ready to share my story, I still told it through tears. Even though I am terrified that the events we host or the content we put out are not going to resonate with people, I still do them.

When I think about success for Diversability, I center my thoughts on this: Did *one* person attend this event and find it transformative? Did one person change how they viewed their disability? That's what matters.

Living in San Francisco, I'm surrounded by people who talk to me about success and growth only in terms of money and technology. But tackling bias and changing people's minds, which are just as important or even more so, happen in one-on-one conversations. If my imperfect outputs impact just one person, that's enough, and it's still worth showing up—even when I don't feel ready.

Diversability at New York City's Disability Pride Parade.

Since telling her story for the first time as a senior at Georgetown, Tiffany has become a three-time TEDx speaker, as well as a presenter at the World Economic Forum Annual Meeting in Davos and at institutions such as Singularity University, Harvard, and Stanford. In 2019, San Francisco mayor London Breed appointed Tiffany to serve on the San Francisco Mayor's Disability Council. She has been named to more "Women of Color to Follow" lists on all the major platforms, accelerators, and publications than we can keep track of, on the tails of her leadership within the disability, Asian American, mental health advocacy, and creator communities.

Further information and resources:

- To engage Tiffany and her team at Diversability® for speaking engagements, disability expertise, sponsored events, and community, check out *MyDiversability.com* or *@diversability* on all social platforms.

- Since we spoke to Tiffany for this interview in summer 2020, she's been named to the inaugural list of 15 Asian and Pacific Islander Trailblazers on TikTok! Check out Tiffany's TikTok *@imtiffanyyu* for her show titled The Anti-Ableism Daily.

CHAPTER 16

FIGHTING HARASSMENT AND HATE

The story of *Tammy Cho*, a serial entrepreneur turned community leader and CEO of *Hate Is A Virus*

INTRO Growing up, Tammy Cho never imagined she would dedicate her life to helping others, let alone mobilize her communities for systemic change. Like many other first-generation kids, she wanted to stay discreet, become successful, and provide for her parents one day. But because of the injustices she faced through her experience of founding a successful tech startup at age nineteen and selling it just two years later, she took a step away from the glitzy path of serial tech entrepreneurship. Instead, she turned her attention inward, to reflect on herself and her identity as an Asian American woman, and learn how to reconcile the two with her life's work.

The thing I remember most about my childhood is waking up to the smell of delicious food. Even though my parents went to work from five in the morning to midnight seven days a week, my mom somehow managed to prepare a feast every single day: kimchi jjigae or some other Korean stew, spaghetti, galbi, and all kinds of banchan. My mom made no distinction between what kind of food was suited for breakfast, lunch, or dinner—we mixed and matched them all. Amid the clashing furniture in our cramped two-bedroom apartment, we would sit on the floor around the coffee table, eat, and chatter over the Korean TV channel playing in the background. When we finished, my mom would pack the food in containers for my sister and me to eat throughout the day.

As much as our home life represented the ultimate comfort to me, I grew up with a complicated relationship with my identity as a first-generation Korean American woman. My parents, who barely knew any English, had been in their thirties with young kids when they immigrated to Orange County from South Korea. For lack of other options, they owned a liquor store for ten years and then a dry-cleaning business for the next nine.

Seeing them othered by the rest of the community was one of my first tastes of being Asian American. Every so often, I would witness an angry customer yell at my parents, call their dry-cleaning business a Chinese sweatshop, and write slanderous reviews on Yelp. My parents would barely react, let alone stand up for themselves, which infuriated and confused me as a kid. My dad was a US Army vet, yet people still felt compelled to call him a chink? Still, my parents fully subscribed to the mentality of putting their heads down and working hard to provide for us.

At home, my sister and I took turns translating English to Korean for them. We went through a stack of mail every day, and we occasionally needed to jump on phone calls with the cable company and wait on hold for two hours. I would then use my deepest voice to somehow convince people that I was a fifty-five-year-old man displeased with our latest bill. My sister and I wanted to help them as much as possible, and we were constantly thinking about how we could provide for our parents one day. But as the demands in our own lives grew, it was hard not to feel occasional resentment over this uniquely first-gen chore.

My parents used to say to me, "We're always going to be disadvantaged because we're not white."

In many ways, I wanted to prove them wrong, that you *don't* have to be white to succeed. At the same time, I internalized their words.

I looked around my high school, which was 75 percent Asian and included a large population of first-gen Korean Americans like me—my beloved community—and decided that I needed to distance myself from it. As I evaluated which college I wanted to go to, one of my top criteria was which schools would have the fewest Asians. I chose Georgetown University in Washington, DC.

With my beloved sisters who inspire me to pursue my passions and the work I do.

Left to right: Robin Byunga Cho, Sally Young-Ah Cho, Soa Cho, Tammy Whe-Ah Cho

A typical day at work with my mom and dad at our dry cleaning and alterations shop in Orange County.

"Seeing [my parents] othered by the rest of the community was one of my first tastes of being Asian American."

. . .

I entered the startup world unintentionally, the summer before my senior year of high school. Because I couldn't afford the summer programs and SAT prep classes that my peers were attending, I interned at a startup that helped nonprofits design their websites, resource pages, and other marketing materials.

My first taste of startup life taught me how to work with a small team, pitch clients, and build design skills that I would use for years to come. By the end of the summer, the founder and I realized that we worked well together and would both be going to Georgetown. We decided to work on another project there, but as cofounders.

At Georgetown, we prototyped a tool that would help nonprofits turn stories from their volunteers into email newsletters for donors—like Mailchimp, but before that existed. We started building it as a casual side project, until different mentors and advisors began telling us that the idea could have serious promise if we added a tech component to it. They encouraged us to apply to accelerator programs in the area.

I had no experience with tech up to that point, but the idea of "scaling impact" excited me. We applied to a four-month accelerator program, which accepted us—with one caveat. They loved and believed in us, but they thought our idea sucked. By the end of the four months, we had to have a new product for the Demo Day pitch. Until the last month of the accelerator, we stuck with our idea. But when we finally concluded, in defeat, that even the nonprofits that loved our product had no budget to pay for it, we decided to pivot.

Instead of concentrating on nonprofits, we decided to focus on marketers, since my co-founder had numerous contacts in the marketing department. Tag-teaming over the next week, three of us co-founders interviewed over a hundred people with any connection to marketing and mapped out the pain points we learned about on a whiteboard.

First day of Acceleprise with the Encore team (June 2013).
Left to right: Felipe Lopes, Tammy Cho, James Li

This was 2014, and multiple people had told us that social media was beginning to inundate brands with noise. As a result, a restaurant might miss that a customer tweeted about finding a roach in their food (a PR disaster in the making) or a major sports team might miss a tweet from an influencer that they could create a special package for (a missed opportunity).

To bring a solution to life with no time to code, the three of us sat hunched over Twitter screens twenty-four-seven for the next week. By the end, we'd read through thousands of tweets on a prospective client's page, plugged the best three into an email, and sent it off as a test.

The trial was a success. *This is exactly what we're looking for*, the client replied. *We're willing to pay six thousand dollars a year. When is it available?*

It wasn't actually available yet, but they were nonetheless willing to sign a contract to enter a four-month waiting list. When we shared the news on Demo Day, we were able to kickstart our seed round and raise nearly $400,000.

At that point, I had to make a decision: stay in school, or leave to focus on the company full time. I knew in my heart that we had a useful product and a great team. Still, my decisions up to that point had revolved around providing for my parents and de-risking my future for them. The overwhelming decision to drop out and forgo my full ride to Georgetown took months, and even an eighteen-page plan that I had to submit to my mom. I wrestled with my guilt for ages, but ultimately, it served to motivate me and drive me to excel and take care of my parents regardless.

. . .

I was twenty-one years old when our tech startup got acquired, two years after its founding. Our team had grown from three cofounders to eight team members, and we joined the acquiring company for the next year.

As much as I learned from building our company, and as much as I felt that we were creating a valuable tool for other companies, I still felt a disconnect. Tech is a powerful tool that allows you to magically build something that people can use on a large scale, but I wanted to apply this leverage to a project that would create more social impact. I wasn't sure what was next for me, but I jotted down directions and ideas and even considered going back to school to finish my degree by transferring to Stanford.

My next step came unexpectedly. In early 2017, a woman named Susan Fowler published her viral blog post titled "Reflecting on One Very, Very Strange Year at Uber." In it, she detailed various episodes of sexual harassment, discrimination, and retaliation that she'd experienced as a software engineer at Uber.

I read her story while sitting in my office, and a flood of experiences rushed through my head, including an uncannily similar harassment incident with a botched HR response. I was floored, not just by how much her story resonated with me, but by the number of comments and tweets of people sharing similar personal stories. For the first time, I realized I wasn't alone. In fact, as I'd later find out in a study, one in three women report having been sexually harassed at work, with 71 percent never reporting the incidents.

After reading the article, I went to lunch at the local teriyaki shop with my coworker Grace. Both of us were absolutely livid, because she also knew what I'd gone through at my company. One by one, we started pointing out the similarities.

From there, it didn't take me long to start revisiting all the other times I'd experienced sexism in the tech industry as a female founder. I thought of the many moments, early in our journey, when we went to startup conventions and people would assume that I was somebody's wife or the intern or a booth babe—then comment on my looks or even ask to take a photo with me. I remembered the times that I considered leaving my own company, because I felt like I was becoming a liability for our team's ability to raise money.

I often had to defend my equity in the company during discussions with investors, who were concerned that I was just tagging along for the ride. Investors always tried to negotiate my equity down, and at one point, they actually succeeded. I had started out equal with my cofounders, and by the end of the negotiation, I had the lowest equity. I had literally co-founded the company from before day one—and alongside my cofounders, I had designed the whole product, managed it from beginning to end, made the pitch deck that the investors had open in front of them, and influenced every piece of the company they were seeing. Still, my identity as a "young, female college dropout" always seemed to overshadow everything else, never mind the fact that any male founder who dropped out of college would have been celebrated as the next Bill Gates or Mark Zuckerberg.

My cofounders and I were unfamiliar with the dynamics at play in that room, so I didn't fight for myself. Instead of recognizing these issues as systemic, I internalized everything. I didn't even tell my cofounders, who otherwise would have advocated for me no matter what.

" I had literally co-founded the company from before day one—and alongside my cofounders, I had designed the whole product, managed it from beginning to end, made the pitch deck that the investors had open in front of them, and influenced every piece of the company they were seeing.

Still, my identity as a 'young, female college dropout' always seemed to overshadow everything else, never mind the fact that any male founder who dropped out of college would have been celebrated as the next Bill Gates or Mark Zuckerberg."

Various thoughts had flown through my head then. Maybe if I wore more tomboyish clothes and presented myself in more of a masculine way, folks would respect me more. Maybe I had overestimated my ability to be in this industry. Maybe I had brought this treatment upon myself. Though I felt upset, maybe I didn't deserve to be.

After reading Susan Fowler's story, a completely new fire arose in me. Grace and I decided to reach out to more women in our circles. As I shared my own experience with harassment, others felt more comfortable opening up about theirs, then introduced us to even more women who had experienced something similar. Our circle continued to widen, until Grace and I had spoken to over three hundred people. By then, we had a strong sense that many faced common emotions in the aftermath of gender-based workplace harassment: shame, overwhelm, and confusion from an overabundance of unvetted information on the internet about what they should do next.

With the skill sets that Grace and I had, we felt confident that we could create a website as a first step in righting this wrong—a resource that would reassure survivors that they were seen and heard, educate them on their rights in the workplace, and guide them on next steps they could take. With the help of therapists and employment lawyers, we pulled together information that would cost hundreds of dollars to access one-on-one with professionals, and we launched it on BetterBrave.org.

We never intended to create an organization, but when the #MeToo wave began later that year, the guide spread faster than we could have imagined. Susan Fowler tweeted it to her thousands of followers. And though I had started school as a transfer student at Stanford by that point, I found myself taking the train from Palo Alto to San Francisco every single day to work on BetterBrave.

After two quarters at school, I knew my heart was completely with the organization, and I realized I had to drop out of college again. My parents had been so excited that I'd made it to Stanford. I was scared to tell them about my decision, but this time, I felt more confident making this bet on myself. With the success of my first startup, I had been able to fulfill my dream of providing for them for the first time, and I knew it wouldn't be the last.

Ever since I've been able to devote more attention to Better-Brave, it has achieved national reach as a nonprofit, and folks from abroad have sent me their thanks as well. Seeing people share that the guide made them feel less alone has motivated me to keep doing the work. I'm also proud that we had multiple opportunities to make significant money as a for-profit organization—one investor was about to help us raise a million dollars in funding for it—but Grace and I turned these down. Of course, the prospect of doing another cool tech startup was glamorous and exciting. But fundamentally, having companies fund BetterBrave would create a conflict of interest with the integrity of information that we would be able to provide. Today, it continues to be a free resource that I'm honored to keep running.

Presenting BetterBrave to attendees of TechCrunch Disrupt 2019.

"After purposefully extracting myself from Asian communities five years before, I had felt like something was missing from my life—and at the Cosmos Retreat, I realized it was my community."

Behind the scenes of an NBC Asian America interview with Grace Choi, my BetterBrave co-founder.

. . .

A few months after starting BetterBrave, I hunkered down in a Seattle Airbnb with twenty other Asian American women. We were attending the inaugural Cosmos Retreat, a three-day weekend retreat hosted by the founders of the Cosmos, Cassandra and Karen, whom my co-founder Grace had known in college. The Cosmos had formed around the same time as BetterBrave, in the wake of an outpouring of responses to the founders' 2017 Medium article titled "What Does It Look Like for Asian Women to Flourish and Thrive?"

After purposefully extracting myself from Asian communities five years before, I had felt like something was missing from my life—and at the Cosmos Retreat, I realized it was my community. As we sat in circles and discussed our experiences as Asian women, many shared familiar stories: they had grown up translating their parents' mail, their families used toilet paper rolls as napkins, and nearly all of us had experienced that particular brand of Asian guilt when it came to making any decision that would affect our parents. We had pushed back on our identities, adopted behaviors to imitate dominant culture, and yearned to be who we really were in ways that felt true to us.

This became another turning point where I realized that I wasn't actually alone in this journey and didn't have to push back on my identity. That our cultural identities were part of what got us here too.

The Cosmos marked the moment when I began to embrace my identity as an Asian American woman, which changed nearly everything about how I showed up in the world. Before, I had to calculate how I presented myself for every occasion—T-shirt and jeans for the startup world, heels next to my cofounders so that I didn't look like tiny, and so on. I'd also thought that emulating the white men around me was the only path to success, so I had to force myself to be more charming and charismatic than what was comfortable, given my natural tendency to be on the quieter side. But I threw those considerations out the window. Over time, I've come to recognize that we can fully embrace who we are and lean into our unique experiences as our strengths. I now nurture the fact that I'm empathetic, caring, and collaborative in the workplace, rather than aggressive and forward. Most importantly, I'm no longer afraid to stand up for myself.

I've been developing this muscle of being able to look at situations more objectively. There's value in being able to see how much of something I can actually improve, versus how much is the result of fundamentally broken systems or biases that other folks have. I used to shame myself in order to make others more comfortable, but now I am completely comfortable making them uncomfortable. I feel justified—and confident—in speaking up.

Collage of Hate Is A Virus supporters and community members.

"I used to shame myself in order to make others more comfortable, but now I am completely comfortable making them uncomfortable. I feel justified—and confident—in speaking up."

That's why, when I began seeing story after story in early 2020 about hate incidents against Asian Americans at the onset of COVID in the US, I felt compelled to do something about it. My parents had already moved back to Korea after shutting down their dry-cleaning business a couple of years ago, but I couldn't stop thinking about what they would be facing if they had stayed.

In April 2020, I launched a campaign called Hate Is A Virus with Michelle Hanabusa of UPRISERS and Bryan Pham of Asian Hustle Network, after the three of us connected over one of Michelle's Instagram posts. We started a local initiative to support Asian-owned small businesses when fears and misinformation around COVID caused a major drop in their sales. When lockdown began, we turned into a digital movement because we recognized that there was still a major lack of awareness around these issues, even within our own circles.

We didn't plan for Hate Is A Virus to be anything beyond a social media campaign at the time—but similar to how both my first startup and BetterBrave had gone, one thing led to another. Bryan mobilized a strong community through Asian Hustle Network, I leveraged my experience running nonprofit campaigns and my connections to community leaders and organizers, and Michelle created eye-catching branding, designs, and infographics that attracted attention across social media and in-person rallies.

In our first event in early 2020, our team of volunteers pulled together and organized a virtual rally in just four weeks, raising $17,000 for Asian-owned small businesses. Today, we're a nonprofit organization actively raising funds to support local community organizations. We've hit our initial $1 million goal, and plan for this to be a longstanding fund, connecting donors with the people and organizations doing directly impactful work on the ground. Our vision is to mobilize the Asian American community to stand up not only for our own community but for other communities of color as well.

Though our Asian American community has a long history of community organizers and activists fighting for change, there are so many of our friends and community members who find activism intimidating. We see Hate Is a Virus as an organization that's especially focused on reaching Asian Americans like these, who want to speak out but don't know where to start. We want to spread the message that activism can look different for each individual, whether it's being onstage at a rally, creating artwork that contributes to the movement and expresses how they feel, reading a book about Asian American history, or healing their own relationship with their identity and community. Creating resources for those who have struggled to use their voices in the past—a group I include myself in—is a significant factor in why Hate Is A Virus has resonated.

I think of myself as a creator, sometimes more so than an entrepreneur. If I see a problem, I normally think, *What's one first step that I can take to address this issue?* For me, that first step is usually building something. Many people think that you need to have the vision of what an organization should look like in its final form before you can even start, but that's never been true for me. I usually take one small step at a time, and it always starts with listening. Every program and product I've created has been guided by the playbook of the community and the people I am building for. I never stress about the outcome of a particular project. If it grows into something big, that's great. But even if it remains one simple website or social media campaign that was valuable for the community in some way, I'm more than happy with that too.

Building these organizations has been not only my way of serving the community but also a way of personally healing and learning about myself. I'm grateful to those who have shared their stories with me, and I hope to listen, learn, and grow, as well as serve the community for the rest of my life.

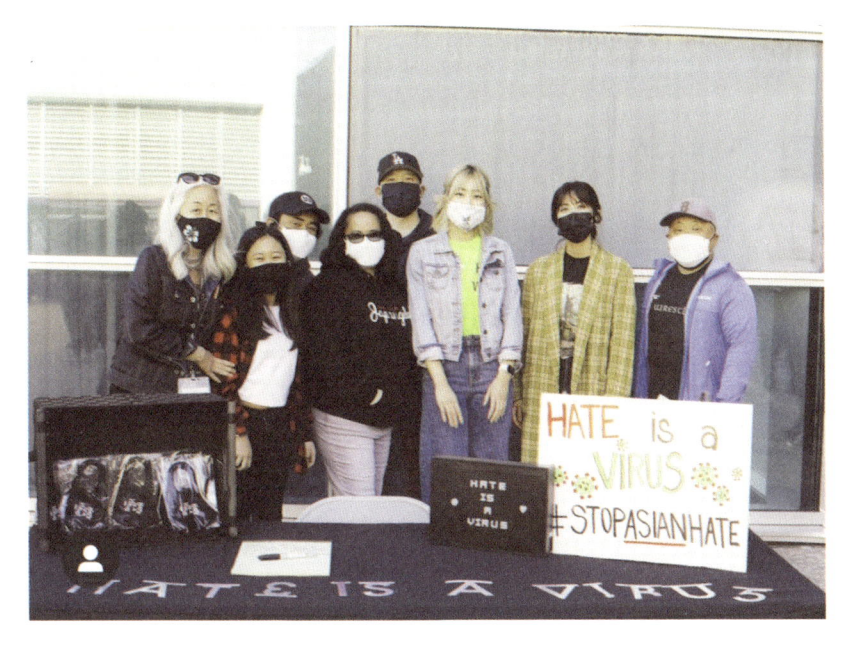

Here with my extended family at the Love Our Communities event hosted by various grassroots organizations in Los Angeles.

Left to right: Karen Kimura Joo, Sydney Joo, Quincy Joo, Rowena Joo, JJ Joo, Tammy Cho, Michelle K. Hanabusa, Sam Joo

---

Tammy knows that her life's work is to dismantle hate in all its forms. Today, she does that by serving as CEO of BetterBrave and CEO of Hate Is A Virus, though she's open to whatever form her work may take in the future. She is invested in making sure that no one feels alone in their struggle. Step by step, every day, she's moving through a lifelong journey of creating more space for love, joy, and liberation in our communities—and in our relationships with ourselves.

Further information and resources:

- Follow Hate Is A Virus at *HateIsAVirus.org* and *@hateisavirus*.
- Check out BetterBrave at *BetterBrave.org* and *@wearebetterbrave*.
- The Cosmos is a space for Asian women to care for themselves, their community, and their world. You can learn more about it at JoinTheCosmos.com and read about their origins and inaugural retreat in the May 2019 article in Paper, "The Cosmos Is Creating a Safe Space for Asian Women."

CHAPTER 17

SABOBATAGE

The story of *Eric Y. Chen*, founder of *Sabobatage: The Boba Card Game*

INTRO In his mid-twenties, Eric Y. Chen nearly died in a car accident. People often assume that overnight, that accident transformed him (a risk-averse middle-class suburban kid) into the successful serial entrepreneur he is today. But that's not exactly what happened. While certainly traumatic and painful, the accident passed and Eric's life went on. Through the stops and starts that accompany any journey of growth, Eric felt like his progress was barely perceptible. . . until one day, five years after the accident, he woke up, and he had invented a boba card game.

Most of my creative ideas come to me in the shower, but the idea of a boba card game came to me on the toilet. Mindlessly scrolling through Instagram, I tapped through a video of someone drinking boba, followed by someone else playing poker. *This person's drinking boba. This person's playing a card game. Wait... Boba, card game. Boba... card... game. WHOOOAAAA!*

For anyone who enjoyed the burgeoning boba life in California in the early 2000s as a middle schooler or high schooler, boba is so much more than just a playful, delicious drink. Boba represents hanging out with friends, joy and indulgence, and community—so much so that my sister and many of my close friends try to drink it every day.

Though I was exhilarated by my toiletside revelation, I mulled over the idea in private for three whole months. After five years of running multiple businesses with a ton of failures and only a few minor successes, the last thing I wanted was another halfhearted, half-baked project that would leave me right back where I started.

...

The first business that I decided to start, two years into my first job in sales, was a sales bootcamp for people trying to pivot from more old-school, corporate sales jobs into the tech world. While researching how to start it, I stumbled across a company called Always Hired that was already building the same thing. They were much further along in the journey than me, with two cohorts of students signed up for their program.

As someone who grew up in a middle-class family in a middle-class suburb of the Bay Area called Fremont, I always played it safe. The minute my fears started running through my head—*you have no entrepreneurial experience; and what if you fail all alone?*—I decided to tag along the *actual* risk takers at Always Hired instead. After working 9-to-5 at a sales dayjob, I would drive up to San Francisco to teach sales classes alongside the

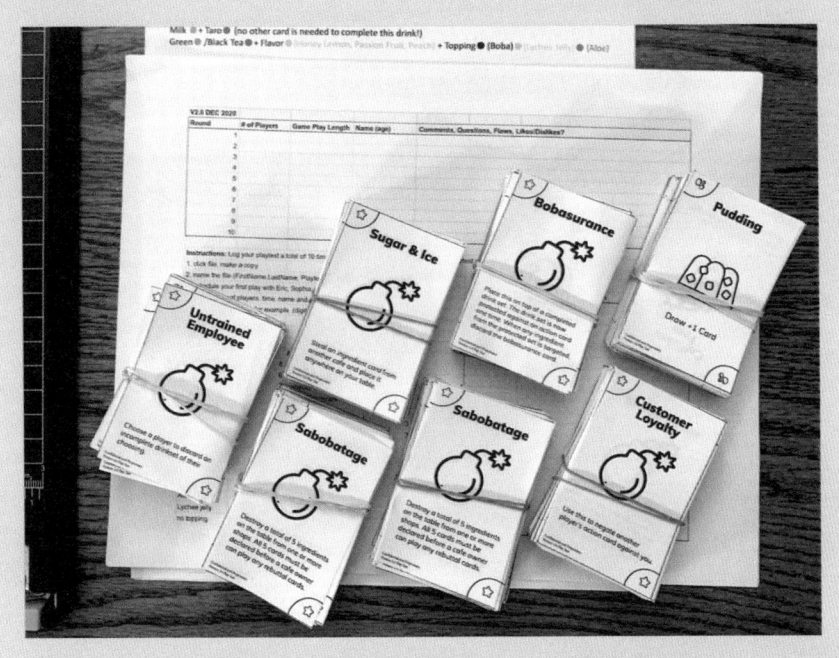

Early Sabobatage
prototype test units
sent out to friends.

A near completed
rendition of Sabobatage:
The Boba Card Game.

Always Hired founding team from six to ten in the evening—then for eight-hour sessions on Saturdays and Sundays.

Young Eric CEOing on a fake computer and keyboard. Little did I know this would be me 20+ years later.

At the nine-month mark of working both my dayjob and my night job, I went out for dinner in San Francisco with friends. When it came time to carpool back to Fremont, we elected a completely sober friend to drive us home. We made it down the 880 and turned the corner into the sleepy streets of Fremont at around three in the morning. Maybe it was the feeling of being so close to home that caused my friend to suddenly fall asleep at the wheel. Less than one mile away from home, his head slumped—and before we realized it, the car had swerved off the road, crashed into a tree at thirty-five miles per hour, and crumpled on the passenger side, where I sat.

All I remembered was waking up in the hospital. My seatbelt had pulled so hard on my stomach that it had severed my intestines in two. After the doctors cut me open and reattached my innards, I recuperated in bedrest for two months.

People ask me all the time if that accident transformed me, and they're surprised to hear that it didn't—at least, not right away. It was such a traumatic and painful memory that I tried to minimize it, desperate for my life to go back to normal. I went back to my job as soon as I could, but all I did was sit in a head fog for weeks—with no energy to perform any of my duties. I decided to put in my two-week notice and focus on my recovery.

When I felt ready to go back to work, I got a sales job at Google. As a kid who'd grown up in Silicon Valley during the tech boom, getting hired at Google felt like a dream. I put aside my earlier dreams of running my own business and vowed to work my ass off to become a VP of sales one day.

It was through selling Google Ads to online businesses that I first discovered the consumer product world. The moment I met Dave on the other end of the phone, I got chills. The solo founder of an online shop called GetKombucha.com, Dave made revenue in the high six figures just by selling a kombucha-making kit. His website was nothing like I expected of a successful, slick ecommerce business—it simply featured a photo of Dave holding up a box of kombucha and saying, "Start making kombucha from your home now!" Another company, which sold shoe insoles online, had a four-person team generating $25 million in sales.

A one-person team can do around $750,000, and a four-person team can do $25 million? You don't have to be a huge corporation to make money like that? As my slumbering dreams of starting my own business began resurfacing, I started revealing my actual curiosities in our sales calls. "How did you start your business anyway?... Tell me more about how it all works..."

In my first quarter at Google, I achieved over 300 percent of my performance quota and became the number two sales rep in the company.

But by the end of that quarter, I was back on a stretcher in my hospital gown. Apparently, my reattached intestines were growing ulcers and bleeding out due to stress. Yet, because my internal organs didn't feel any pain, I thought, *What the fuck? I'm literally bleeding out of my ass.*

If you don't know what a colonoscopy entails, take a moment to ask your parents or anyone over the age of forty-five. Three in

CHAPTER 17

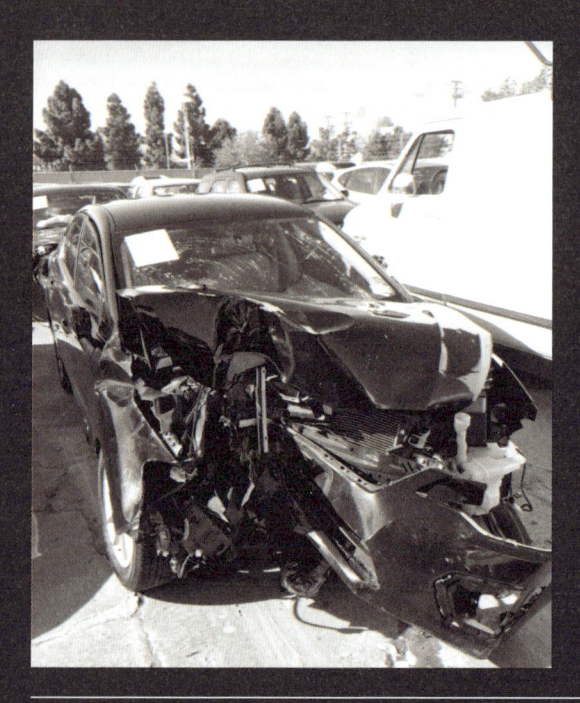

The indent of the tree can be seen on the right side of the hood, primarily on the side of the passenger seat where I was sitting.

> "*What would I do with my life if I could ever have my 'normal' body back, and a second chance to do it all over again?*"

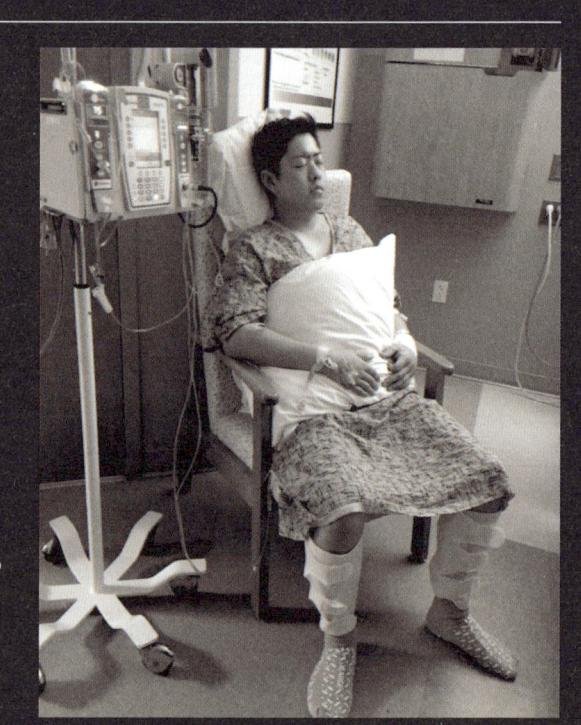

Exercising my core strength after having my stomach cut open to reattach my intestines.

a week is next-level pain. You're flushing out your system, severely dehydrated, newly anemic from having so much blood drawn, and getting probed and prodded constantly (up the butt).

The hospital Wifi was terrible, and I could only get lost in my books for so long. Back to being bedridden for eight days, I had time to think. *What would I do with my life if I could ever have my "normal" body back, and a second chance to do it all over again?*

The doctors had diagnosed the causes of my internal bleeding as overwork and stress. It was then that I made up my mind: if I was to stress myself out to the point of hospitalization again, let it at least be over the pursuit of my own dreams—not someone else's.

When I got discharged from the hospital, I gave Google a three-month notice. I decided to kick off my journey with a stint of digital nomadship as I'd read about in Tim Ferriss's *4-Hour Work Week*: traveling the world, pondering my life from quaint cafés, and popping random businesses out of my laptop keyboard on some sunny beach, piña colada by my side.

That spring, I invited all my friends to a goodbye party. In my backyard, amid streamers and a big banner that read *GOOD LUCK ERIC!!!*, I hugged my friends goodbye. "This is gonna be indefinite," I told them sentimentally. "In fact, I don't think I'm ever coming back."

. . .

I saw the Northern Lights in Norway with my best friend, hiked through Cinque Terre in Italy, backpacked around Prague, Budapest and Berlin, and fell in love with Spain so much that I canceled my upcoming itinerary in Denmark, England, and Ireland just to soak it in.

While I sat in cafés, trains, and hostel beds, I read about how to start an ecommerce business on Amazon FBA (Fulfillment by Amazon), a common entry point for ecommerce entrepreneurs.

Amazon FBA is essentially about reverse marketing, or observing what products are already selling and then selling the same or similar with your own twist.

After researching a few options, I'd come up with my product criteria, which I called "the toilet paper theory"—essentially, what's something that people would always have to come back and purchase more of when they run out?

Itching to get started, I bought a spontaneous flight to Guangzhou, China for the largest import and export convention in the world, the Canton Fair. By the end of the trip, I'd placed an order for my first product: a few thousand sets of splatter targets, or thick, colorful papers with a black silhouette to indicate targets at shooting ranges. One box of samples would arrive back home in Fremont, and the main inventory would go to Amazon's warehouses and launch straight away.

When I returned to Fremont and opened the samples, my heart sank. The bright neon ink on each paper had already start-

In the early pursuits of entrepreneurship, I set off to China to visit the Canton Fair to source products.

ed crusting and flaking off. I had a flashback to my chummy handshake with the factory owner, feeling such naive camaraderie just to be doing business with another Asian person. Deep down, I knew I should have ordered samples before signing a Purchase Order for $7000 worth of product on the spot, but I'd also thought, *It's just paper… what could possibly go wrong?*

Over the next few weeks, customer complaints came in. The only thing left to do was to drop the prices to sell through. All in all, I had racked up a loss of $10,000, but I decided to try again. In my second FBA attempt, I sold pencil grips, those ones that prevent kids from getting calluses on their fingers. For a little while, I was making a thrilling $150 profit a day. But the company with an expired patent on the product sent a cease and desist, and after much back and forth, I decided to shut it down.

To the extent that I'd mapped out my brand new entrepreneurial life in the hospital, I had pretty much checked everything off my bucket list. When it came down to it, I realized I sucked at living out of a backpack and being a beach bum. How productive can you really be when you're on the beach with shoddy Wifi, anyway? I didn't know how all the Youtubers seemed to pull it off with such ease. (Spoiler alert: I met them, and they struggle just the same.)

I decided to stay in Fremont and dig deeper into the physical product world. Amazon FBA was really heating up back in 2017, with thousands of new third-party sellers starting FBA side hustles every month. I linked up with a business partner around that time who was running his own seven-figure FBA business, and the two of us started informally helping friends with their own e-commerce ventures. As our connections and consulting opportunities grew, we spun out a full-fledged product accelerator company called Startpad in partnership with a manufacturer in the Bay Area.

 Clients would come to us with their product ideas, prototypes, or patents, and we would help them manufacture their products, launch crowdfunding campaigns, and run their mar-

> "When it came down to it, I realized I sucked at living out of a backpack and being a beach bum. How productive can you really be when you're on the beach with shoddy Wifi, anyway?"

keting. Among hundreds of clients over nearly three years, we helped a mattress company scale from $20,000 to $180,000 in monthly sales. We helped another client bring their consumer electronic patent to market and start grossing $90,000 in monthly recurring revenue after four months.

The hypergrowth excited all of us in the beginning. Clients paid us thousands for consulting and referred new leads. We struck partnerships, revenue share agreements, equity deals, and even acquired a new company fresh off its Kickstarter campaign. Our early successes in Startpad gave me my first opportunity to get on the speaking circuit as a product launch expert and host FBA meetups that people flew from all over the country to attend.

Successfully launching various businesses, I was invited to speak in front of 150+ aspiring entrepreneurs with lessons learned from my successes and mostly my failures.

Of course, that's also where our problems started. In the free fall of entrepreneurship, it's easy to catch Shiny Object Syndrome. When you quit your job and start from a blank slate, there really is an overabundance of opportunities: dropshipping, FBA, Print-on-Demand, and other e-commerce options; content creation; becoming an agency or service business. Startpad was literally a lighthouse of Shiny Objects. We'd grown other people's brands to successful six-figure per month products, worked with celebrity-owned brands, and built a global team across the Bay Area, Europe, and China to launch products across every vertical imaginable.

Yet, something felt deeply wrong. I had left Google to start my own business, but for the past three years, I'd somehow climbed into a hamster wheel growing other people's businesses. I had ultimately been too scared to make a bet on myself. Instead, I was hedging my chances of failure by latching onto other people's dreams and successes.

Two and a half years into Startpad, I exited the company. To give myself a fresh start, I moved to LA. Soon after, I came up with the concept of Sabobatage: The Boba Card Game.

> "...something felt deeply wrong. I had left Google to start my own business, but for the past three years, I'd somehow climbed into a hamster wheel growing other people's businesses.
>
> I had ultimately been too scared to make a bet on myself. Instead, I was hedging my chances of failure by latching onto other people's dreams and successes."

. . .

After a few months had passed and I found that I was still excited about a boba card game, I started floating my idea with friends cryptically. "Hey, I have this idea and I'm gonna tell you in three words," I'd say. Then I'd do jazz hands over my head in an arc as I said with extra drama, "Boba. Card. Game."

"Huh?" Most people responded with blank stares. Some business mentors understood the concept, but they said, "That's such a novelty idea, it's got to be worth a couple thousand dollars, tops."

A boba card game could have looked like an infinite number of variations, depending on the inventor. If someone who liked Dungeons and Dragons had created a boba card game, the game would more likely be a board game. Ultimately, I knew I wanted to create a highly portable game that could be played in just around twenty minutes in a boba shop—about the time it takes for a group of friends to down their boba drinks.

I studied the strategic elements of games that I loved, like Settlers of Catan and Monopoly. I stood in front of the game aisle at Target and took in the designs. I envisioned something cute, but not classically American, nor cute in an Asian, kawaii way—instead, I visualized little boba characters in my own interpretation of an "Asian American" aesthetic.

On a set of index cards, I penned rough sketches of boba ingredient cards: toppings like boba, aloe, and grass jelly; teas like oolong, earl grey, and jasmine; and combinations like milk, passionfruit, and taro. Players would need to draw random cards and assemble complete drinks from these elements. Then I drafted our first action cards: *Lactose Intolerance*, which allows a player to trash a Milk in someone else's shop, *Customer Loyalty*, which allows a player to protect their drinks, and *Sabobatage*— the ultimate sabotage card that allows a player to discard five whole ingredients of other players' boba shops.

Once a week, my roommates and I played the game and discussed how to improve it. Around iteration number ten, I turned the index cards into a printable PDF and sent this "playtest kit" to sixty friends.

Over the month of December, I observed my friends playing the black-and-white printer paper version over video chat. Anytime their body language showed confusion or engagement, I'd take note of the tweaks I'd need to make. Whenever I witnessed the subtle yet oh-so-delicious disintegration of relationships over my manufactured boba drama, I'd smile inside.

Confident finally at the 30th iteration of the game, I onboarded a team from my previous product launches, complete with an artist, designer, and operator. A few volunteers who wanted to launch their own products in the near future also decided to join my team to experience launching something in real time.

For the six weeks that we pulled together our Kickstarter campaign, a high-production commercial, and our marketing strategies, I was feeling an entirely unfamiliar aliveness. I was completely wired, sleeping three to four hours a night to keep our planned launch date after Lunar New Year, yet feeling entirely peaceful inside for the first time I could remember. The final days leading up to the launch passed by in a blur of finalizing our artwork for Bo (the main tapioca pearl character), preparing our pre-marketing, visiting boba shops in the area for pre-sales, and priming everyone on my team for their role during launch.

I set a public goal of $10,000, with an internal moonshot goal of $250,000, for the 30-day Kickstarter campaign. Having launched multiple Kickstarters for others, I knew that crowdfunding alone would be enough to secure funding for small passion projects—up to a few thousand dollars—but to raise a six-figure amount, it would take a solid investment into marketing. In my case, I budgeted a total of $30,000 for my initial production run, my team, and marketing.

The game that we launched a week after Lunar New Year was the thirtieth iteration of Sabobatage: The Boba Card Game. On the first day, we reached our public goal and raised over $20,000 for the minimum production run. Over the 30-day campaign, we raised over $148,000 from over 4000 backers. A huge continent of supporters came from the Asian American and boba-obsessed communities, and people outside of the Asian community also backed the project. For me, the best feeling was seeing people from all corners of my life come out to support me. Ultimately, as we grow the company and sell into boba shops, it is my goal to create bonding moments and memories with friends to accompany the already warm feeling of friendship that boba brings. And finally, after five years, I built a business that I'm truly proud to call my own.

Me holding up my final product, ready to share this box of joy, Sabobatage, and hoping to bring happy memories to households across the world.

On set filming the Kickstarter commercial with me as the talking head. The entire production was scripted, planned, shot, edited in less than 3 weeks. Shoutout to Taylor Chan and his amazing crew.

Eric delivered his first production run of Sabobatage: The Boba Card Game to his Kickstarter backers in July 2021, and fans will begin seeing it pop up in their favorite boba shops, too. In the backdrop of building Sabobatage, Eric is also building NeedThat.com, a media company where budding content creators write about the products that they most recommend to friends and earn commissions. Not only does Eric hope to continue paying forward these opportunities for emerging entrepreneurs, but he also plans to build out NeedThat.com as a platform to launch his future product innovations—those gems he decides to develop from those unpredictable moments of genius from the shower, or from the toilet.

Further information and resources:

- Check out Sabobatage at *BobaCardGame.com* and *@sabobatage* on Instagram.

- Check out *LaunchBrandGrow.com*, where Eric continues to consult individuals and companies on branding and launching products to market.

CHAPTER 18

BUILDING ASIAN HUSTLE NETWORK

The story of *Maggie Chui* and *Bryan Pham*, cofounders of *Asian Hustle Network*

INTRO

Many people in the Asian diaspora grow up estranged from their Asian identities and communities, only to rediscover them later in life. Not so for Maggie Chui and Bryan Pham, though. Even though they grew up in two different cities, both of them were surrounded by Asian Americans from their birth to their young adulthood. So when they met in their late twenties, started a business together, and started frequenting entrepreneurship and self development summits, meetups, and conferences, they couldn't help but notice that the lack of representation felt weird, rather than normal. Where were the other Asian. . . attendees, let alone speakers?!

Searching but not finding existing, accessible communities that were specifically geared toward developing entrepreneurial leadership within Asian communities, they started their own. In November 2019, Maggie and Bryan launched Asian Hustle Network, which has since become the largest online community for Asian aspiring and established entrepreneurs around the world. Today, Asian Hustle Network numbers over a hundred thousand members who share their stories to inspire and connect with each other every day.

PART 1: MAGGIE CHUI

At the Meiji Shrine in Tokyo, one of the most famous Shinto temples in Japan, there is a section of the beautiful grounds where visitors can write down their deepest, heartfelt wishes on wooden wishing tablets called ema (絵馬). After leaving their prayer hanging from a little string alongside thousands of others written by people from all around the world, the shrine's priests and priestesses will individually pray for each and every wish to come true, and for the person to feel unburdened.

For hours, Bryan and I stood rooted in the peaceful, silent space, reading and absorbing the wishes of those who had come before us. A wish for a family member to recover from illness, a wish to be accepted into a certain college, a wish to be forgiven for a specific incident, a wish to be a good parent. . . Each wish was deeply relatable, as is anything that comes from the most vulnerable places in our hearts.

When we finally took our own placards to hang up, I wrote, *I wish to find my voice.* We took a final look, bowed, and left.

. . .

Ever since I could remember, people have been telling me that I'm "extremely quiet." I sat in the back of the classroom at school, never raised my hand to ask questions, and even kept quiet at the dinner table with my family rather than recount my day. Part of that comes from being an introvert—if I'm in social situations lasting over an hour, I typically like to recharge through solitude, and I easily get lost in my thoughts and analytical personality. But I also feared speaking up because I was raised in a culturally Chinese household that values "saving face." In many Asian cultures, "face" is an important value: we save face to guard our reputations and maintain dignity, and we lose face when we attract humiliation—and sometimes, the safest way to save face is to simply stay quiet.

Unlike when I heard the same feedback later in my life, I never saw being quiet as an issue. I grew up in a tight-knit community in San Francisco's Sunset District, where nearly everything in my life was within walking distance: every school I attended including college, the Century Theater and Classic Bowling Center and Fuddruckers where everyone I knew would host their birthday parties, my Chinese Bible School, the Polly Ann Ice Cream joint where I would stand on a stool to pick my flavor since I was toddler, and even the local real estate boutique where I worked my first job.

When I got that job, my parents jumped for joy that I'd secured a stable job with steady pay. The two of them had immigrated to California from Hong Kong in the 70s, and for the near-fifty years between then and now, they truly put everything into providing the best life possible for my sisters and me. My dad worked in a printing company for almost over forty years to put the three of us through college, and my mom commuted an hour and a half from Oakland to Sacramento to work in various restaurants, garment factories, and electronics companies while going to school. Once she had her second child and realized that

" In many Asian cultures, "face" is an important value: we save face to guard our reputations and maintain dignity, and we lose face when we attract humiliation—and sometimes, the safest way to save face is to simply stay quiet."

My mom, dad, and me at my middle school graduation in June 2002.

babysitting services would be more expensive than her income, she decided to became a stay-at-home mom. As a kid, I loved listening to their stories of immigrating to the US, but it didn't register until I was around the age that they were when they immigrated, just how much they had really sacrificed for the sake of their children. Over the years, I'd internalized their hopes for my own success, which equated to the security that they'd maintained their whole lives—it would take a few more years for my eyes to gradually open to the world of entrepreneurship.

. . .

In 2017, I met Bryan, who had just moved to the Bay Area, dropped out of law school, and started flipping houses. Given our overlap in real estate, we wanted to experiment with a business partnership. I've always been interested in interior design, so I proposed that we start a staging company—a service company that furnishes houses on the market to look more appealing in listing photos and open houses.

We registered our company with the Secretary of State and got to work. With two business models open to us, we could rent all of our furniture for each job, or we could purchase and store it. Since furniture rental companies slap on all kinds of fees, we decided to purchase all of our inventory. Over three months, we visited over fifty different furniture stores in the Bay Area, applied to professional programs to access wholesaler and stager deals, and surveyed warehouses for storage. Luckily, one of Bryan's investor friends owned a half-vacant home in Santa Clara and let us store our furniture there. (We played Tetris countless times, trying to fit five sets of three-bedroom houses' worth of furniture into a single living room.)

Initially, we staged Bryan's own flips, until other real estate agents and sellers requested our services. Without the capital to purchase our own truck or hire our own movers, Bryan and I rented a Budget truck and moved the furniture ourselves. I'm

4'10" and Bryan's 5'10", so when we carried furniture up and down multiple flights of stairs every week, our initially smooth communications would often devolve into chaos as the top of my head disappeared from view behind the armrest of a 3-seater sectional sofa. Over time, we got better and better with our communication, systems, and operations, and we designed layouts and furnished listings up and down the Bay Area nearly every weekend.

After a year, we put a halt to the business, because frankly, our backs hurt.

But it had been my first taste of entrepreneurship: building relationships with clients, managing inventory, finding deals, and setting my own rules. I loved the feeling of excitement and creative freedom that I'd never experienced in the corporate world. And as I dipped my toes more into the world of entrepreneurship, I noticed that my idea of what was possible for my life was growing.

"After a year, we put a halt to the business, because frankly, our backs hurt."

Me sitting on an ottoman after a finished staging project in October 2018.

By the time we shut down the staging business, I was working a government job, providing supportive services to people in need in San Francisco. While I enjoyed the work and the social impact, my career had stagnated after a few years and we were never able to effect legislative change. I decided to pivot from government to tech—at the very least, to gain insight on how to build, manage, and scale a company.

> "With the two of us increasingly observing how Asians were underrepresented at the [events] we frequented every month, we started searching for existing communities that connect Asian American professionals or entrepreneurs."

Every night for a month straight, I forced myself to sit down and apply to at least ten companies. Once I secured a position in a company's finance department, I kept my eyes open to learn the ins and outs of how the business operated, how to market the product, what the business strategy was, the risks involved with onboarding third party vendors, and all the transferable skills that could be helpful if I were ever to build my own business.

That opportunity came nine months after Bryan and I returned from our trip to Tokyo. With the two of us increasingly observing how Asians were underrepresented at the professional business conferences, real estate industry events, and personal development summits that we frequented every month, we started searching for existing communities that connect Asian American professionals or entrepreneurs. The ones that existed tended to require hefty membership fees or elite qualifications (like having exited an eight-figure business at least once). *What would an inclusive and representative community actually look like for us?* We felt our way back to a memory of the ultimate belonging and camaraderie: among the silent and anonymous crowd that accompanied us at the Meiji Shrine, reading and writing their life dreams into reality on their prayer placards.

. . .

In the first month of Bryan and I designing the systems and processes of Asian Hustle Network to replicate the combination of vulnerability, hospitality, and mutual care of the placard experience at the Meiji Shrine, the group grew from our initial friend group to nine thousand members sharing their stories. Two months in, the community doubled to twenty thousand. Members around the world were not only sharing and relating to each other's stories—whether about business, career, or the personal life that's inevitably involved in both—but they were also connecting outside of the group, forming meaningful relationships, and hungry to meet in real life.

We hosted the first live event for Asian Hustle Network in January 2020, two months after founding the group, at a swanky cocktail bar in the middle of the Financial District of San Francisco. I remember it so vividly because we had no idea what we were doing. We posted to the Facebook group asking for sponsors and immediately received inquiries: *Where can I sign up?*, *I'd like to sponsor the event!*, and *Finally, the FIRST AHN event!* Without any marketing budget, we secured over fifteen sponsors that day. When we made our final announcement on the day of the event, members were coordinating carpools in the comments—"I'll be leaving from San Jose at 4:30pm, so if there's anyone who'd like a ride, let me know!" I was amazed to see the trust that people had built among themselves, even though they hadn't met in person.

So much planning and preparation goes into a community event, and no one on the team had any event planning experience. From securing a venue space to creating an events listing page, pricing ticket sales, scheduling announcements, securing sponsors, finding a photographer and videographer, finding a DJ, setting up signage, signing up volunteers, creating name tags and flyers, figuring out the VA system, securing guest speakers, determining merchandise to sell, hand-filling swag bags for our guests, convincing the security we wouldn't violate building fire codes—

not to mention all the food we had to prepare for our guests—the single biggest mistake we made in the end was forgetting to confirm whether there would be garbage bins at the location. I mean, who really thinks about that? Guests were holding onto their plates of chicken and rice until the end of the night, hours after they'd finished their meals. Only when the last guests had left, we finally found the time to retrieve garbage bags from a bar owner and pick up the plates, neatly strewn along the thin tables of our sponsors and the floor.

For our second official event in Southern California a month later, countless volunteers helped plan the logistics. Sponsors again stepped forward to offer their services or products for the event pro bono. Again, we paid $0 in marketing and ads, because news of the event spread completely through word-of-mouth. Lo and behold, we had almost 500 people attend, including some who flew in from other states and abroad!

The magic of bringing like-minded people together at the SoCal event was in how people shared their dreams and goals so openly with each other—something that people often feel the need to keep private because there can be shame associated with transcending our limiting beliefs, thinking big, or wanting to become more. As different speakers came onstage to share their stories, the crowd nodded and clapped, taking in the variety of stories of people who looked and sounded like them and, as a result, reflected their own experiences in some way.

To me, the SoCal event defined the ethos of abundance and "give first" that Asian Hustle Network exists to cultivate in our community. Even as a co-founder, the raw, electric energy pervading this event opened my eyes to the true power of coming together to support each other and serve our community. In the month between that event and Covid-19 forcing us into virtual events, we continued hosting events from California to Boston, DMV, New York City, and even Melbourne.

"The magic of bringing like-minded people together at the SoCal event was in how people shared their dreams and goals so openly with each other..."

Photo taken by Angelina Hong for AHN's first feature for the *LA Times* in December 2019.

. . .

Since leaving my 9-5 job seven months into this journey, I've considered myself to be a constant work-in-progress. Many nights I feel like I have a whole community behind me, and many nights I've felt intensely alone. Like many entrepreneurs, I was often unable to share what I was going through. My friends and family had fully supported me when I told them that I quit my job to pursue this side hustle full-time, yet I hesitated to discuss my problems with the people closest to me, because I didn't want them to think I'd made the wrong decision.

Even after half of my lifetime of trying to break the generational limiting mindset of saving face and often advising community members to do the same, I would sometimes still find myself failing to follow my own advice. Over many months, I started training myself to constantly think about my why. *Why am I doing all this anyway? What will all this amount to?*

Slowly, I've stopped thinking so much about what others would say, because the impact we can create by growing Asian Hustle Network is so much more important. In the short year and a half since its founding, I've helped create this safe space to cultivate countless relationships and business connections—many that we're not even aware of. From the beginning, we minded the smallest details, like responding to members' direct messages nearly every minute of the day, making sure that Bryan or I greeted each newcomer personally when they joined, and logging feedback from the group constantly. We put in work behind the scenes to demonstrate that we would proactively develop the community with the help of others. And by personally onboarding more women moderators to the group, organizing women entrepreneurs in my network to share their stories on the platform, and hosting events specific to Asian women's experiences with entrepreneurship, we rebalanced the ratios of the group from 70-30 to 53-47 men to women and non-binary.

It's not perfect, and improving on how we run the community will be a constant process. Still, I'm proud to have seen members who pivoted their businesses in the pandemic post their new products in the community and receive such great feedback that they sold out within the next couple of hours. I'm proud when I see service professionals build enough of a client base through AHN that they can quit their jobs and start their own practices. Members have raised money for personal causes and crowdfunding campaigns, sourced entire teams of freelancers and suppliers to support their product launches, published books that feature chapters about other AHN members, found their significant others and business partners, and even located long-lost relatives through the group! Through it all, the impact that sits closest to my heart is seeing members start their own businesses from scratch because they read about others who did the same, and they believe in the power of the community to support them when challenges inevitably crop up.

I never would have imagined that in my life, I would be up on a stage speaking in front of even five people, let alone hundreds. The first time I did it, it was surreal to take the microphone in my hand and feel my fears fall away. I didn't prepare a speech, but I looked into the crowd, felt the energy flowing through the room, and spoke words from my heart: that through AHN, we're doing more than just managing a Facebook group—we're observing a movement. A movement for Asians to own their voices and their stories, to support each other's various paths towards their most personal dreams in life—and what better medium for both of those challenges than the topsy-turvy, interdependent, emotional rollercoaster of business and entrepreneurship?

"Through it all, the impact that sits closest to my heart is seeing members start their own businesses from scratch because they read about others who did the same, and they believe in the power of the community to support them when challenges inevitably crop up."

AAPI Charity Dinner in San Francisco benefiting AHN and HateIsAVirus in May 2021.

PART 2: BRYAN PHAM

The 2010 census showed that the 626 area, also known as the San Gabriel Valley in Southern California, was populated by over half a million people of Asian descent—more than the Asian American populations in San Francisco, Los Angeles, Chicago, and forty-two US states. When I was growing up there, people came from Asia to seek a better life or to escape the Vietnam War, like my parents. The 626 offered a level of comfort: no matter where in Asia you had come from, someone would speak your language and share your culture.

My high school was around 80 percent Asian and 10 percent Latinx, with only three white people total. We never called ourselves Asian Americans back then; we identified as Viet, Chinese, Korean, Japanese, Filipino, and so on. Growing up, I felt ashamed to be Vietnamese, because I always thought that we brought all the crime, gambling, and other negative stereotypes to the Asian community. It wasn't until I was older that my dad explained that we were seeing only the cream of the crop from other Asian countries because they weren't escaping war. Still, we sat with our own groups at lunch and distanced ourselves from others. After all, our home countries had all been fighting each other not so long ago.

Sidewalks were cracked, vacant lots abounded, and most of the business signage was written in Vietnamese or Chinese. The smell of incense wafted out of Chinese restaurants on every street corner. Hoarding was the norm at any friend's or relative's house, with every inch of space filled with possessions, many of them packed up and ready to be taken at a moment's notice. People were always picking up cans, cleaning the street of trash, showing respect to one another, and aiming high, despite their lack of education. I rarely met parents who were US-educated, if they went to college at all, and they were all blue-collar workers.

When we first arrived in the 626, my dad took an array of odd jobs: delivering furniture, dishwashing at restaurants, and working at car washes. Inspired by a late-night infomercial, he enrolled in technical school to learn how to fix used appliances. For the next year, he sat in night school with my baby sister in one arm while he took notes with the other, struggling to understand just two English words per sentence that came out of his teacher's mouth. While he went to school full time, my family's savings dwindled to twenty-five dollars, which the five of us stretched for a whole month by subsisting on instant noodles. That was one of the origin stories my parents told us when we had to get through more difficult times later on.

At first, my dad operated his store out of our 600-square-foot, two-bedroom house. My siblings' mattresses covered every inch of the living room floor. With no space in the house, we studied in the backyard or on top of the car. I tagged along for all of my dad's deliveries and asked him how to fix refrigerators, stoves, washers, and dryers, but he was tight-lipped in his responses. "I don't want this life for you," he'd say. "You can do better. You know English."

Tony Pham (left), me (middle) and our mom (right). This picture was taken in 1998.

> "Our visions of success were simply figments of our parents' imaginations mixed with our own."

My brother Tony and me as kids.

Do what, though? We had no idols. Scarcity mindset abounded, understandably so, because 95 percent of the people in the 626 were escaping something: persecution, war, extreme poverty. Our visions of success were simply figments of our parents' imaginations mixed with our own. There was always a huge emphasis on education, but never on entrepreneurship. The typical goal was to do well enough to take care of yourself and your family, but not to go any further than that.

As a kid, I always knew I was going to do something great in my life. When I got my first C in elementary school, I told my mom that it was nothing and that it wouldn't define me. I never let setbacks, grades, or other people tell me what I could or couldn't do. I don't even know where that mindset came from, other than being an automatic defense mechanism against the pessimism that surrounded me. No matter what I said I wanted to achieve, everyone around me would always tell me I couldn't do it. No one ever told me that I *could* do it, so I programmed myself to be my first believer, no matter what. That's stuck with me throughout my entire life. Even with starting Asian Hustle Network, when people told me it didn't sound like a good idea, I would think, *I've been hearing that since I was a kid. I don't need you to tell me. I'll just try it out myself.*

When I was young, I'd save my allowance for packs of Magic: The Gathering cards and Yu-Gi-Oh! cards, five bucks at a time. I entered weekend tournaments and won $500 awards and new boxes of cards, until I had leveled up into an elite circle of players. Those were the first kids from wealthier families that I'd ever met.

When they invited me to their homes, I saw their gated communities and BMWs. I learned that these kids thought they could be anything they dreamed of: doctors, astronauts, scientists, you name it. When my new friends and I would finish playing Magic, I would always amble over to their kitchens and try to sneak in conversations with their parents.

"Mr. Pan, did you do all this by having a job?" I said to one friend's dad, gesturing at his cavernous kitchen and his BMW M3 in the driveway.

"No, of course not," he said. "I do stocks and real estate too."

"Wait, aren't stocks really risky, like gambling? That's what my parents say."

"Not really. If you do it right, it's not gambling. It's very strategic."

Another friend's mom, a VP at Nike, said the same thing. I was fifteen at the time, and I realized that I needed to learn about stocks too. That would be how I'd rise above my social status.

"No matter what I said I wanted to achieve, everyone around me would always tell me I couldn't do it. No one ever told me that I *could* do it, so I programmed myself to be my first believer, no matter what."

The grand opening of Tony Appliances in Pasadena, CA. My dad, mom and younger brother, Tony Pham.

. . .

I went to college near home at UC Irvine. During my first job at the campus bookstore, I trained myself to stack fifty to a hundred boxes of books in two hours, when it would normally take eight. With my remaining six hours, I would spend three of them studying, two hours reading manga, and one hour sleeping somewhere in the library. (They didn't have security cameras.)

When my boss noticed my efficiency, she asked if I could start working on data entry in addition to stacking books. Thinking it would take forever, I figured out how to write simple code to autosort everything in fifteen minutes. Secretly, as I sat behind the computer, I was researching random facts all day: *How do stocks work? How does Amazon work? How do you get rich through real estate?* For two years, I learned about money and investments.

I knew I'd be the first working kid in the family, and I wanted to pay for every single one of my parents' expenses the minute I could. After calculating what they would need to have to support their own life, my life, and my sister's PhD, I wrote the number on a page and circled it: $250,000 a year was my goal. Knowing that, I overloaded myself at school and graduated in two and a half years with a computer science degree, a political science degree, and premed—just in case. I didn't stack degrees to impress anyone; I was scared. Graduating during the recession, I saw how my parents' business was suffering, and my older friends were saying things like "Yeah, we applied for a hundred jobs and got one interview."

When I started my first software engineering job at IBM, I was so grateful to even be employed that I vowed to be the best worker possible for the company. I coded for sixty to seventy hours a week while side-hustling on Amazon, selling all the free swag I got from my job and other knickknacks from Alibaba. I used to bring a whole grocery bag of inventory to work and run down to the post office during lunch to mail out fifty people's packages at once.

> "I knew I'd be the first working kid in the family, and I wanted to pay for every single one of my parents' expenses the minute I could. After calculating what they would need to have to support their own life, my life, and my sister's PhD, I wrote the number on a page and circled it: $250,000 a year was my goal."

I didn't know how the post office worked, and the guy told me it'd cost $7.99 per package for expedited shipping. I'd purposely chosen to sell only tiny products to reduce the shipping costs—earbuds, gaming discount codes, and blank CDs from China you could burn media on—so that was way too expensive. He told me the cheapest option was to mail packages with stamps, but because they took a whole month to get to customers, I ended up with terrible reviews. I sold out inventory every time, but the headache that followed wasn't worth the profit. I started looking for other products to sell, spent ten to twenty grand purchasing weird items that no one wanted to buy, and ate even more losses—basically all the money I had.

We were still in an economic downturn at that time, and one year into my job, my company started laying off my coworkers, including some who had been there for decades. That's when I realized that there's no such thing as loyalty to any company. On top of that, there's no such thing as easy, fast cash. I pivoted from selling on Amazon to real estate investing instead, and vowed to avoid building a flimsy business like I had with Amazon reselling. I spent a whole year building my fundamentals while working my job.

BiggerPockets is the biggest real estate investing community online, with thousands of members posting stories and advice in their forum. For a year, I posted three questions every day to the forum, no matter how basic: *What is equity? How does interest work? What is compounding over this time period?* Those dumb questions mattered to me, and people answered them. To this day, my account still has nine hundred posts from that time. BiggerPockets also has hundreds of podcast episodes, which I chugged at 2x speed to get through five of them every day. When I finished those, I finished three hundred episodes of another podcast about out-of-state rentals in two weeks.

From the podcasts, I got information, but from networking on the forum, I got confidence. If everyone on the BiggerPockets forum went there because they hated their job and found that real estate was their way out, then there had to be a viable path for me too.

Three years into my software engineering career, I could barely stand going into work every day. My weeks were disappearing in my state of numbness. As I glanced around, I saw that my coworkers who had been there for fifteen or twenty years all looked like me—as if they'd lost track of time. I was terrified of becoming like them.

Even though I'd studied real estate diligently for a year, the idea of taking the first step terrified me. Part of me worried that I still didn't know how much I didn't know. I thought law school was the answer, that maybe if I learned how to read contracts and protect myself first, then I could finally take that next step in business.

I studied for the LSAT for two years, got accepted to law school in the Bay Area, and moved up from LA five months before the start of the semester. That's when I moved in with Sean, a peer that I'd met in a different Asian frat at my college.

"Why would you go to law school?" he asked. "You're gonna work long hours and make less money than if you did something like real estate."

Hearing that from a hypercompetitive guy like Sean, who was my age but from an educated and successful family, I treated his words like a challenge. I told myself that if I could get one deal going before law school, I would drop out and pursue real estate seriously.

I found my first opportunity through the BiggerPockets forum in 2016. I read through the numbers and thought that I was replying to the guy who posted it, but I actually messaged a different person with the same name. He responded, *Hey, this is actually my first flip too. Do you want to partner? If you have time to fly down to LA, I have this deal that I want to get under contract.*

"I didn't even know this person and had just sent him my entire life savings. I couldn't sleep for four days afterward. I kept alternating between thoughts of *I fucked up. Shit is not good!* and *If I lose money, I won't die! If I lose money, I won't die!*"

The two of us agreed to go in fifty-fifty, and we signed the flimsiest possible contract with just two paragraphs in it, built on nothing but trust. All he had was $60,000, and all I had was $60,000. I met him online on a Tuesday, flew down to LA that Friday to see the property, got it under contract on Sunday, and wired him the money on Monday. I didn't even know this person and had just sent him my entire life savings. I couldn't sleep for four days afterward. I kept alternating between thoughts of *I fucked up. Shit is not good!* and *If I lose money, I won't die! If I lose money, I won't die!*

Once we needed to get contractors, we had to take a hard money loan. I didn't know how hard money worked or how much interest we had to pay on it. *That's* what got me hella scared—we had to finish this project fast because hard money is outrageously expensive.

We rushed the contractor to finish the project in three months. I wasn't sure if we did a great job on the property, but it was the result of pure panic. As soon as the flip was finished, we listed it and got an offer three days later that was $100,000 over the asking price. Within five months, I'd gotten my investment back, plus $200,000 net.

I dropped out of law school, as I promised I would, and fully pivoted into real estate while working my software engineering jobs on the side. The second and third time I flipped properties, I gained confidence. I started branching into out-of-state rentals and larger apartment complexes, until I had seventeen rentals at one point. That's when I was able to buy my parents' house for them, the same one they'd been renting all throughout my childhood.

> "I didn't want to end up like the people I saw fifteen years ahead of me in real estate, many of them lacking a purpose beyond money-hungriness, which had been my motivator until this point."

By the time I was twenty-eight, I felt like I was getting pretty good, but that was also the year the market turned. You don't buy anything when the market turns, so I spent time reflecting on my life instead. I'd finally reached my money goals and could provide for my parents, but now what? I didn't want to end up like the people I saw fifteen years ahead of me in real estate, many of them lacking a purpose beyond money-hungriness, which had been my motivator until this point.

When contemplating the next phase of my life, I thought about the place I'd always turned to whenever I felt lost, depressed, or at a crossroads: role models and stories. I've long been in tune with other people's stories, but I kept wondering what other Asian people were thinking. I'd been incessantly curious about the Asian diaspora ever since I left the majority-Asian bubble of my childhood. The Asians I'd grown up with were tough and confident with each other, but when I later met Asians outside of where I grew up, I learned what a vast range of lived experiences people of Asian descent really have. There were those who had grown up as minorities, those who weren't proud to be Asian, those who saw themselves as Asian American rather than fractured along ethnic divides. The more Asian people I met all around the country, the less I felt like I belonged in the Asian community of my hometown. I wanted to surround myself with people who were more aware and who wanted to do more for each other.

That was on my mind leading up to starting Asian Hustle Network. I also recognized that I've always been down to hustle hard for my connections and to find stories that inspire me—these things were never given to me. But I wondered what would happen if those connections and inspirations were abundant to everyone, including those who didn't have the desire to hustle for them. What could we achieve as a community?

In 2019, Maggie Chui and I created the Asian Hustle Network Facebook group. Between the two of us, we invited 1,500 people. The thought of sharing my own story was my greatest fear because I was terrified by the possibility that people would Google me and see that I went to UC Irvine for undergrad instead of Stanford, Harvard, or any of the other schools that CEOs and leaders seemed to attend. That imposter syndrome was always plaguing me, but I finally got over it. I had just turned thirty, and I decided that I had nothing to hide. I wrote a blurb about myself in the group and explained that our intention was to create a safe, supportive space for Asian entrepreneurs to share their stories.

Maggie and I logged off and went to the gym. After a couple of hours, our first members started inviting their friends, who started inviting their friends. Within the first three days, we reached one thousand members, who started posting their stories.

We had planned for AHN to get big. On the first day, we onboarded fifteen moderators, friends who covered every time zone across the world. We read and reviewed every post that came through, then liked and commented with *Hey, thank you for sharing your story and welcome to Asian Hustle Network*—even when the number of posts increased to hundreds per day.

We wanted everyone to feel welcomed, and we saw the evolution of the community close-up.

Within three months, AHN grew to ten thousand members, and by the end of the first year, we approached one hundred thousand across Facebook, Clubhouse, Instagram, and our membership website. In that time, volunteer committees all around the world—in Canada, Australia, and different countries in Asia—have sprung up to organize in-person meetups and local chapters of Asian Hustle Network. Members can meet like-minded people who are looking for more and who can support them on what's often a lonely journey as a founder or business owner.

Nearly two years into the journey of building AHN, my biggest takeaway is that the Asian community is even more amazing than I thought. It blows my mind how integrated we really are in society, but I simply don't know about it. We're in C-level executive positions, government, advocacy work. We're also naturally willing to support each other. While the earlier generations had to worry about survival, we have the opportunity to bridge our community with the digital tools we never had before.

Because we're based on the idea of creating an environment for entrepreneurs to share their stories, you would think that the majority of our events would be business focused, but at least half of them are actually about Asian identity and mental health. There's enough information out there on entrepreneurship tactics and strategies, but there are few spaces for us to discover who we are and who our community is. That's the main reason why our engagement has always been tremendously high: we need space to talk about all the shit happening in our community, to cry, to be upset, to be angry. We've created spaces that people weren't finding before. Knowing this, I keep focusing on growing bigger because I don't want people to feel alone.

To me, the power of storytelling is understanding how much commonality really exists between us. When I used to talk to my friends' wealthy parents about their success, I always asked them what their upbringing was like and how it shaped their world-view and beliefs. Hearing their answers would always bring up this thought: *Why not me*?

So, why not you? Why wait for someone to tell you that you can do it, that you can take control of your own destiny too? I'm telling you now—don't wait. Go out there and get it.

My parents during AHN's first LA event watching me speak on stage.

ACKNOWLEDGEMENTS

Thank you to the Asian Hustle Network team, which met for thirty to sixty minutes every single Wednesday afternoon for fifteen months to make this vision a reality: Makayla Gessford, Nick Shen, Eric Y. Chen, and Galina Lang. Thank you to each of our interviewers for entrusting us with your stories, which was gutsier than it may sound, given that none of us knew what we were about to create when we were first going into this project. Thank you to Maggie Chui and Bryan Pham for being the greatest partners to have ever taught me about partnership and, obviously, for being the reason this project exists.

Thank you to our professional services providers, who turned a very average-looking Google Doc written in 12pt Times New Roman into a hip, hype, and soulful object that stands a chance of being beloved, dog-eared, and timeworn. Gabrielle Widjaja (aka Gentle Oriental) designed every inch of *Uplifted* with love, care, and color. Reinhardt Kenneth's creative direction, Matthew Freiheit's video production, Michael Purwagani's photography editing, and Priscilla Chung's lifestyle photography gave *Uplifted* a visual world of its own, captured people's imaginations on Kickstarter, and made our first print run possible.

Thank you to everyone who guided *Uplifted* through four rewrites (some of which were complete rebirths). Thank you to Joel ben Izzy for his storytelling coaching, without which *Uplifted* may not have reached the finish line at all. Thank you to Evelyn Anderson and Albert Chen for delivering honest feedback in the earliest, most vulnerable phases of *Uplifted*'s editing process. Thank you to early volunteer readers within Asian Hustle Network who provided feedback and thought partnership: Kate Lee, Thi Nguyen, Christopher Shue, Tania Wu, Christopher Truong, William Kun, Cecilia Liu, Eric Om, Evan Lessler, Linh Nguyen, Mandy Wong, and Tony Lee. Thank you to Crystal Shelley of Rabbit with a Red Pen Editorial Services for expert copyediting and sensitivity reading. And many thanks to loved ones who edited without even being asked, and provided the final polish towards the end: Alison Gwinn, Jane Won, Dan Niven, and Raina Sun.

Thank you to many more loved ones for your wisdom, love, and feedback in this process—in no particular order: Alexandra Caturano, Kyle Michelson, Bea Kim, Emily Gao, Simone Hudson, Jaclyn Marcatili, Katie Kramon, Maggie Zhang, and Alina Liu.
Thank you to my parents, Yifeng Chen and Zhenhai Chen, for loving and trusting me completely and thus setting the standard for me to love and trust myself completely. Thank you to my parents-in-law, Brenda Wong Aoki and Mark Izu, for paving a beautiful legacy for Asian America in the arts, and for teaching me about what it means to be Asian American when I was still an ambivalent, reluctant student. And to their son and my husband Kai Kāne Aoki Izu, who helped with literally everything about *Uplifted*: thank you for everything all the time.

UPLIFTERS

Thank you to our Uplifter Tier for contributing to our Kickstarter campaign in August 2021 and making our first print run possible:

Bernard & Christine Moon
Andy Chen & Nissana Akranavaseri
Loose Leaf Boba Company
Sanzo
Ernie McNabb
Brenda Chen
Dave Liu
Kai Kāne Aoki Izu
Nanxi Liu
D.Wang
Ryan Yan
Stacy Chui
Eric J. Chang
Jenn M Choi
Tai Anh Doan